9/05

MAN THE HUNTED

MAN THE HUNTED

PRIMATES, PREDATORS, AND HUMAN EVOLUTION

Donna Hart
University of Missouri – St. Louis

Robert W. Sussman
Washington University

A Member of the Perseus Books Group
New York

Copyright © 2005 by Westview Press, a Member of the Perseus Books Group.

Published in the United States of America by Westview Press, A Member of the Perseus Books Group.

Find us on the world wide web at www.westviewpress.com

Westview Press books are available at special discounts for bulk purchases in the United States by corporations, institutions, and other organizations. For more information, please contact the Special Markets Department at the Perseus Books Group, 11 Cambridge Center, Cambridge, MA 02142, or call (617) 252-5298, (800) 255-1514, or email special.markets@perseusbooks.com.

A Cataloging-in-Publication data record for this book is available from the Library of Congress.

ISBN 0-8133-3936-7 (hardcover)

Drawings by Christina Rudloff

The paper used in this publication meets the requirements of the American National Standard for Permanence of Paper for Printed Library Materials Z39.48–1984.

10 9 8 7 6 5 4 3 2

CONTENTS

FOREWORD

Students of human evolution (like hapless skiers attacked by mountain lions) have always held equivocal views about the place that *Homo sapiens* and its predecessors have occupied in the food chain. And as a result they have tended to straddle or shuttle between extremes when attempting to reconstruct the behaviors and lifestyles of our earliest ancestors. Two diametrically opposed traditions in the artistic representation of early hominid lifeways run right back to the very beginnings of paleoanthropology in the mid-nineteenth century. Some of the many artists of the nineteenth and early twentieth centuries who specialized in re-creating prehistoric scenes typically depicted small groups of puny and vulnerable early humans huddled nervously around a campfire while big cats circled, awaiting their opportunity to pounce. Others preferred to represent the noble savage, proud and erect and usually armed with a hunting spear or a stone axe (and sometimes with a dog at his heels), striding out in search of quarry. The discovery in 1879 of the astonishing animal images adorning the ceiling of the cave of Altamira, Spain, taken early on to consist of straightforward if powerful and stylized representations of the prey animals of the Ice Age hunters who made them, gave a huge impetus to interpretations of the latter kind. Still, the duality of interpretation lingered well into the last century, possibly because both interpretive schools had in common a tendency to emphasize the importance among humans, then as now, of social cooperation, either as an essential ingredient in defense against predators or as an integral component of successful hunting. Another frequent element in these rather anecdotal scenes displayed the use of intelligence and guile by hominids to compensate for their relative lack of strength and of such inbuilt weapons as dagger-like canine teeth. Understandably for those days when the human fossil record was tiny, ancient and extinct kinds of humans were most commonly viewed somewhat as junior-league versions of ourselves, with at least echoes of our own vulnerabilities and strengths.

Perhaps unexpectedly, when serious scientific attention began to be turned specifically to the matter of how early hominids had lived and thrived within their environments, this attention was focused not on the lifestyles of humans in the late Ice Ages, but rather on the behaviors of truly ancient human precursors. During the second quarter of the twentieth century, Raymond Dart presented the first diminutive hominid bipeds as "murderers and flesh hunters," whose violent proclivities had inevitably led to the "blood-spattered, slaughter-gutted archives of human history." Based largely on an interpretation of patterns of bone and tooth breakage at ancient "australopith" (archaic, small-brained hominid biped) sites in South Africa now known to date between about 3 and 1.5 million years ago, Dart's vision of humanity's origin in a group of vicious, tool-wielding predators seized the public imagination in mid-century when it was popularized by the scenarist Robert Ardrey in his beautifully crafted book *African Genesis*. Significantly for the recent history of the human sciences, this dramatic view of "Man the Hunter" influentially held the stage during the period when many of today's senior figures in paleoanthropology and primatology were being trained.

Inevitably, though, the Dart/Ardrey view of mankind's bloody birth ultimately produced a reaction that swung interpretation toward the opposite end of the spectrum of possibilities. Studies by Bob Brain during the 1960s and 1970s of South African australopith assemblages clarified how the fossils came to be jumbled and fragmented as elements washed into underground cavities, or as body parts accumulated by predators or scavengers, rather than as a result of murderous breakage by hominid killers in their lairs. Dramatically, Brain demonstrated that twin punctures in a skull fragment of a juvenile australopith were perfectly matched by those of a fossil leopard, whose relative had doubtless dragged the hapless hominid's body into a tree, as leopards still do with the corpses of impalas and other unfortunate prey.

Still, some of the South African australopith sites, notably that of Sterkfontein, cover a period of well over a million years. And in his detailed examination of this site in his 1981 book *The Hunters or the Hunted?* Brain suggested that while at about 2.5 million years ago "the cats apparently controlled the Sterkfontein cave, dragging their australopithecine victims into its darkest recesses," by a million years later hominids "had not only evicted the predators but had taken up residence in the very chamber where their ancestors had been eaten." This set the stage for a more nuanced view than Dart's of early hominid lifestyles, and one which emphasized the vulnerability of the small-bodied early hominids who first quit the shelter of the forest and ventured out into the expanding woodlands and grasslands. Still, Brain's book envisaged an almost inexorable progression by hominids toward predatory behaviors.

In the 1990s, with increasing knowledge of the ways in which our closest living relatives the great apes behave, the pendulum began to swing more emphatically. Beginning with the assumption that early hominids were more in the nature of evolved apes than of unperfected humans (though the conclusions need hardly have differed either way), some primatologists began to point to the fact that apes have been documented to behave in some pretty nasty ways, up to and including what has been characterized as "genocide" (as when the males of one chimpanzee community in Tanzania systematically wiped out those of a neighboring one). Thus became popularized the notion of the "demonic male," whose extreme and enduring hunting proclivities have been turned inward, toward members of his own species, and to whom by extension we owe many of the less endearing traits we human beings display today. These include the male domination of women and mayhem of all kinds. The latest wrinkle on this re-energization of the notion of Man the Hunter has been the claim that it was the regular cooking (initially of tubers, but by extension of meat) that spurred the origin of our genus *Homo* at around 2 million years ago, and that this in turn was responsible for our modern, Western (though not universal) pair-bonded social system and a slew of other human behavioral peculiarities.

Well, all of this makes a good story, even though there is precious lit-tle evidence of the regular domestication of fire before about 400,000 years ago (or maybe, according to the latest reports, a little more). But are all good stories necessarily true? And more specifically, is this one true? If you are inclined to believe the chorus of reports in the press, which is fa-mously receptive to reductionist explanations of almost everything, you might readily conclude that behaviorally speaking we are indeed the pris-oners of our genes: that the way we human beings behave today is the re-sult of millions of years of fine-tuning by natural selection, deep in our evolutionary past. But if we look at the archaeological record, the archive of the behaviors of our predecessors, it is readily evident that significant behavioral innovations over the course of human evolution have been both sporadic and rare. The pattern we observe, whether physically or behaviorally, is certainly not what one would expect from a generation-by-generation process of improvement via natural selection. Further, it seems that in (rather recently) acquiring its unique symbolic reasoning processes, mankind made a qualitative leap: a leap that was not simply an extrapolation of trends that are discernible earlier in human evolution. For example, a small window of time in our recent history points toward an adoption of true big-game hunting, yet millions of years of our early history indicates that we were mainly a prey species. Clearly the unprece-dented qualities of our species are the result of an emergent event, and there is indeed something truly *different* about the way we *Homo sapiens* behave that seems to distinguish us from even our closest ancestors. And as a result, it is evident that we cannot attribute the ways in which we be-have directly to our genes or even, more indirectly, to our history, as a bee or an angel fish might much more plausibly do.

So what can we reasonably say about our ancestral heritage, and more specifically about the roles of our ancestors as the hunting or the hunted? And what, if anything, is the relevance of all this for the mysterious ways in which members of our peculiar species act today? For an accessible and innovative appraisal of these issues I cannot think of a better place to turn than to this elegantly accessible book by Donna Hart and Bob Suss-man. These gifted primatologists recognize that to inquire whether the place of humans in nature is properly as hunters or as hunted is to create a peculiarly human paradox. For of course, at one time or another, we are and were both. This is particularly significant because, in a very real sense, in our present incarnation we are interlopers into the web of nature, our forebears having very recently taken an entirely new ecological turn. And although we are neither condemned to be a predator as a leopard is, nor to be constantly preyed upon as a wildebeest must be, elements of both conditions nonetheless linger within most human beings. Insulated as most of us are today from the practical dangers of predation, we are nonetheless (often) meat-eaters who are still haunted by atavistic fears, and Hart and Sussman eloquently explain why.

Crammed with captivating anecdotes, but always with its feet firmly on the scientific floor, this intensely readable volume explains how the intricate web of nature is constructed, what we can reasonably say about how our predecessors fitted into it, and how our past has contributed to our sometimes rather uncomfortable place in the world today. And, most importantly, it tells us how predation upon our species has significantly molded its history. *Man the Hunted* presents the first comprehensive synthesis of the information available about predation on humans in both ancient and recent times, and it combines the insights thus gained with a penetrating survey of an extraordinary range of data on human fossils, primate and human behavior, ancient habitats, the archaeological record, and a host of other topics relevant to the understanding of human origins. The result is a revolutionary but convincingly documented perception of the origins of our earliest ancestors not as fearsome killers, but as another primate prey species. If you are looking for a truly unusual and innovative perspective upon the human story, read on.

—Ian Tattersall
New York City
June 2004

PREFACE

"Man the Hunter". . . popular buzzwords, almost shorthand during much of the twentieth century to describe the human ancestral condition. And, as we settle into the new millennium, the idea that humanity blossomed forth from an oppressive killer-ape stem is a notion still embraced by many and challenged by few.

This book is a completely different look at human origins. As the title indicates, a change of just one letter in those buzzwords—to Man the Hunted—offers an entirely refitted perspective on who we are and how we got here. Does the *Homo sapiens* flower at the end of the killer-ape stem still contain dark seeds from ancestors who slew giant beasts with rocks and bashed each other's heads in during routine bloody torrents of violence? Well, that's a very *convenient* excuse for the unpleasant aspects of our human condition, but evidence points to quite contrary circumstances. That effectual, but ugly, proto-human growling, swaggering, and bashing its way through the epochs of prehistory isn't pretty, but at least it's powerful. What we have to suggest in this volume is perhaps a less powerful, more *ignoble* beginning. Consider this alternate image—smallish beings, not overly analytical because their brains were not huge, possessing the ability to stand and move in a vertical plane, spending millions of years as . . . basically, meat walking around on two legs. Meat on the plantigrade foot . . . bipedal edibles . . . saber-toothed cat cuisine . . . giant hyena chow . . .

crocodile comestibles . . . plain, unadorned food for predators. Early humans as a preyed-upon species is an abstraction that reveals our origins as just one of many, many species that had to be careful, had to depend on other group members, had to communicate danger, and had to come to terms with being merely one cog in the complex cycle of life.

But isn't this what we always discover about the truth behind the myth? Our inglorious rootstock, however, doesn't need to undercut our evolutionary status as currently large-brained and remarkably opposable-thumbed beings. It just makes us very much like other animals that have evolved through a long period of fits and starts, some of them making it and others dying out.

Our theory of Man the Hunted builds on the work of those in the paleoanthropological community who've made assertions that the hackneyed, but eternally popular, view of our ancestors as meat-eating, megabeast hunting killers is a totally erroneous concept. What if we didn't start out as killers, but instead originated as tasty primates that were being caught and eaten by a whole host of predators? There's been fossil evidence that points to our vulnerability, but what has been missing until now is evidence that other primates besides humans also lay squarely in the category of prey. Notably, if our closest relatives—the chimpanzees, the gorillas, and the orangutans—were exempt from predation, then it might be reasonable to assume (fossil evidence notwithstanding) that early hominids were also fairly free of this pressure.

We, the authors, have been working to trace the extent of predation on our primate cousins for over a decade. RWS developed this interest and passed it on to DH when she was his graduate student. The subsequent data compiled by DH for her dissertation quantified the evidence of predation on primates through meta-analysis. Having secured the non-human primate foundations of predation, we were then able to proceed with integrating that new knowledge into the fossil evidence. This combination of two approaches leaves no doubt that we as humans were a species that developed behavioral, ecological, and morphological adaptations as an outgrowth of predation.

Early hominids—the ones who lived between 7 million and a few hundred thousand years ago—probably were subject to predation at the same rates at which living primates existing under natural conditions are today. These frequencies are compatible with many so-called typical prey species—the ones we picture grazing on the African savanna, but also including hoofed animals inhabiting the Indian subcontinent, giant rodents of South America, southern and eastern Africa's unique and ubiquitous hyrax (tiny fourth cousin to the elephant), and the forest antelopes of Central Africa. All of these tasty items are consumed by the standard lineup of predators—leopards, eagles, lions, tigers, jaguars, hyenas, pythons, crocodiles—the same ones that prey on our primate cousins.

As further evidence to substantiate Man the Hunted as a reasonable portrayal, we have pulled together countless references to the relationship between modern humans and predatory animals. Currently, humans living near pristine (and even not so pristine) natural areas fall prey to the same predators that eat our non-human primate relatives.

What we've described is the nature of life, and nothing about past or present predation on humans should be construed as implying that we need to cleanse the world of dangerous creatures. As author David Quammen has affirmed so eloquently in *Monster of God: The Man-Eating Predator in the Jungles of History and the Mind*, great predators (the ones we admire and fear) are part of the ecological and psychological context in which our identity as humans arose.[1] We (and we're limiting this accusation to those of us enculturated by Western concepts of nature) have huge blind spots. The major one encompasses a previously mentioned problem; to be exact, realizing we humans are woven into the mesh of life. For example, what is more beautiful than a tiger?—almost everyone agrees, tigers are truly magnificent animals. What is a tiger?—a predator. What do predators do?—they eat other creatures. What would happen if you were walking through a forest inhabited by tigers?—they might eat you. Does this mean tigers should be eradicated?—no, it just means there are places where humans do not hold ultimate power. Here's another example: In twenty-first century North America we are fortunate enough still to have bears and mountain lions roaming in certain domains. Bears and mountain lions can and sometimes do eat people—so people should stay away from where bears and mountain lions are trying to make a living. Don't expect the bears and mountain lions to understand the rules that have been promulgated in the last few thousand years—they're living by the rules that have been in effect for tens of millions of years. We can't help it if we look tasty to predators; predators can't help it that they might want to eat something tasty.

Modern humans have nearly swept the planet clean of large "great" predators in the past 50 years. Rather than dwell on the fact that the remaining ones might attack us, we advocate using every tool available to preserve those that remain. Think of the areas where large predators exist as fragile natural works of art that must be preserved at all costs. Humans were spurred to evolve a larger brain because we were prey—and eventually that large brain seriously altered the world. Let's use those smarts we evolved to prevent the ruination of the planet for ourselves and all the other species.

One last major point we want to make in this book—we humans are not slaughter-prone assassins by *nature*. We often act badly, maliciously, cruelly, but that is by choice and not by our status as bipedal primates. We can state this because our closest relatives use cooperation and friendship as the most expedient method for gaining what they need and want. Yes, just like humans, chimpanzees occasionally act brutally wacky—usually because of stress, resource shortages, or unknown factors that evict them from their comfort zone. Sound familiar? Isn't that exactly why we humans get crazed? Let's quit accepting our spurious heritage as Man the Hunter to excuse why we start wars, torture others, and scorch the earth.

Humans are by nature highly social animals. Who among us doesn't want to be liked? Who doesn't desire a guaranteed route to social comfort? We owe those desires and needs for sociality to countless evolutionary adaptations forced upon us during our past. That evolutionary past, to a large extent, consisted of being a prey species. This book is devoted to setting the record straight, debunking the myths, and proposing that our earliest ancestors were not the hunters . . . but the hunted.

1

JUST ANOTHER ITEM
ON THE MENU

On the second day of January 2001 something occurred that has happened uncountable times before . . . something that has been happening, in fact, for millions of years . . . something that has influenced the way we humans act and the way we evolved.

A woman was cross-country skiing along a popular lake trail near her home in Alberta, Canada. Rangers say a 132-pound cougar lay hidden under an evergreen. It watched her pass, then stealthily zigzagged behind her for nearly 150 feet. The woman was probably totally unaware of the cat until just moments before it killed her.[1]

Man-eater! The word conjures up a latent human nightmare. It shocks us; it scares us badly. It seems to frighten us down to some deep collective subconscious. It's gruesome . . . macabre . . . downright ghoulish when a human being is killed by a predator. Newspapers report the event, books are written, movies are made, eyewitnesses are interviewed for more snippets about such an aberrant deed.

A quick browse of the internet comes up with over a hundred websites connected to the word "man-eater." There is even a book entitled *Maneaters* that "explores the wide world of man-eaters—creatures who regard *Homo sapiens* as just another noon-day snack."[2]

During the relatively short period of written human history—with weapons ever more efficient and living areas secured behind barriers to the natural world—we have come to think we should be exempt from attacks by carnivores, birds of prey, and reptiles. Those of us living within the rarified atmosphere of Western civilization presume that our superior position in the hierarchy of the animal kingdom is unquestionable. And, truth be told, modern humans in the industrial world have suffered relatively little at the claws and teeth of predators.

The human species excels in duality of thought. This comes as no surprise to anyone who has read the work of the famous anthropologist Claude Lévi-Strauss.[3] He theorized that all human cognition was based on dealing with binary contrasts or oppositions—left versus right, low versus high, night versus day, them versus us. We also seem to carry this duality into our feelings about predators. On the one hand, we humans—or at least those of us in Western cultures—have a conception of ourselves as superior entities who exist on a plane above the rest of the animal inhabitants of our world. And yet—and here is the duality—we worry ceaselessly that inferior beings, such as predators, may harm us.

Modern humans, with the help of technology, are able to ward off predation effectively, and mask our vulnerability as a species. As cited at the beginning of this chapter, there are times when people meet their demise from predators: The solitary jogger or cross-country skier attacked by a cougar . . . a tiger or leopard that preys on villagers in India . . . the two lions, made famous in the film *The Ghost and the Darkness,* that savaged railway workers . . . newspaper reports of crocodiles consuming humans from West Africa to Indonesia.

The bizarre realization that humans get eaten comes hard to the Western mind. However, much current ethnographic evidence points to the fact that large predators are often a major and well-recognized problem in regions of the world where villagers are in near contact with big cats or large reptiles. Perhaps there's more truth than we in the Western world would like to acknowledge that "the ultimate horror of being eaten alive is very real [by] sharks, lions, leopards, tigers, bears, wolves . . . jaguar and puma."[4]

In South Asia—India and Bangladesh, in particular—there is a long history of dealing on a daily basis with predation by tigers and leopards. Before World War II and prior to independence for India,

British colonial records listed 1,500 human deaths from tigers *per year*, and these statistics excluded the numerous Princely States. One tigress was responsible for an incredible 436 human predations.[5]

The Sundarbans delta of the Ganges and Brahmaputra Rivers—a huge area of over 3,800 square miles of mangrove forest and islands that spans both India and Bangladesh—is notorious for its man-eating tigers. John Seidensticker, tiger expert at the Smithsonian Institution, commented in a speech he made at an academic meeting: "Tigers kill people. They don't kill people in every part of their range and that might be interpreted as great restraint on the part of the tiger considering the abundance of this very vulnerable potential prey species. One area where tigers do eat people on a regular basis is the Sundarbans."[6]

During one decade near the end of the twentieth century (between 1975 and 1985) 425 people were killed by tigers on the Indian portion of the delta and another 187 on the Bangladesh side.[7] Plastic face masks—constructed to be worn on the *back* of the head—have been distributed by the Indian authorities. Locals wear them as a deterrent to tiger predation while they are boating through the swamps in the Sundarbans delta. These masks help reduce tiger attacks because big cats like to stalk prey that are unaware of impending danger. The wide-eyed, staring mask on the back of a human head is interpreted by the tiger as a fully *aware* prey and, therefore, not a potential meal. Dummy humans set in boats and wired with electric shocks are also used to deter tigers from the enticement of human flesh. The theory is that once a tiger has been literally and figuratively shocked by pouncing on an electrified "human," that particular item will no longer be so appealing. Some of the other, more traditional Indian and Bangladeshi means to counter tiger attacks include fireworks, special shrines, and priests.[8]

Why specific animals become predators on humans is complex. Predators are after the simplest avenue to a meal, and modern humans— even those in the undeveloped world—are usually dwelling *in* villages, *inside* houses, *with* weapons, and seldom make a simple target. We do not in any way want to portray carnivores (or reptiles, or birds of prey) as rapacious fiends that must be eliminated for the good of humankind. All predators are critical and necessary parts of healthy ecosystems. If we are going to save any of the wild places on earth, predators are the keystone species that must be protected.

In the Sundarbans delta, India, local inhabitants wear masks on the back of their heads to deter tiger predation. (Ragui Rai/Magnum)

FOSSIL EVIDENCE AND LIVING PRIMATES

Having noted that (outside the West) predation on humans happens—and not all that infrequently—we are confronted with a number of questions: Was this always the case? What about the 99% of human evolution from which we have no written records? Does the occasional unsettling instance of an attack by a predator accentuate the long history of humans as simply one more link in the food chain?

Were early humans bold hunters or were they fearful prey? Has *Homo sapiens'* evolution been molded by hunting ability or by survival techniques developed to avoid being eaten?

We only have two sources to draw on if we want to fill in the millions of years before historical times. These are the *paleontological remains*—a sparse but fascinating fossil record—and the *living primates*—who are our closest relatives.

There are caves in South Africa where bones of early hominids (humans and their ancestors) lie in piles. Researchers study how bones came to be buried in the earth and preserved as fossils, thus shedding light on how these ancient humans lived. Early hominids, using rocks and branches as weapons the way many living primate species do, had (presumably) the same ability as other primates to ward off predation—that is, not much except a slightly larger brain–body ratio than other mammals and the ability to communicate between group members when danger was sighted. These were not superb weapons if the predator managed a surprise ambush or just outran or outclimbed its hominid prey.

Paleontological evidence supports the conclusion that both hominids and other primates, such as baboons, were frequent meals for ancient predators. Both australopithecines (one of the groups of early hominids) and baboons are found together in the prey-remain assemblages of true saber-toothed cats, false saber-toothed cats, hunting hyenas, spotted hyenas, and leopards. Fossil evidence from South Africa supports theories of extensive predation by leopards on both early hominids and baboons between 1 and 2 million years ago.[9]

One skull of a fossil hominid found in a South African cave has a set of puncture marks. Two round holes about the size of dimes are spaced several inches apart on the skull. If a leopard caught one of the australopithecines and dragged the prize up a tree for eating, the cat's upper

Fossil evidence from South Africa documents predation by leopards on our early ancestors. (C. Rudloff, redrawn from Brain 1981)

canines would have drilled deep into the frontal part of the brain directly
above the eyes, and the lower canines would have grasped the prey on the
back of the skull. When paleontologists reunited a fossil of this ancient cat
with the fossil hominid skull, there was a perfect matchup between the
two puncture holes in the skull and the two huge lower fangs of the cat.

The famous "Taung child," a two-million-year-old *Australopithecus
africanus* skull, was discovered in 1924 by Raymond Dart, an early and
influential paleontologist. Dart had an arrangement with a limestone
quarry in South Africa; all intriguing fossils were extracted intact and
shipped to him. One of these boxes of limestone rubble contained a veritable jewel of paleontology—the skull and mineralized brain of a very
young child, a child that died 2 million years ago. Were violent circumstances involved in the child's death? Unlike the other skull from a
different site in South Africa, the Taung child did not bear the marks of
carnivore teeth but instead exhibited deep rakings. More oddly, the
mandible, or lower jaw, of the Taung child was still attached. (The remains of carnivore meals most often have detached mandibles. Big-cat

fangs tearing away at small hominid skulls would rarely result in a still-attached jaw.)

What was going on? If not ancient cats, then what might have caused the death of the Taung child? It took another 70 years for an answer to this mystery. In 1995 paleontologists Lee Berger and Ron Clarke published their detailed findings about the predator who killed the Taung child.[10] Birds of prey, technically called raptors, include living species of eagles with enormously robust feet and talons. These adaptations enable the eagles to kill antelopes and monkeys many times the birds' own weight. Berger and Clarke found that marks on the Taung child were identical to the marks that modern African eagles leave on the bones of *their* prey. The Taung child was no doubt the prey of a very large and very strong extinct eagle.

Two million years ago, the Taung child was no doubt the prey of a large eagle. (C. Rudloff, redrawn from Zihlman 2000)

The most exciting fossils of early *true* humans—individuals who can be classified in our own genus, *Homo*—were uncovered beneath a medieval town called Dmanisi in the Republic of Georgia within the past few years. Besides astounding the world of science with the age of *Homo* specimens found *outside* of Africa—a whopping 1.75 million years old!—the remains of six individuals include another verification of hominids as prey.[11] Again, telltale round holes were found in one of the skulls. This time saber-toothed cat fangs fit neatly and perfectly into the two punctures.

David Lordkipanidze is the Georgian scientist who worked the Dmanisi site. He has speculated that simple chopping and scraping tools unearthed with the fossils may indicate that these ancient humans sometimes scavenged off kills of the big cats. The idea of early hominids as scavengers, rather than the more traditional vignette of humans as big-game hunters, also has been advanced by Pat Shipman at Johns Hopkins University. Shipman suggests that Man the Scavenger is not nearly as attractive an image as Man the Hunter, but hominid-made cut marks that overlay carnivore-made tooth marks occur on the same fossil bones.[12]

We propose that a choice lies not between *hunting* man and *scavenging* man at all—the reality is more likely that *hunted* man took advantage of predator kills. Recent research by John Cavallo suggests that early hominids (adults, at least) were able to protect themselves from predators fairly capably during the daylight hours. But when nightfall came, it was a different story altogether. Leopards, especially, ruled the night. Early hominids may have been in competition with leopards to scavenge tree-stored kills during the day, while they themselves became leopard prey at night.[13]

If we look at the behavior of other primates today, such as baboons, we see the same phenomenon of day–night shifts in primate–predator clashes. Male savanna baboons bare their teeth and rush at predators during the day. Actually, there are even quite a few cases in which male baboons have killed predators. Out of eleven aggressive retaliations against leopards by baboons that are written up in scientific papers, the leopard was killed in four instances. One scientist even observed a single dominant male baboon maim or kill four large dogs when they attacked his troop.[14]

But baboons retreat to trees and cliffs at night where they are virtually helpless after dark to protect themselves and their young when lions or leopards are on the prowl. After primatologist Curt Busse switched to nocturnal observations in his study of baboon populations at Moremi, Botswana, he saw an entirely different picture of primate defensive skills. Based on night observation hours during which Busse followed the screams of his terrified baboon subjects, he calculated that at least 8% of the baboon population was killed annually due to predation by lions and leopards.[15]

PREDATION AND PRIMATE STUDIES

Busse feels strongly that primatologists may get a skewed and misinformed representation of predation by studying primate behavior and ecology only during daylight hours. To accomplish an accurate appraisal of predation, Busse has challenged his fellow researchers to make significant changes in field methods, such as including night observations, as well as studies of the predators of primates (along with the primates themselves).

Predation is acknowledged to be an issue of fundamental importance in the study of primates. However, while predation has been discussed in broad theoretical terms, little quantified data have existed on the subject. There has been little attempt to recruit research carried out on various predators as an aid to understanding the impact of predation on primates. In this book we have combined the research of primatologists with the findings of their colleagues who study large and small predatory mammals, raptors, and reptiles to assemble both empirical and anecdotal overviews of primate deaths due to predation. Perhaps combining these data may sound like a natural, very standard process. However, the multidisciplinary approach had not been extended previously to merge the world of primatology with the world of predator research. When we did combine data from both primatologists and predator researchers, we found that a clear picture emerged of primates as prey.

Current examples of predation on primates can be used to infer the rates of predation on our hominid ancestors. Because paleoanthropologists have been unaware of the extent of predation on living primates, they have tended to analyze hominid fossils and construct theories without integrating predation as an important factor in human adaptations.[16] Some of the past analyses of fossil assemblages require reinterpretation using this approach.

AN ACCURATE APPRAISAL OF PREDATION

A continuing academic debate concerns whether primates, in general, are important as prey species. Furthermore, the debate has now entered into the scientific literature on hominid evolution. Our premise is that primates, including early humans, have been the prey of many carnivores, reptiles, and even birds of prey and that being *hunted* is integral to our hominid lineage. In this book we propose that much of human evolution has to do with the fact that we—along with other primates—are prey species.

This aspect of human evolution and its implications for modern humans is a controversial departure from more traditional theories. We are not the first nor the only ones to arrive at this theory. Well-known paleoanthropologists have drawn the same conclusions as we have about early humans and predation, for example C. K. Brain, Lewis Binford, and Matt Cartmill.[17] (Brain, in fact, coined the phrase "Man the Hunted.") But combining the fossil evidence regarding levels of predation on early hominids with comparisons to predation on living primates has not yet been done. By merging the two kinds of evidence, we hope to accomplish a long-overdue synthesis of the theory we call Man the Hunted.

Our theory on human evolution is based on the only two sources of information there are—fossil evidence and living primates. We will present the case for a radically different view of human prehistory, one that places us squarely in the animal kingdom as a smallish bipedal (walking on two legs) primate without many defenses except a brain that was being stimulated to increase slowly in size. We will present the evidence for predation as an evolutionary force, a force that may well have been one of the prime stimulators to that increase of brain and even to our need to stay in groups and be a social animal. *Not* getting killed is a powerful force to deal with each day—it stimulates evolutionary adaptations that no scientist or layperson ever questions, such as the swiftness of the gazelle and the protective armor of the turtle. Why then would it not have as deep an impact on a smallish bipedal primate?

Our contention is that for 7–10 million years of hominid evolution, predators were a factor shaping evolution—and remnants of those predator-prey interactions still occur. They occur where "civilization" has not swathed the landscape in asphalt and concrete, preceded by a century of purposeful extermination of predators. And they occur psychologically every time we feel the primitive chill up our spines because one of our species has succumbed to a wild animal.

2

DEBUNKING
"MAN THE HUNTER"

Why are we the way we are? What makes us think and act the way we do? Birds fly and snakes slither because they must. What are we impelled to do? Well, humans walk upright, they verbalize language, and they manipulate their environment to suit their needs. But did we start out with those legacies or did they come slowly over time? Yes, most birds fly, but the ancestors of birds were probably terrestrial dinosaurs. Snakes slither, but the skeletal remnants of hind legs are found in primitive snakes. Considering these strange and drastic developments over time in other animals, we might well question in what state of nature we humans may have started out. To look generally at our past and specifically at our position in the food chain—predator or prey?—we need to study our roots; we need to get down to the very beginnings of the first steps on the human path.

The evolution of our species—*Homo sapiens*—is a story told in fits and starts, through new fossil discoveries and breaking headline news. *Missing Link Found* is often the lead in any media report about new findings in our hominid line. The "missing link" has not yet been found and is—in scientific terms—a quite inappropriate term. *Missing Common Ancestor of Chimps and Humans Found* would be the correct (but not nearly as generally exciting) headline that would stun the world of paleontology. That would be *the* find! The one sought by every researcher who spends years raising research money through grant-writing and then years more painstakingly grubbing in out-of-the-way locations for fossils—the elusive creature at mile-marker zero of our evolutionary highway whose progeny took two different forks in the road. One road led to modern chimpanzees and one led to modern humans. In no way did "we" (modern humans) pass through a stage in which we were chimpanzees. The chimps are as modern in their approach to life in the trees of tropical Africa as we are in our two-legged wandering all over the earth.

The question that drives paleo-detectives to distraction is *when* did that fork in the road appear?

First, a cautionary disclaimer. As has been the case with every volume published that contains theories of where, when, and what constituted our beginnings, this chapter may be overridden by a new discovery of a fossil hominid that changes the whole story line once again. One irrefutable statement, though, is that our hominid lineage begins much farther back in geologic time than science estimated a decade ago. Even in the 1990s, 4-million-year-old petrified remains were considered close to the seminal divergence from a common ancestor with chimps. Now, six-to-seven-million-year-old fossils have been discovered in the African nations of Chad and Kenya. Newly discovered finds appear to be hominid species that lived sometime after the chimpanzee and the human lines diverged from a common ancestor because they show evidence of upright walking, or bipedalism—which is a trait of humans but not of chimpanzees.

It is only fair to state that the oldest known hominid fossils have their detractors. The major controversy revolves around whether the fossil remains do indeed indicate bipedality, which is the initial and singular characteristic most indicative of hominid lineage. Pelvis, knee, and leg bones will answer this question quite nicely, but what if those are not among the retrieved remnants of long-deceased kin? Well, if cranial (skull) bones are found, one of the indicators of bipedality is the placement of the foramen magnum, the large hole at the base of the skull through which the spinal cord attaches to the brain. Picture how the back and head of a quadrupedal animal—like a horse for example—is oriented; the spine is on a horizontal plane so the foramen magnum, the entryway to the brain, is positioned high up on the back of the skull. Now visualize a bipedal animal whose spine is on a vertical plane; the foramen magnum is located as far down on the base of the skull as possible. Currently, it is the sense of the anthropology community that the fossils we will discuss here imply *obligate* bipedal hominids; in other words, they had upright bodies and hips that made bipedal striding the most comfortable form of locomotion and this necessitated the placement of the foramen magnum at the bottom of the skull.

WILL THE FIRST HOMINID PLEASE STAND UP?

Asking for the identity of the first hominid should be an easy entreaty, right? We just mentioned that upright walking was the litmus test of human ancestors. But, even the technical categorization of a hominid has now become more enigmatic than a few years past. Taxonomists—the scientists who immerse themselves in Latin nomenclature to classify species and devise the relationships of all living creatures one to another—have added another layer of stupefaction. First, all monkeys, apes, and humans are primates—that's a given. The latest taxonomic blueprints, however, group orangutans, gorillas, chimpanzees (that is, all the so-called great apes), and humans in the same taxonomic family—designated by the Latin term *Hominidae* (commonly anglicized to "hominid"). Gorillas, chimps, and humans are subsequently grouped together within the same *sub*family level. Why? Because, currently, based on DNA similarities, it is only at the descending level of our genus—*Homo*—that taxonomists can separate our genetic building blocks from our ape relatives.

Despite total acceptance of this powerful DNA evidence, we realize that the new blueprint, combining humans and apes into one taxonomic family, exponentially increases the bewildering jungle of taxonomy. So, for the sake of ease in reference to our subject matter and to avoid potential esoterica as much as possible, we will continue throughout this book to employ a more conventional approach and distinguish as *hominids* only those species that diverged from the human-ape stem some 7–10 million years ago and were bipedal. The alternative is repeatedly to identify forerunners to modern humans by their individual Latin names (*Australopithecus, Paranthropus, Kenyanthropus, Ardipithecus, Orrorin,* and

Sahelanthropus), a decision that would cause this book to be much longer than intended.

Some of those Latin monikers may sound familiar and some are so new they are just entering the most recent editions of college textbooks on hominid evolution. We'll start with *Sahelanthropus tchadensis* (not a name that exactly ripples off the tongue, but a celebrity nonetheless) because it is the oldest fossil hominid so far discovered. What makes it a paleontologist's dream—and nightmare simultaneously—is that its existence stretches our human history back to between 6 and 7 million years, while at the same time refuting a slew of theories concerning the location and habitat of hominid origins.

Nicknamed *Toumai*, or "hope of life" in the local Goran language of the Djurab Desert, the fossil was unearthed in the African nation of Chad. *Sahelanthropus* is represented by a cranium, a jaw fragment, and several teeth. It was found in 2001 by a team of French and Tchadian paleoanthropolgists led by Michel Brunet of the University of Poitiers and his colleague Djimdoumalbaye Ahounta. The landlocked equatorial nation of Chad is bounded on the north by Libya, on the south by the Central African Republic, on the east by Sudan, and on the west by Niger, Nigeria, and Cameroon. As is apparent from the geographic description, Chad's location is smack in the center of Africa. The discovery of *Toumai* was a bit like finding medieval Christian artifacts in the middle of Australia. Fascinating, but how can you reconcile it with traditional theories? And traditional theory had it that Central Africa is a peculiar place to find hominid fossils because it is the "wrong" side of the Rift Valley.

The Great Rift Valley, which stretches from Mozambique in the south up through Ethiopia in the north, is a monstrous gash in the East African landscape. If you are peacefully driving north from Nairobi, Kenya, to Lake Nakuru National Park, at one point you will see an innocuous 12-by-12-inch sign that reads, "Beware the Escarpment." Before you have time to think what that decorous command may imply, you are hurtling over the edge of the Great Rift Valley on a switchback road that seems to angle downward at 45 degrees. Below you lies the valley, stretching endlessly and shimmering in the dry heat. Until the excavations in Chad, all of the earliest hominid fossils have been found on the east side of the Rift Valley (Ethiopia, Kenya, and Tanzania to be specific). One neat, and now retired, theory stated that when chimps and hominids evolved from their common ancestor, the chimp line stayed in the trees of the forested region to the west of the Rift Valley and the hominids began—successfully and bipedally—to colonize the drier savannas of the east. This ceased to be a viable theory when hominid fossils started popping up in places on the west side of the Rift, like Chad.

The Great Rift Valley of East Africa is shaded. To date, only two early hominid fossils have been found west of the Rift Valley. (C. Rudloff)

As often happens behind closed doors, when the startling fossil description of *Toumai* was published in *Nature* in July 2002, pundits tended to remark something on the order of "It'd be better if they had covered it back up!"—echoing the frustration of fitting this new piece into the paleo puzzle. And who is to say that fossils are not to be found in other unexamined areas of interest to anthropologists. For instance, Malawi in southeastern Africa, said to lie in a "hominid corridor" between the fossil-rich eastern and southern regions of the continent, has been tossed out as a fresh, new location to investigate for ancient hominid bones.

The second oldest of the hominid finds (represented by the thigh bone, teeth, and lower jaw of an individual estimated to have lived 6 million years ago) startled the world of anthropology likewise. French researchers Brigette Senut and Martin Pickford discovered *Orrorin tugenensis* (called "Millennium Man" because of the relic's unveiling at the dawn of the new age) in the Tugen Hills, Baringo region of Kenya. Senut and Pickford had only a short interval to revel in finding the 6-million-year-old fossil and publishing their findings before the more ancient *Toumai* from Chad was stealing the show.

As we work our way forward over the millions of years from the beginning of smallish bipedal beings to the present, another character in the geologic drama walked on stage. We next encounter *Ardithpithecus ramidus* ("ardi" meaning ground and "ramid" translating as root in the local Afar language), unearthed in Ethiopia in 1993 by Tim White and Alemayehu Asfaw. This was the first of the excavated hominid remains in excess of 4 million years of age. Bones and teeth of 17 individuals, while highly fragmentary, have been dated at 4.4–5.8 million years ago and a new find of the same species, measured at 5.2–5.8 million years, confirms the great age of this hominid.

Having briefly glanced at these three hominids who we know lived approximately 6 million years or more prior to the present, let's continue meandering through the various life-forms that preceded our own species. Meave Leakey of the famous Leakey clan of paleoanthropologists *par excellence*—we'll talk about her husband's, father-in-law's, and mother-in-law's stunning discoveries a little later—found *Kenyanthropus platyops* (this translates as "flat-faced Kenyan man") in the area of Lake Turkana where the Great Rift Valley exits northern Kenya. The emphatically vertical plane of this fossil face motivated Leakey to suggest *K. platyops* as a direct ancestor to modern humans. (Jutting jaws are considered a trademark of those hominids less likely to be in the direct human ancestry; flat faces are more "human-like.") *K. platyops* represents a 3.5-million-year-old skull from what Leakey claims may be an entirely new branch of the early human tree.[1]

All the extinct hominid species we have described so far preceded the legendary "Lucy" (a.k.a. *Australopithecus afarensis*) found in Ethiopia by Donald Johanson in 1974. Lucy is a hominid fossil with personality. Her discovery was celebrated in the field with a rollicking party that boomed pop music through the desert night. She was named after the Beatles' song "Lucy in the Sky with Diamonds," and Johanson and his colleagues truly rock 'n' rolled the world of science when they presented the nearly complete post-cranial (below the skull) skeleton of a young female hominid who lived 3.2 million years ago. Lucy is thought to have stood upright at 3 and one-half feet (males of her species may have been as much as a foot taller). She was bipedal but had long feet with an exceptionally powerful big toe that was divergent like our modern human thumbs and could be used to grasp and climb trees. She may have exploited the forest fringes, using those grasping toes to evade predators by shinnying up a tree.

Two relatives of Lucy left their footprints in newly fallen ash at another spot in East Africa called Laetoli (these immortalized footfalls constitute another Leakey family find—Mary, the family matriarch, this time). A pair of australopithecines, possibly male and female from the difference in how their respective weights imprinted the ash, were walking side by side over 3 million years ago. Their footprints give a tantalizingly personal nature to australopithecines as individuals. Where were these two going? Were they a mated pair? What might they have been leaving or going toward on their journey?

A "robust" relative of Lucy (*Paranthropus boisei*) had been discovered at Olduvai Gorge in Tanzania by the incomparable first-generation husband-and-wife team of fossil-hunting Leakeys—Louis and Mary—in the 1960s. The "robust" appellation doesn't refer to any gigantic stature of the prehistoric hominid but to the incredibly large jaws and huge molars possessed by this particular branch of the family tree, making them capable of grinding hard, fibrous plant material. Another robust species of early hominid was

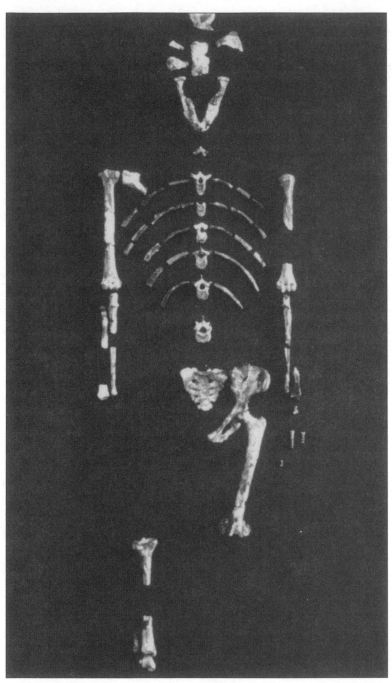

Lucy—the fossil skeleton of a young female hominid who lived 3.2 million years ago. (Used by permission of Institute of Human Origins)

found by Richard Leakey (son of Louis and Mary), who is not only a world-renowned paleoanthropologist but a giant in the field of wildlife conservation and the Kenyan political scene. The younger Leakey commenced a dig at Lake Turkana, Kenya, and disinterred the famous "Black Skull." This mineral-stained cranium is the most extreme example of the robust branches on the family tree found so far. Although no teeth accompanied the Black Skull, it's estimated that the molars for this individual were four to five times the size of a modern human's teeth.

The elder Leakeys also discovered the earliest member of our own genus, *Homo habilis* (baptized "handy man," although a penchant for dreary labor hardly seems the case for any of the Olduvai residents). Evidence in the form of simple stone tools at the gorge left clues of this early human who lived about 2.3 million years ago.

During our whirlwind tour of early hominids we must not forget the very first of the African hominid fossils to be discovered—the one that *should* have thrown the world of anthropology into a tailspin in 1924 but didn't. Raymond Dart, a young anatomy professor at the University of Witwatersrand in Johannesburg, South Africa, had issued a standing request to the foreman at a limestone quarry called Taung (the Setswana word for "place of the lion") to bring him anything that might be a fossil. When Dart gleefully utilized his wife's knitting needles to chip the breccia (cemented limestone, sand, and bone) off a putative fossil, the brain and face of a young (but obviously not human) toddler appeared—the "Taung child" (*Australopithecus africanus*)—and the modern era of paleoanthropology began. Until Dart's breakthrough, the human lineage was assumed to have been European or Asian in origin. None other than Charles Darwin had suggested that the African residence of gorillas and chimpanzees might be the key to human evolution, but great skepticism greeted all who thought of African human origins during the racist colonial nineteenth and early twentieth centuries.

This might be a good time to mention that there has always been a lot at stake in concepts of human ancestors—more than objective science, more than impartial pursuit of truth. Especially in the late 1800s and early years of the twentieth century, we—humans and our ancestors—had to be on the top of the species heap. We had to be the smartest species. We had to be special and powerful and above other animals. And very importantly, humans had to be ranked in a hierarchy of races with European humans at the apex. With the development of

the theory of evolution through natural selection, Darwin put humans in their place with the rest of the animal kingdom, subject to the same laws of nature. However, in so doing, even Darwin visualized a spiritual and intellectual gap between humans and their closest living relatives, the apes. As he stated: "There can be no doubt that the difference between the mind of the lowest man and that of the highest animal is immense."[2] What separated the biology and behavior of all humans from other animals was the presence of a large brain. Late nineteenth-century theorists took the amount of gray matter residing in our modern brains as the truly "human" aspect and looked for early human fossils that fit the big-brained expectations.

Slipping forward past the tangled morass of inchoate relatives, our evolutionary tale gets a little clearer with what may be an immediate predecessor of modern humans, *Homo erectus*. In 1891 this early representative of our genus, initially known as Java Man, was stumbled upon by a Dutch physician named Eugene Dubois who was stationed in Indonesia on military duty. He thought the island of Java was a logical place to look for fossils since Asia at that time was hypothesized to be a possible site of origin for the human species. Later in the 1920s more *H. erectus* fossils were found in a cave outside of Beijing, China.

Java Man was an acceptable human ancestor to the late Victorian fossil hunters—certainly more than anything from Africa—but nothing would be as satisfying as a European origin for humanity. The English scientific establishment found what it desired in "Piltdown Man." In 1912 an amateur fossil hunter discovered pieces of a cranium and jaw in England. The greatest men in British science put the puzzle pieces together and marveled over the extremely large brain case combined with a primitive jaw. This was hard to explain, but explain it they did in a burst of chauvinistic pride. Their explanation? Encephalization (increase in brain size) was the forerunner for all other hominid features in ancient Europeans.

As with all scientific shrines built on ideology alone, this one had a spurious foundation. About 40 years later, it was revealed that Piltdown Man was an utter hoax. If practical jokes were awarded the Nobel Prize, than surely Piltdown's perpetrator deserves the honor. The best minds in the field of anthropology did not recognize that the wonderfully brainy fossil was an amalgamation of a modern orangutan jaw and a modern human skull, both stained to look ancient.

A Messy Bush

You may at this point have a surreal feeling of drowning in names, places, and millions of years . . . of sinking down, down, down into a bottomless pool of *anthropus*—this and *pithecus*—that . . . and, omigosh, we've still got millions of years to go! You have every right to suffer the headache of how untidily complex our family tree is growing; you are not alone—the experts are often just as confounded by the constantly fluctuating nature of this branch of science.

Ian Tattersall of the American Museum of Natural History has been a prestigious fixture in the analysis of paleoanthropological finds for several decades. So when Tattersall suggests the need for a mental paradigm shift concerning our hominid past, people tend to listen. There has been a tendency to portray the human ancestral line in a neat linear diagram—one early hominid with primitive features slowly evolving into a more human-like successor and so on and so on.

Tattersall, instead, sees our hominid past as that of a messy bush—branches and twigs sprouting in all directions. That is, he sees in the fossil record a great diversity of hominid species, many of them living at the same time, if not in the same place. The human "family bush" contains many dead ends—extinctions—mostly because of environmental changes. In fact, extinctions are the rule rather than the exception, with the result that there is only one hominid—modern humans—alive today.

Another eminent authority, Bernard Wood of George Washington University, postulates that the ancient fossils being found now in Chad and other places are just the tip of the metaphorical iceberg. He thinks that fossil ape-like creatures were diverse and prolific—and that there will be evidence of wide proliferation of numerous ape-like creatures, including the common ancestor of humans and chimps, in a bewildering array that cannot be imagined today.[3]

And on the messy bush occurs one branch that managed to survive as the only still-living hominid—anatomically modern humans. As Tattersall eloquently states: "In pondering our history as human beings we should never forget that we are simply the sole surviving twig on this ramifying bush, rather than the products of a slow, steady, and single-minded process of perfection."[4] Where did all the other branches on the messy hominid bush go? Smallish, bipedal primates came and went for possibly 7–10 million years. Some were successful—consider the 1-million-year-plus reign of *H. erectus*—but nothing in our history points to a starring role for one branch over another. A fascinating question that science ponders endlessly is why so much diversity existed in our past and yet now only one hominid species inhabits the earth.

WANDERLUST

One last example of how important it is to keep a flexible attitude toward our ancestors involves our eventual exit from Africa. Previous to 2002 it was accepted as fact that no hominid emigrated from Africa until we arrive at the relatively large-brained direct predecessor to humans, *Homo erectus*. As mentioned earlier, *H. erectus* fossils have been found in China and Indonesia for over a century. The large leap in cranial capacity between *H. habilis* (the first known member of our genus) and *H. erectus* is substantial: a jump from under 700 to over 1,000 cubic centimeters (cc) of brain mass. The length of the leg bones and, therefore, of walking stride between the short-limbed *H. habilis* and the long-legged *H. erectus* is also significant.

In an example of the exciting and unpredictable twists and turns in the world of paleoanthropology, *habilis*-like fossils were recently uncovered in the Republic of Georgia, overturning the theory that hominids stayed put in Africa, the continent of origin, until *H. erectus'* long strides and larger brain carried him/her out sometime after 1.75 million years ago.[5]

At some point the size of the brain must have reached a critical mass that enabled more and more manipulation of the environment through complex communication and tool making. At such a point it seems feasible that early humans would begin their colonization of the world. Nevertheless, the pioneers who traveled thousands of miles to decidedly different biomes may have been small, short-legged hominids with cranial capacities of 680 cc. Hardly the imagined progenitor of our human wanderlust.

Man the Hunter?

The question "Why is man man?" has been posed since literal biblical origins gave way to scientific inquiries. "Because man evolved as a meat eater" is one answer to the question. Robert Ardrey stated in one of his series of immensely popular books of the 1970s, *The Hunting Hypothesis*:

> If among all the members of our primate family the human being is unique, even in our noblest aspirations, it is because we alone through untold millions of years were continuously dependent on killing to survive.[6]

There are several misconceptions included in this proposal of human hunting singularity. First, we are not the only primate that hunts for living prey. Hunting is a common feeding strategy throughout the primate order. Baboons are adept at capturing infant antelope; chimpanzees, especially, excel in hunting and eating monkeys. Even different methods and approaches toward hunting have been observed in different chimpanzee populations. At Jane Goodall's field site, Gombe Reserve in Tanzania, the male chimps hunt as lions do—the more individuals involved the greater the success rate, but no coordinated team effort is manifested. In the Tai Forest of Côte d'Ivoire the chimps hunt like wolves, each individual playing a key role in a team effort.[7]

Whether hunting could have been the main food-procurement venture for early hominids is also subject to anatomical constraints. We need to look carefully at teeth and digestive systems, the critical parts of human anatomy that lend themselves to answers about early hominid dependence on hunted meat. Intestines do not fossilize, but teeth make up a good portion of the fossil remains of australopithecines and their dentition is not that of a carnivore.

So, where did the Man the Hunter idea come from? When did the certitude that humans were too busy *killing* to *be killed* arise? Who were the proponents of the myth of fierce and dangerous hominids? When you consider the reality, what a public-relations coup!—a fangless, clawless, smallish bipedal primate gets a reputation for being Godzilla wielding an antelope jawbone!

Raymond Dart with his discovery, the Taung child, the first of many early hominid fossils to be found in Africa. Dart initially described this fossil in 1924. (F. Herholdt)

In some sense the Taung child is the key to the Man the Hunter theme. Taung child was the first fossil in a series of australopithecine finds. It is somewhat ironic that Raymond Dart's painstaking reclamation of this fossil—probably the young victim of a predator—was so instrumental in creating a trend toward "killer-ape" status for human ancestors.

To view the inception of Man the Hunter's forceful accession and acceptance, we need to go back and fill in the people who inhabited the rather small and esoteric world of paleoanthropology in the 1920s. As emphasized earlier, Africa was not then the important arena for fossil humans. The English had their Piltdown Man, reassuring the white European experts that large brains came before flat faces. The Neanderthal finds in Europe were augmented by Java Man and Peking Man from the Far East. What did it matter if an obscure anatomy professor in South Africa had found a skull and fossilized brain that didn't look like a chimp but whose brain was way, way too small to be considered human?

In the atmosphere of the day it is no wonder that the Piltdown Man, with its ape-like jaw and large cranium, was immediately accepted as the earliest hominid ancestor, while the small-skulled, ape-like australopithecine discovered by Raymond Dart was considered a pathological specimen or a mere ape. While Piltdown supporters were busy explaining the intellectual endowments of our large-brained ancestors, Dart was convinced his small-brained creature was the first ape-man, and he developed a theoretical picture of the behavior of this transitional form. At first Dart believed that australopithecines were scavengers barely eking out an existence in the harsh savanna environment; a primate that did not live to kill large animals but scavenged small animals in order to live.

Few cared what Dart believed, however, because few took his ape-man seriously. In fact it was not until a quarter of a century later, with the unearthing of many more australopithecines and the discovery in 1953 that Piltdown was a fraud, that students of human evolution realized our earliest ancestors were more ape-like than they were modern-human-like. This led to a great interest in using primates to understand human evolution and the evolutionary basis of human nature.[8] With these discoveries began a long list of theories attempting to re-create the behavior and often the basic morality of the earliest hominids.

By 1950 Dart had developed a wholly new and different view from his former scavenger model. His ponderings about strange depressions in the crania of fossil australopithecines eventually flowered into a full-blown theory about killers who murdered their own kind. Given the game animals with which australopithecine fossils were associated and the dents and holes in the skulls of the australopithecines themselves, Dart became convinced that the mammals had been killed, butchered, and eaten by the ape-men, and that these early hominids had even been killing one another.

Dart once believed that the australopithecines had been forced to scratch out a meager existence on the savanna once they abandoned the trees of the African forest. But Dart now saw that hunting, and a carnivorous lust for blood, actively drew man-apes out of the forest and were together a main force in human evolution. He stated more than once that "the ancestors of *Australopithecus* left their fellows in the trees of Central Africa through a spirit of adventure and the more attractive fleshy food that lay in the vast savannas of the southern plains."[9] Dart was himself influenced by a University of London professor, Carveth Read, who suggested in 1925 that human ancestors were similar to wolves; they hunted in packs and lived off the meat of large game. Read suggested that the name *Lycopithecus* (literally, "wolf-ape") would be descriptive of early hominids.

The discovery of baboon skulls mysteriously bashed in on the left side of the skull inspired Dart to conclude that only the australopithecine ancestor of humans could have killed with such precision. Since no stone weapons or tools were found in the South African sites, Dart postulated that the unusually high frequency of thigh bones and jawbones from antelopes must have been the weapons of choice. His "osteodontokeratic" culture—that early man had used the bones, teeth, and horns of his prey to kill even more prey—provided the means by which these killer apes accomplished their bloody work.

In 1953 Dart published a paper entitled "The Predatory Transition from Ape to Man." In it he hypothesized that the dentition and geography of australopithecines precluded any type of diet other than heavy reliance on meat. And not only did they eat meat but they armed themselves with weapons to hunt large prey. None of the well-known journals would accept the article, so readership within the scientific community was sparse. Robert Ardrey, a successful playwright, visited Dart in South Africa and was convinced that this theory would revolutionize the science of anthropology. Ardrey spent 5 years between 1955 and 1960

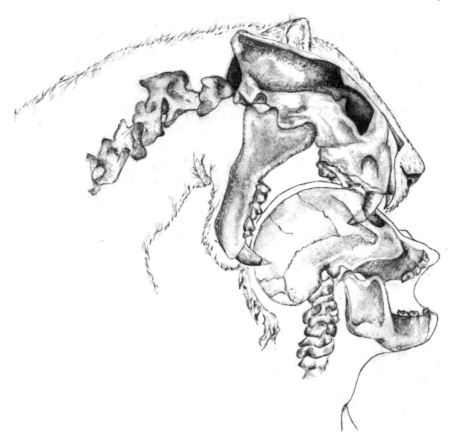

Holes in the skulls of some early hominid fossils match perfectly with big cat fangs. (C. Rudloff, redrawn from Cavallo 1991)

researching and writing *African Genesis*—a popular account of our beginnings as killer apes.[10] The book was a best-seller and had tremendous influence both on the general public and the scientific community.

By the mid-1970s Dart's claim that a hominid with a brain no larger than our ape cousins expertly fashioned weapons and went on the hunt because it was easier than scavenging was fully accepted. But, Dart's *evidence* for Man the Hunter was not good, and his particular vision of the human hunter/killer hypothesis did not stand up to rigorous scrutiny. C. K. Brain, a South African specialist in how fossils are formed by natural forces, was skeptical of the baboon-killing theory from the first. Upon examination of the evidence, Brain noted that the bones associated with the man-apes were exactly like fragments left by leopards and hyenas.[11] He saw the holes in the baboon skulls and the similar indentations in *A. africanus* as oddly similar to the tooth patterns of living African carnivores. He set about measuring the distance between the lower canines of African big cats and found that the space between the lower fangs of leopards fit precisely into the fossil skull holes.

Round holes that match perfectly with fangs of leopards. It seems that the australopithecines were likely the hunted and not the hunters. Fossil bones of early hominid origin were found with baboon remains in South African cave excavations at Swartkrans, Kromdraii, and Sterkfontein, places that have become famous for their australopithecine remains.[12] Brain hypothesized that baboons and early hominids slept in caves, providing an excellent opportunity for leopards to kill them and drag the carcasses farther into the caves for feeding.[13] The Mt. Suswa lava caves in Kenya provide a current analogy to the paleontological record in South Africa and lend significant credibility to the hypotheses. Mt. Suswa is a favorite sleeping site for baboons, and leopards in the area subsist almost entirely on these primates.[14]

MAN THE DANCER!

The next widely accepted version of the recurring Man the Hunter theme was presented in the late 1960s by Sherwood Washburn (the father of American field primatology) and his colleagues. They claimed that many of the features that define *men* as hunters (more about why the other 50% of the species was not defined will be discussed later in this book) again separated the earliest humans from their primate relatives.

> To assert the biological unity of mankind is to affirm the importance of the
> hunting way of life. It is to claim that, however much conditions and cus-
> toms may have varied locally, the main selection pressures that forged the
> species were the same. The biology, psychology, and customs that separate
> us from the apes—these we owe to the hunters of time past. And, for those
> who would understand the origin and nature of human behavior there is no
> choice but to try to understand "Man the Hunter."[15]

Like Dart, Washburn related human hunting to human morality, both of which had their biological basis in our evolutionary past. What he

Using the nineteenth-century anthropological concept of cultural survivals, "Man the Dancer" explains early hominid behavior just as well as does "Man the Hunter." (C. Rudloff)

termed the "carnivorous psychology" of the australopithecines resulted in a human species that takes pleasure not just in the chasing, hunting, and killing of other animals, but in dark depredations on fellow humans. The public spectacles of torture and suffering in "most" cultures are for the *enjoyment* of all humans. This interpretation led him to the conclusion that only careful *un*training of our natural drives can lay a veneer of compassion for others on top of naturally human "carnivorous curiosity and aggression."[16]

Again, much like Dart before him, Washburn did not amass a large amount of evidence to support his theory and seemed to have recognized that evidence to the contrary existed.[17] Rather, he relied upon a nineteenth-century anthropological concept of cultural "survivals."[18] These are

behaviors that are no longer useful in society but that persist as leftover survival mechanisms from a time when they *were* adaptive. Washburn saw a
connection between the ease with which modern sports (including hunting)
are learned and the pleasures they confer, and the survival mechanisms of a
bygone age. Because successful ancestral humans were those who hunted
best, their genetic legacy is an easy and pleasurable acquisition of hunting-
like behaviors.[19]

Using a similar logic, we have developed an alternative (sarcastic,
yes—but no less feasible) theory to challenge Man the Hunter. We call
our theory "Man the Dancer." After all, men *and* women love to dance,
it is a behavior found in all cultures, and it has less obvious function in
most cultures than does hunting.

Although it takes two to tango, a variety of social systems could develop from various types of dance: square dancing, line dancing,
riverdance, or the funky chicken. The footsteps at Laetoli might not represent two individuals going out for a hunt but the Afarensis shuffle, one
of the earliest dances. In the movie *2001: A Space Odyssey*, it was wrong
to depict the first tool as a weapon. It could easily have been a drumstick,
and the first battle may not have involved killing at all but a battle of the
bands. Other things such as face-to-face sex, cooperation, language and
singing, and bipedalism (it's difficult to dance on all fours), even moving
out of the trees and onto the ground might all be better explained by our
propensity to dance than by our desire to hunt. Although we are being
facetious with our Man the Dancer hypothesis, the evidence for dancing
is certainly as good and no more preposterous than that for hunting.

WE WERE NOT "CAT FOOD"!

Between 1961 and 1976, the playwright Robert Ardrey popularized the
then-current version of the Man the Hunter myth with a number of
best-sellers. Ardrey believed that it was the competitive spirit, as acted
out in warfare, that made humans what they are today: "the mentality of
the single Germanic tribe under Hitler differed in no way from that of
early man or late baboon." Because of a lack of a competitive territorial
instinct, gorillas—Ardrey believed—had lost the will to live and with it
the drive for sex. He argued that gorillas defend no territory and copulate

rarely. And their story "will end, one day, not with a bang but with a whimper."[20]

African Genesis may well have been the starting point for the public popularity of Man the Hunter, but the prominence brought to paleo-anthropology by the patriarch of the Leakey family was the strong suit that clinched the public's acceptance. The great Dr. Louis S. B. Leakey, a larger-than-life personality, was the premier paleoanthropologist of the mid-twentieth century and the personification of the fossil-hunting field scientist. His dynamic personality and exciting ideas took the quest for human origins to the heights of media coverage, catching the public's imagination. Inquiring minds finally *did* want to know about our origins! Along with his wife, Mary, who accomplished much of the actual discovery and reconstruction of the fossils, the Leakeys became worldwide celebrities. From their home base at the Kenya Museum of Natural History, they made Olduvai Gorge in Tanzania synonymous with human origins. Leakey also gave the world an eventual look at our closest relatives through his support for Jane Goodall's research on chimpanzees, Dian Fossey's work on mountain gorillas, and Birute Galdikas' study of orangutans. He was particularly thrilled when Goodall identified hunting and meat-eating in chimpanzees.

And Leakey's endorsement of Man the Hunter gave it the academic credentials that Ardrey's popular books lacked. In a famous defense of Man the Hunter as fearless and bellicose, Leakey stated that we were *not* "cat food," and the ramification was a change in perception of human origins for the entire Western world.[21]

The designation of early humans as Man the Hunter rapidly attained axiomatic status. Our ancestry as fearless hunters and remorseless killers of our own and other species has been the generally accepted perception now for nearly 50 years. And not just the layperson, but academics as well, fall easily into using this paradigm. Here's a common example from an evolutionary psychologist, Charles Crawford of Simon Fraser University in Burnaby, British Columbia. Crawford lamented in an arti-cle about human evolutionary adaptations gone awry in modern times: "I used to hunt saber-toothed tigers all the time, thousands of years ago. Now I sit in front of a computer and don't get exercise."[22]

We think it's time to put this particular myth to rest. Tweaking Charles Crawford's theme, our hominid ancestors probably got plenty of exercise from desperately trying to *avoid* saber-toothed cats, not from blatantly suicidal attempts to hunt them. Instead of Man the Hunter, we contend that Man the Hunted is a more accurate snapshot. For smallish bipedal primates, we envision a whole host of predators were licking their chops with anticipation.

WHO'S EATING WHOM?

3

One thing's for certain: there's nothing in a Stephen King novel that will beat the gruesomeness out there in the archives of the print media. It was quickly apparent as we gathered material for this book that entire volumes could be filled with gory exploits of man-eaters garnered from newspapers and magazines around the world. These bloody events are commonly given high profile in newspapers, and they often make the front page in a city that is thousands of miles from the predation itself. For example, "India Fighting Plague of Man-Eating Wolves," screamed a headline on the front page of *The New York Times* in 1996.[1] Would this situation really be relevant to the average *Times* reader? Or, more precisely, would it be *more* relevant than an article about 300 million citizens in India who suffer from malnutrition (a tragedy which does *not* appear in headlines in New York or anywhere else in the United States)? Certainly, in today's world deaths from car accidents, heart disease, cancer, toxic chemicals in our environment, malnutrition or starvation, and warfare hugely outnumber deaths from predators. Even in areas of the world where predation on humans happens regularly, the paucity of predators compared to ever-expanding human numbers makes the impact of predators on overall human populations miniscule. When current-day predation is posed as a mortality factor to a global population in excess of 6 billion people, the percentage of humans killed by wild animals may not even be worth recording.

So, why the heightened media coverage? Might it be that we are fascinated by a deep recognition of what predation by other species has meant in our long evolutionary history? Hans Kruuk, a famous animal behaviorist and authority on predators, feels that our revulsion, our curiosity, our fascination with gory stories of man-eaters is based on a hardwired instinct that these events are *very* scary to our whole species—scarier than many of the more obvious killers in our midst.[2] After all, we evolved for *millions* of years being hunted and eaten by other animals, but we have only had to fear automobile accidents for 100 years (just a few generations). Tigers, bears, and wolves touch off much deeper neural pathways than Toyotas, Fords, or Volkswagens.

We readily admit that the relative fright levels of certain species of animals versus certain makes of cars might bring up accusations of purely speculative logic. The big question for us as anthropologists is: How do we get past speculation about the long-term evolutionary effects of predation on humans and into the domain of empirical data when the critical epochs in which we are interested were many million of years before historical records? As mentioned earlier, there are only two factual avenues that trace the path of hominid evolution—the fossil record and our closest relatives, the primates. The fossil evidence for predation on our species is pretty impressive, and we will go into detail about it. But first, we'll take a look at primates—our taxonomic cousins—to see if they can shed light on our big question.

A TALE OF TWO FAMILIES

Let's consider two tales of predation: The first appeared in a popular journal called *Asiaweek* in April of 1998.[3] It concerned a mother's nightmare in the Auri district of Garwhal, a region in northern India. This mother was carrying an infant while her other offspring, an 8-year-old, trailed behind. They were making their way home when a leopard came out of the darkness and grabbed the eight-year-old by the leg. The big cat began to pull the child while the mother frantically tried to hold onto the baby and her older youngster's arm. The mother's grip loosened as the leopard pulled them all down an embankment in a macabre tug-of-war.

Shrieking, the mother lost her hold on the child and heard the youngster's cries as she was carried off into the night. The half-eaten body of the 8-year-old subsequently was found under a bush by villagers who tracked the dried bloodstains.

The second tale was told by Walter Baumgartel, a "white hunter" in colonial Africa (specifically in what was then the Belgian Congo).[4] Baumgartel wrote a book containing another description of a family stalked by a leopard. The father was attacked unawares while asleep, but he had tried to fight off the leopard and in so doing had tumbled down a slope. His lifeless body was taken to Makerere Medical School for an autopsy. Two days later, the leopard was found feeding on another member of the family, a youngster. She had been killed in the same fashion as her father with a gash in the groin that severed an artery and, according to medical opinion, had resulted in instant death. Over a period of several months, more bodies from this same family were found, sometimes fresh, sometimes partly decomposed.

The first tale involved *Homo sapiens*. In the second tale, the family was a close relative—the mountain gorilla (*Gorilla gorilla beringei*). These two accounts serve to depict how parallel are predation events of humans and other primates.

We contend that a true understanding of ourselves as prey is enhanced and expanded by how our closest relatives are affected by predation. Our research has established that quantifiable evidence for predation on primates exists, including ample evidence of predation on all of the great apes—gorillas, orangutans, and chimpanzees. Gorillas, a species much larger than modern humans and several times bigger than early hominids, are prey to leopards weighing half as much. Anecdotal data describing leopards preying on gorillas, as our tale above, are supported by current scientific research in Central Africa. Michael Fay, primatologist *cum* conservationist whose daring trek across unknown areas of tropical rain forest recently was featured in *National Geographic*, carried out his dissertation research on lowland gorillas in Nouabalé–Ndoki National Park, Republic of Congo. Pygmies in this area held firmly to the fact that leopards preyed on gorillas (and chimpanzees and humans, also). Mike and his colleagues subsequently published evidence of predation on gorillas. The substantiating evidence they presented were intact gorilla *toes* found in leopard feces—the last remnants of a feline meal.[5] The toes have since been

Leopard scat that contained two gorilla toes was found by researchers in the Central African Republic; one intact toe has been removed from the fecal material and is clearly visible on the right. (Used by permission of Michael Fay)

sent to the Field Museum of Chicago and were examined before our writing began. Eerie is the only word that aptly describes these arti-facts—relics of predation that are startlingly human in appearance.

The famous zoologist George Schaller reported eyewitness narratives of predation on mountain gorillas in his landmark monograph, *The Mountain Gorilla: Ecology and Behavior*.[6] Schaller's information came from, among others, the same colonial hunter we mentioned earlier, Walter Baumgartel. Baumgartel resided at the time in the famous Virunga Mountains, where Rwanda, Uganda, and Democratic Republic of Congo meet, the only home of the mountain gorilla. He later transcribed his ad-ventures in the heart of Africa in a book entitled *Up Among the Mountain Gorillas;* in it he tells of the leopard, recounted above, who stalked and killed an entire family group of mountain gorillas.[7] Baumgartel also wrote that the same or a similarly disposed leopard continued the killing spree until there was a single group of only two mountain gorillas left in the Congo portion of the Virunga Mountains.

The great red ape of Asia, the orangutan, is an elusive creature who, unlike the majority of primates, does not live in social groups. Authentication exists that this species is prey to both tigers and the reclusive Asian wild cats called clouded leopards.[8] Once in the 1970s a clouded leopard happened on a conservation project in Sumatra set up to reintroduce seven juvenile orangutans back to the wild. The cat repeatedly raided the project's camp until all seven orangutans were killed. Tigers, being much larger and stronger than clouded leopards, can and do kill even brawny adult male orangutans.

Nevertheless, to reveal the ancient hominid state, we find the most compelling evidence in the substantial predation rates on chimpanzees. Chimpanzees share 98% of human DNA; they make tools, they learn and transmit unique behaviors (thus fulfilling for some the definition of culture), they—along with other great apes—learn American Sign Language and will use it to convey concepts.[9] Significantly, over the course of past decades, chimpanzees were assumed to be far too much like humans to be preyed upon. But this has since been dramatically disproven.

Even in the relative safety of Gombe National Park in Tanzania, the site of Jane Goodall's famous chimp families, human researchers have frequently seen anti-predation behaviors directed against the occasional transient leopard.[10] The reality that chimps in Gombe are almost always in the company of armed humans, along with the fact that visits by leopards are extremely rare, may make the park an artificially safe environment for chimpanzees. It was noted several decades ago that a "safe environment" is definitely *not* the case in the Parc National du Niokolo Koba, located near Mt. Assirik in Senegal, West Africa. French primatologist Caroline Tutin headed a team that found suspiciously cautious demeanor among the chimps of Mt. Assirik.[11] First, Tutin's team ascertained that a full complement of predators were active both day and night—lion, leopard, spotted hyena, and wild dog all coexisted with the chimpanzees. These chimps had a healthy respect and fear for the carnivores they encountered, and their behavior reflected it. Compared to the relatively protected chimpanzees at Gombe, chimps at Mt. Assirik built nests higher in the trees, never engaged in hunting forays for monkeys or the small forest antelopes called duikers, and behaved nervously when traveling as a group on the ground.

Other, more focused studies have since taken place to measure the degree of natural predation by large cats on chimp populations. The results definitively clarify the relationship between chimps and predators. Two examples are pertinent: The chimpanzee population of the Mahale Mountains, Tanzania, has been the subject of long-term demographic research by Japanese primatologists. Predation as a mortality factor for chimps was assumed to be negligible. No researchers had guessed that any of the Mahale Mountain chimps fell prey to the king of beasts until the Japanese team noticed lion feces containing a lot of familiar black hairs. An analysis confirmed the presence of chimpanzee hair, bones, and teeth in four out of eleven samples of lion feces collected over widely spaced periods of time.[12] As it turned out, lions annually killed an estimated 6% of the chimpanzee population studied by Takahiro Tsukahara in the Mahale Mountains during his research period.

In the Tai Forest, Côte d'Ivoire in West Africa, the level of predation on chimps by leopards is much the same. Swiss primatologist Christophe Boesch has tracked leopard predation over the years on the Tai chimpanzee population he studies. In 1985 he first noticed two or three sharply cut parallel wounds on an adult male chimp that could only have been from a leopard. He was soon aware that leopard predation was a constant factor for the chimps: "The tremendous power of the leopard's bite makes him a rapid killer and, if taken by surprise, even an adult individual seems unable to prevent it from the fatal biting. Thus, all age-sex classes may suffer from predation by leopards."[13] Boesch found that the presence of humans was not much of a deterrent to the leopards; one chimpanzee was attacked only 30 yards from where the researchers were working. Boesch calculated that leopards kill more than one in twenty individuals (5.5%) in his study group of chimpanzees each year.

THE PREY FLEE, THE PREDATOR PURSUES

It might be a good idea at this juncture to take a few moments for a discussion on what is known about predator–prey interactions. Stated succinctly, within the constraints of habitat and population density of prey animals, predatory behaviors are shaped by the forces of natural selection to maximize nutrient intake.[14] In plain language—predators hunt when they are hungry, and they are unlikely to kill more than they will eat. There is no predation just for fun. The act of predation is costly in terms of time spent, calories expended, and possible injuries sustained. No smart predator is going to use up precious energy stalking and killing unless hunger is pushing her buttons to feed herself or her dependent young.

Conventional wisdom would picture predators formulaically thinning the size of their prey population—mountain lions eating just the right numbers of deer to keep the deer, in turn, from overpopulating. But that's just the short-term view, and natural processes don't operate over short time spans. Under natural conditions (that is, in environments devoid of human perturbations caused by agriculture or technology), it is the prey populations that delimit the ultimate size of predator populations.[15]

One of the most elegant studies of predator–prey relations was carried out by George Schaller, the zoologist. His study involved the lions of the Serengeti Plain and the animals (including baboons and vervet monkeys) they ate. He concluded that predation is not an important limiting factor on prey populations. It actually has little impact on the populations of prey because predators like lions most often take the surplus animals destined to die anyway from malnutrition or disease.[16] Naturally, the chances are better at securing an easy meal than one that may outrun you, leaving you not only hungry but too worn out to pursue the next prey. (Or, to put it in suburban terms, when you need milk at 10:00 P.M. and your gas tank is nearly on empty, why drive to a faraway shop when you can guarantee your milk needs will be satisfied at the corner all-night mini-mart?)

Should we then worry that too many chimpanzees might be obliterated by their natural predators? Absolutely not. Any substantive and long-term drop in numbers of prey will arise from lack of resources. In other words, prey have a finite amount of food they can eat and when there are too many of them for each to get the proper amount of food, there will be deaths. The resource-induced decline in prey populations will eventually set off a decline in predator reproduction: fewer predators will seek mates, fewer matings will take place among those that do, and fewer young will be produced at longer intervals when the prey population drops. The prey population will rise when the food supply rejuvenates under the decreased pressure of fewer animals, and eventually the predator population will do likewise. The population level of the predators simply lags behind and follows the status of the prey species they eat, and the prey species they eat are regulated by the amount of food available to them.

Nonetheless, predators are responsible for many aspects of the morphology (form, shape, and size) and behavior of the animals on which they prey. There is basic asymmetry in the evolutionary rate of prey defenses and the predatory mechanisms challenging them. Behavioral ecologist John Endler named this imbalance the "life versus dinner" principle: A missed predation attempt saves the *life* of the prey, but only loses a *meal* for the predator, so defense mechanisms of prey species are more strongly selected for than are predator counterdefenses.[17]

Coevolution between predator and prey is a case of "the deer flees, the wolf pursues." In other words, if prey evolve a new way to elude predators, predators evolve in the direction of overcoming that new strategy. Any major destabilization in the balance of predators and prey comes about because the prey have evolved some new way to elude predation; the predator then has to counteradapt or give up eating the newly elusive prey.[18] We contend that these same natural principles were in place as our human ancestors emerged. Hominids evolved new ways to elude predators and those adaptations include many of the most basic human behavioral traits. Predation is an important source of evolutionary change.

We find the coevolution that occurred between predators and their non-human primate prey is visible in the behavioral and anatomical adaptations of some species of monkeys. Adaptations are even traceable to specific predators. For example, aggregations of two or more different species who feed, travel, or rest together occurs with many New World monkeys and African forest monkeys. Nonetheless, these "polyspecific associations" only exist in geographic regions inhabited by monkey-eating raptors—harpy eagles of South America and crowned hawk-eagles of Central and West Africa. The birds of prey have provided a strong evolutionary incentive for monkeys to cluster into the largest groups possible.[19] Harpy eagles have exerted such strong selective pressure on many Neotropical (Central and South American) primates that the effects are manifested in large body size in some species and in behaviors such as group living and cryptic concealment (freezing to avoid detection) in others.[20]

To reiterate, if anti-predator defenses have evolved in prey species in response to predators, populations of prey species will not be unduly affected by predation under normal environmental conditions. If, however, the slow process of coevolution has not occurred between predators and prey (specifically in the case of exotic or foreign species introduced into an ecosystem by humans), prey species may lack proper defenses and could suffer high mortality to the point of extinction.[21] There are, unfortunately, hundreds of examples of these human-arranged debacles. The current endangered status of all Hawaiian ground-dwelling birds is a result of the importation by European settlers of pigs, cats, and mongooses to the islands where no terrestrial carnivores had ever lived. A lesser-known situation is the high mortality inflicted by domestic dogs (and feral cats to some degree) on primates living in many parts of Asia and South America.

WHO ARE THESE PRIMATE PREY?

Inhabiting the world currently are more than 250 other species of primates besides humans. Non-human primates are a diverse-looking bunch; their physical differences are staggering. Primates range in size from a couple of ounces to nearly 400 pounds. (The gorilla, at 390 pounds, appears to have no outward resemblance at all to the tiny, aptly named mouse lemur, weighing 2 ounces.) Some primates actually resemble cats; in fact, during any given time period watching primates in a zoo setting, you will hear visitors mistaking ringtailed lemurs for cats. Some primates resemble rodents; the mouse lemur at first glance looks very much like a wide-eyed gerbil. Some primates resemble no other living creatures—the tiny 4-ounce tarsier has a combination of enormous eyes (each eye weighs as much as its brain) and exceedingly long, powerful hind limbs. The tarsier also moves its head 180 degrees in each direction instead of moving its eyes, just like an owl. Perhaps the most bizarre of the primates is the aye-aye of Madagascar, which has evolved colossal rodent-like gnawing incisors with a consequent dwindling and disappearance of other teeth; in addition the species has one long crooked digit on each front limb that is used to dig out insects from rotted wood, much like a woodpecker's lifestyle. The great eighteenth-century classifier of plants and animals, Linnaeus, included bats and colugos (commonly

A selection of representative prosimians: (a) fat-tailed galago; (b) slow loris; (c) sifaka; (d) ringtailed lemur; (e) mouse lemur; (f) ruffed lemur; (g) aye-aye (not to scale). (C. Rudloff, redrawn from Napier and Napier 1985)

called flying lemurs) in the primate order, and until quite recently tree shrews had been mislabeled as primates also.

Indeed, it was not until the mid-twentieth century that the British anatomist W. E. Le Gros Clark provided a modern definition of the primate order.[22] Le Gros Clark characterized primates by the retention of generalized limbs tipped with five grasping digits; the replacement of some claws by nails; expansion and elaboration of the brain; emphasis on vision as the primary sense with subsequent de-emphasis on smell; loss of some teeth from the ancestral mammalian state; delayed maturation; and reduction of litter size to a single offspring that receives a high degree of socialization from adults. As primates, humans fit this description just as well as the other 250 or so species.

Sixty-five million years ago, the first almost-primates were probably small, arboreal, nocturnal insect- and fruit-eaters, resembling present-day tree shrews.[23] As primates evolved, some became terrestrial, some diurnal, some became fruit-eaters, some specialized their diets even more and became leaf-eaters. Throughout millions of evolutionary years, the solitary early primates adopted complex social structures. Last but not least, body size increased along with these other adaptations. Modern prosimians—the earliest primates to evolve (the lemurs, galagos, and lorises)—are thought to be more like the first primates 65 million years ago than are monkeys and apes. Many of the prosimians are found only on the island of Madagascar, although the galagos and a few other prosimians inhabit Africa and lorises live in tropical Asia. Prosimians depend more on a sense of smell than the rest of the primates. (In fact, their wet nose, or rhinarium, is a trait shared with dogs and cats.) Many prosimians are nocturnal and arboreal, and their social groups generally are not as large or complex as the monkeys or apes.

New World monkeys include squirrel monkeys and capuchins (think organ-grinder monkeys), the tiny tamarins and marmosets that can easily fit in your hand, and the large spider and howler monkeys. All New World monkeys, except the owl monkey, are active only during the day, and many have a prehensile tail that acts like a fifth limb during treetop travel and feeding.

Old World monkeys range throughout tropical Africa and Asia. Baboons and macaques are the most numerous of these primates. Macaques also have successfully colonized temperate areas in Japan and the mountains of Morocco. The frequently filmed Japanese macaque (or snow monkey) lives at a higher latitude than any other non-human

Representative monkeys and apes: (a) siamang; (b) colobus monkey; (c) tamarin; (d) drill; (e) saki monkey; (f) gorilla; (g) spider monkey (not to scale). (C. Rudloff, redrawn from Napier and Napier 1985)

primate species and has evolved many behaviors such as bathing in hot springs to help it counter the cold climate. Another group of Old World monkeys, the leaf-eating colobines, has adopted the primate equivalent of bovine behavior. Sacculated stomachs (much like the four stomachs of a cow) help digest the roughage in their diets; this makes for a more lethargic lifestyle in these primates than the fruit- and seed-eating baboons and macaques.

Besides the great apes—gorillas, orangutans, and chimpanzees—there are the lesser apes, the gibbons and siamangs. Found only in Southeast Asia, gibbons and siamangs are rather unique. One, they are frequently monogamous, contrary to the generic promiscuous primate state. Two, they are true brachiators—traveling fast and furiously through the rain-forest canopy by swinging hand-over-hand under the branches.

THE DICHOTOMY ABOUT DEATH

Pick a side! Regarding the subject of predation on primates, the primatology community holds entrenched—and divergent—views. Opinions range from a belief that the role of predation has been minimal to theories that predation has been a powerful force in shaping social patterns.[24] Predation as a demographic parameter often is discounted by primate researchers under the assumption that few instances have been observed or recorded.[25] We noticed that variations on the statement "Predation is rarely observed . . . " are frequently employed by scientists as a caveat when the topic of primates as prey is under discussion. It is not an exaggeration to say that the statement has come to be accepted as an axiom within the primatology community and is sometimes used to convey in shorthand that the evolutionary consequences of predation on primates are as incalculable as the unknown magnitude of predation. Furthermore, the significance of apparent anti-predator patterns (physical, social, and behavioral) is disputed because most of these adaptations can also be explained plausibly as responses to sexual selection (the competition between males for available breeding females) or feeding competition.[26] Because observations of predation in the scientific literature have often been anecdotal rather than quantitative, there has been a tendency to minimize both the possible frequency of predation on primates as well as the pervasive influence that predation has had on the behavior and ecology of primates.

However, the pendulum may be slowly swinging. Significant changes in field research methodology have been called for, such as night observations and the study of primate predators along with primates themselves, to accomplish a more accurate appraisal of predation.[27]

THE JAMES CARVILLE APPROACH

Remember how James Carville, the Democratic strategist, kept the Clinton campaign focused before the elections of 1992 and 1996? "It's the economy, stupid!" was the mantra that spelled success. Well, apologizing for any unintended insult, we want to co-opt the James Carville tactic and reiterate: "It's the predators, stupid!"

It is a paradigm in the published research of animal behaviorists (called ethologists) that predator–prey relationships can best be studied from the perspective of the predator. *They* all know this—but primatologists chose to reinvent the wheel where predation was concerned. "Hey, let's pretend that it doesn't count at all. We never see it!" (Small wonder since most predators choose not to attack their next meal in front of people.) "Every other branch of field research looks at the predators, but we'll only look at the prey. After all, we study primates." We don't claim to be tackling something in a brand new way when we state that the integration of research on predatory animals may help to answer some of the myriad questions regarding predation on primates. In fact, it is so elementary that you may wonder why we would make a point of it. So, we humbly mention that a look at primate predation from the viewpoint of current predator research could expand knowledge on this important aspect of primate life history. Many other primatologists have concurred that progress in understanding the importance of predation on primates will come only from this approach.[28]

Observation of only one group of one species (the typical parameters of primate research) provides limited data and often skews the perception of predation, whereas fieldwork on predatory species gives a broad view of several food chain levels. The home range of a solitary predator usually overlaps numerous prey groups and species; while the predator hunts on a daily basis, it may attack the primate group under study only occasionally.[29] For example, the range of an African forest guenon, such as the blue monkey, is approximately 50 square yards; redfronted lemurs in Madagascar have a home range even smaller; while a chacma baboon troop may range just a few square miles.[30]

Compare those relatively minute areas with the predator's frame of reference. Home ranges for predatory species are large.[31] Within the range of the typical leopard there may be not only many *populations* of one primate species, but many populations of *many* primate species, and the leopard may be preying on all of them. Leopard territories have been estimated to be as small as 4–8 square miles or as large as 250 square miles, and one male leopard in the Kalahari Desert had a home range of 500 square miles. Other carnivores hunt in equally vast areas that might contain scores of primate groups. Tigers defend a territory of 20 square miles, spotted hyena clans claim a territory of 6–25 square miles, jaguars hunt over an area of approximately 30 square miles, and a pack of African hunting dogs will range over 400 square miles. Birds of prey, of course, also have huge ranges in which they seek food. A harpy eagle pair may possess a 60-to-120-square-mile territory, Philippine eagle pairs have a home range of 15–30 square miles, and the total home range of a pair of crowned hawk-eagles is approximately 6–8 square miles.

Even a relatively small carnivore, such as a fossa (a relative of civets, genets, and mongooses), is estimated to hold a home range of nearly 3 square miles. Fossa fill the ecological niche of wild cats in Madagascar and were previously misclassified taxonomically as a cat species. By virtue of its cat-like claws, teeth, and jaws, the fossa looks much like a North American cougar and is equipped to kill mammals nearly its own size. Patricia Wright and her research team from Duke University tracked one individual fossa in the rain forest of southeastern Madagascar that was making regular attacks on four sifaka social groups, each separated by at least 1 kilometer. The sifaka is an acrobatic lemur that excels in vertical clinging and leaping. They jump in an upright position, sail loftily through the air, and land upright with all four limbs entwined around the intended trunk or branch. Pat Wright's research team concluded that this particular fossa's home range was large enough that it took 1 year for the fossa to cycle through the four primate territories.

Earlier in this chapter we mentioned the lions that move in and out of the Mahale Mountains National Park, Tanzania, and the chimpanzees that provide part of their diet. While researchers speculated that predation

on chimpanzees could be heavy if the lions would permanently reside in
the park, it may be that the Mahale Mountains are simply one portion of
the lions' home range through which they periodically cycle.

Who's eating whom? Like building a pyramid, we needed to get at
the foundation of predation on all primates before we could discuss predation on early hominids. We couldn't present a theory of Man the
Hunted unless we could get the facts on other primates. If non-human
primates are not prey, then that sets us and our relatives in a special category—so special that the laws of nature and predation do not affect us.

We set to work finding out all we could about predation on primates.[32] Until our research, no comprehensive attempt had been made
to collect and summarize published and non-published empirical or anecdotal records of actual primate predation events in the wild. We
examined the scientific and natural history literature from both the
predator and prey perspectives. From our data we came to the conclusion that primates in general are vulnerable to predators. In fact, the
chances may be just as likely that certain primate species will become
the meal for a hungry predator as the chance that more "typical" prey—
such as gazelles or antelopes—might be selected and eaten.

For all the debate about predation on primates (and by extension,
predation on our hominid ancestors), a *systematic count* of observed predations on primate species had never been attempted. Based on
anecdotal comments from colleagues and an initial cursory look at the
writings of naturalists from the first half of the twentieth century, we
felt there was reason to challenge the rather dubious axiom, "predation
is rarely observed." Nevertheless, our own intuitive judgment that predation was an important feature of primate life was no more solid than
the idea that predation is rarely observed. So we decided to do the sub-
limely obvious—simply *count* in a systematic fashion the number of
times predation on primate species has been observed and described in
the scientific and natural history literature. Published accounts from
field researchers and naturalists who have actually witnessed predation
on non-human primates were collected. These eyewitness accounts of
predation events are dramatic and numerous, beginning in 1895 and
continuing to the present. (Just as with other living primates, modern
humans still fall prey to predators, and anecdotal descriptions also
abound of man-eating lions, leopards, tigers, crocodiles, and pythons.

These unsettling instances accentuate the long history of humans as another species of primate prey.)

After compiling in excess of 550 eyewitness accounts of predation on non-human primates, we felt rather confident that primates occur in the diets of many predatory animals. Approaching the subject of predation on primates from this objective viewpoint, we found it evident that a divergence of views concerning the rarity of predation exists between primate researchers and their counterparts who study those species that eat primates. The evidence for primates in the diets of many carnivores, raptors, and reptiles is considered indisputable to researchers who study predatory animals.

The difference between data gathered from primate and from predator researchers can be dramatic. This was apparent from questionnaires sent out to the two different research communities. Less than 10% of the 227 primatologists who responded to questionnaires had knowledge of more than two predations on their study populations. Contrast this with the responses from predator researchers; known or observed kills by the predator they were studying averaged 20 primates, and one researcher had gathered information on 350 primate kills by leopards.[33]

Predation as a demographic parameter in primate populations has been one of the least studied areas because little empirical information on predation has been available. So, what *was* the exact empirical evidence gathered during our study of predation on primates? We found 176 species of confirmed or potential predators of primates in the four geographic regions inhabited by non-human primates (Africa, Madagascar, Asia, and the Neotropics).[34] These predatory animals include diminutive birds all the way to huge mammals and reptiles. Primates are preyed upon by hawks, eagles, owls, and other predatory birds, and by wild cats, wild dogs, jackals, hyenas, and bears. They are preyed on by little-known species of small carnivores, such as civets, genets, mongooses, tropical weasels, raccoons, the marsupial opossum, large and small crocodiles, snakes, monitor lizards, tegus (Neotropical lizards), and even sharks! These predators range in size from 2.5 ounces (the hook-billed vanga of Madagascar) to in excess of 500 pounds (the Indian mugger crocodile, which measures over 9 feet in length).

We reviewed the scientific literature dealing with these predator species for quantitative and qualitative references to primates as prey.

Questionnaires we sent to field researchers were used to collect an additional set of quantitative and qualitative data. Both of these areas showed that primates may as likely be prey as most other groups of herbivorous or omnivorous mammals.

When describing the data we gathered, support was given to our argument that primates are, and have always been, prey animals. Much of the data collected for our study came from predator researchers who determined the frequency of primates in predator diets through analyses of feces, stomach contents, regurgitations, nest and den remains, skeletal components left at kill sites, and direct observation of kills—information regularly gathered in studies of predatory animals.

These data were drawn from the fieldwork of ornithologists, herpetologists, and mammalogists. We analyzed the data collected through questionnaires and literature searches and used the information on predators to provide a counterbalance to information provided by primate researchers. This, in essence, allowed us to cross-check between the two fields, a technique useful in establishing more accurate estimates of the level and impact of predation.

Known primate deaths, unsuccessful attacks, and suspected predations were tabulated. Data on almost 3,600 separate instances of predation were available from questionnaires and the scientific and natural history literature. Diurnal raptors, owls, and other birds were the top predators on primates (41% of the total), followed by wild cats (35%), wild dogs and hyenas (7%), reptiles (5%), small carnivores such as the fossa (33%). Unknown predators accounted for 9% of the total. Further fieldwork is critical to expand these findings since many of the 176 predator species have not been studied at all in their natural state.

No geographic region could be identified in which primates were free of predation. No variables of body size, night or day activity cycles, or strata (high forest canopy, low shrub, or ground level) could be identified that exempted primates from predation.

The limited data available from questionnaires indicate that adult primates are more often prey than other age groups and that males are more often prey than females. However, infant *survival* rates are identified by many researchers as being very low, and a good portion of this mortality may be due to predation.

Estimated predation rates were as high as 25%. (Predation rate is defined as the percentage of the population removed annually by predators.

A predation rate of 25% means that one in four individuals in a population is killed by a predator in a year.) An analysis of the estimated predation rates of primate species indicates that small, nocturnal, and arboreal primates may undergo higher rates of predation than larger, diurnal, and terrestrial species.

In studies we analyzed, the frequencies of occurrence of primates in predator diets ranged from miniscule to 90%; raptors and wild cats had the highest percentages of primates in their diets.

Eleven predators met our criteria of "primate specialists," defined by us as species that rely heavily on primates as food. These rapacious superpredators are leopards, harpy eagles of the Neotropics, African crowned hawk-eagles, the fossa of Madagascar, Philippine eagles, bateleur eagles of Africa, Henst's goshawks of Madagascar, Madagascar buzzards, Madagascar long-eared owls, African pythons, and reticulated pythons of Southeast Asia. Of these eleven species, four—the leopard, harpy eagle, crowned hawk-eagle, and fossa—were by far the most dedicated to hunting primates.[35]

While we narrowed the whole realm of predators down to these four dedicated primate specialists, none of the four specialists have what you would call a rigidly narrow food base. There are no mammalian predators, for example, comparable in their food selectivity to aardwolves that eat only termites or whales that must strain tiny crustaceans through a baleen filter in their mouths. Therefore, primates are what we have dubbed "generalist" prey. Despite the evidence found to identify certain predators as primate specialists, we take the position that primates are "generalist" prey in the sense that, as a group, they come in all sizes, from very small to very large; they inhabit geographic ranges throughout the tropics, subtropics, and a few temperate forests; they range from totally arboreal to totally terrestrial; and they include both nocturnal and diurnal species. Their successful radiation into many ecological zones carried with it the potential to interact with many predators that will opportunistically feed on a wide range of prey.

For a wider perspective, we also compared primates to other, so-called typical mammalian prey species, such as hoofed animals and large rodents, to ascertain if there were any overall similarities in rates of predation. Traditionally, primates have not been thought of as prey species in the same league as ungulates (deer, antelopes, and gazelles). However, when primates are compared to other species (particularly the grazing ungulates) inhabiting the same biomes and preyed on by the same predators, some similarities in rates of predation became apparent. Primates may be as much a food source for predators as other, more typical prey.

Predation is undoubtedly significant and may be the leading source of mortality in populations of primates.[36] It was the main conclusion of our study that species of primates are influenced to varying degrees by predation and that major physical, ecological, and behavioral adaptations have evolved in response to predators. We hypothesize that some predatory species specialize on primates as a resource base and that many others kill primates opportunistically.

PREDATION RISK VERSUS PREDATION RATE

We like a pithy statement from tropical ecologist John Terborgh who summed up predation rather concisely: "Successful predation is a rare event—at most it can occur only once in the lifetime of a prey."[37] Whatever the overall impact of *successful* predation may be to the species or population, it does not modify the behavioral strategies of an individual primate living at constant *risk* from successful predation.[38] Behavior is predicated on predation risk not predation rate because animals *react* to unsuccessful attacks, but they *die* from successful ones.

Animals strive to reduce their predation risk because it represents the sum total of all past unsuccessful encounters with predators *plus* their perception of the likelihood of future attack.[39] Predation risk involves the entire spectrum of compensations primates must make to offset predation. Direct observation by researchers substantiates that predation risk is constant in the daily lives of primates.[40, 41]

Predation rate, on the other hand, involves the annual mortality of a certain percentage of a primate population due to predators. Predation rates on primates are variable, but as Connie M. Anderson, a physical anthropologist at Hartwick College, noted, "events have a powerful selective effect if the event completely eliminates an individual's genetic contribution to the next generation. . . . [F]or a dead individual, any [predation] rate above zero is highly significant."[42]

Primate species have slow reproduction potential due to long gestation periods, birth of a single infant rather than a litter, and long

The tiny mouse lemur is the smallest primate. It can withstand a high predation rate from owls because of its unusually elevated reproductive capacity. (J. Buettner-Janusch)

intervals between births. John Terborgh postulated that predation was, of necessity, a rare event at the level of a whole primate group. He speculated, for example, that a South American capuchin troop could not sustain more than one loss to predation per year since the replacement level (the birthrate) is only one to two infants per year.[43]

How is it possible then that one-quarter of the little mouse lemurs in Madagascar are eaten each year by various species of owls? This 25% annual predation rate for mouse lemurs[44] seems to belie Terborgh's cautionary comments. Higher predation rates are acceptable, however, if—and only if—the species' potential reproductive rate is high enough to compensate for losses to predation.[45] Unlike the other prosimians, monkeys, or apes, the mouse lemur is able to sustain a predation rate of 25% because the species is rare among primates in having a high reproductive capacity to offset predation. The genus *Microcebus* ("tiny monkey" in Latin) has two "litters" of two infants per rainy season, resulting in an average annual production of four offspring per breeding female. Even with a 50% infant-survival rate, an average of two out of the original four babies per year survive, and this overachievement in offspring provides the mouse lemur with the ability to rapidly replace its population.[46]

But, you may legitimately ask, how does a discussion of mouse lemurs relate to human evolution? We find these predation rates relevant to our central Man the Hunted *not* Man the Hunter theme because of one highly publicized situation that is used as evidence to support conjectures that man (and it *is* limited to the male of our species) is a natural-born killer. The particular situation is the systematic killing sprees by male chimpanzees in Gombe National Park, Tanzania. The chimps' quarry is mainly another primate species, red colobus monkeys; the calculated pressure is a predation rate of 17–33% per year inflicted on the colobus by their chimp predators.[47] The reproductive capability of *Microcebus* makes life with a 25% per year loss to predation possible. Red colobus monkeys do not have this high reproduction rate.

Irwin Bernstein, a highly respected primatologist, has challenged the idea that chimpanzees *naturally* hunt with such gusto.

> The murderous Gombe chimpanzee hunters are said to have killed 30% of the red colobus monkeys each year for twenty years. Even if this was the only cause of death for red colobus, if half the animals were female and 60% were reproductive, then each female would have to have one live birth every year just to satisfy the chimpanzees.[48]

Without a uniquely high (and quite unprimate-like) reproductive capacity, how can such high rates of chimpanzee predation on red colobus at Gombe (up to a whopping one-third of the population killed yearly) be anything other than an aberrant situation? It is, therefore, obvious that this chimpanzee predation on monkeys is a recent and unnatural phenomenon. And, if it is aberrant and unnatural, then much of the punch is taken out of the "killer ape/man the hunter" equation.

Predation risk, not predation rate, nonetheless, is what drives an animal's anti-predation behavior. Low and high predation levels, of course, are relative terms. Nonetheless, scientists have assigned qualitative definitions to low, medium, and high predation risk: Low risk entails the presence of predators but no actual or attempted predation has been observed or suspected; medium predation risk is associated with occasional predation attempts but infrequent predation observed or suspected; high predation risk involves frequent or regular, actual or attempted, predation observed and suspected.[49]

Unsuccessful predation attempts—that is, the failure of predators to catch prey—underlie selection for defense behaviors. Guy Cowlishaw of University College London is one of a handful of researchers who are attempting to measure predation risk in a field setting. He constructed a field experiment to measure perceived versus actual risk in chacma baboons. He found that females in small groups are expected to be at the greatest risk from predators, but males had equal or higher mortality rates. These results suggest that females practice more anti-predator behavior, such as vigilance, and this may compensate for their susceptibility to predators due to their smaller size or pregnancy or infant-carrying. These kinds of insights into the individual and evolutionary impacts on primates from predation will come only from increasingly sophisticated field studies that emphasize the interrelationship between primate prey and their predators.[50]

WHO WAS EATING OUR HOMINID ANCESTORS?

Many scientists will turn ghastly shades of red when arguing against creationism and for evolution, yet they want to hang onto some special classification for modern humans, early hominids, the great apes, and even primates in general as too smart to be prey animals. Surely, they insist, at least humans (that is, Man the Hunter) had to be in control of their environment—they couldn't have been at the mercy of "dumb animals" that ate them right, left, and center. If we believe in natural selection and the theory of evolution, then we must accept our place in the zoological framework of predators and prey. We have established that predation is a fact of life for primate species. A smallish bipedal hominid was as eminently eatable as any other primate.

Barbara Ehrenreich writes in *Blood Rites: Origins and History of the Passions of War:*

> We were not given dominion over the earth; our forebears earned it in their long, nightmarish struggle against creatures far stronger, swifter, and better armed than themselves, when the terror of being ripped apart and devoured

was never farther away than the darkness beyond the campfire's warmth . . . .
The original trauma—meaning of course, not a single event but a long-stand-
ing condition—was the trauma of being hunted by animals, and eaten.[51]

We had millions of years during which we were vulnerable lip-
smacking delicacies. We've had only a flick of an eye during which we
have exerted some domination over the predators. While we may no
longer have the predators to handle, we are still handling things as if we
were prey.

All primates are at risk from predation, as early hominids undoubtedly were. At question is only the *degree* to which predation influences
the life history of the individual or shapes the evolution of a species.
How may predation have affected early hominids, themselves vulnerable
primates living in open woodland?

Now, we turn to stories told in stone—those creatures who we know
were eating our ancient ancestors by the evidence they left millions of
years ago. The fossil record has a wealth of stories to tell about saber-
toothed cats, bear dogs, giant hyenas, fast-moving crocodiles, and
predators who inspired enough fear to shape our evolution.

4

LIONS AND TIGERS AND
BEARS, OH MY!

Africa is a continent in which many humans still live with the realization that predation may be a part of daily life. Probably the most
famous modern man-eaters in Africa were the legendary Tsavo lions held
responsible for the deaths of over a hundred railroad workers during a
nine-month period in 1896.[1] These may also be the only individual wild
animals to be featured in a statement to the British Parliament. The
prime minister of Great Britain in 1896, the Marquis of Salisbury, was
called to explain the delay in completion of the Uganda Railway. His
apology was blunt and typically colonial: "The whole of the works were
put to a stop because a pair of man-eating lions appeared in the locality
and conceived a most unfortunate taste for our workmen."[2]

The railroad construction was stalled for quite some time around
Kenya's Tsavo locale due to these man-eating lions. The body count,
when all was said and done, was allegedly 135 workers devoured.
Chicago's Field Museum of Natural History received the carcasses of the
two man-eaters after an intensive physical and psychological war was
waged against them by British engineer J. H. Patterson—the character
immortalized in the film *The Ghost and the Darkness*. Patterson suc-
ceeded in killing the two lions in 1898; 100 years later scientists at the

Field Museum began studying the remains looking for clues concerning why these lions preyed on humans. The results of their study negate age or ill health as reasons for seeking human prey, although the late nineteenth-century period corresponds with the outbreak of a disease that nearly eliminated African buffalo, the lions' favored food. One of the Field Museum researchers, Julian Kerbis Peterhans, estimates scores of people are killed in Africa annually by lions. "Given the right circumstances," he says, "any lion is capable of attacking people."[3]

Lions and tigers (and even bears as we shall see later in this chapter) really can be quite a hazard for some humans in modern times. Cases of lions attacking humans for food have been recorded from all parts of Africa in which lions are found. The twentieth century has chronicled countless numbers of human mortalities inflicted by the king of beasts. One of the most extreme examples was the case of a single lion that killed 84 people in the vicinity of Ankole, Uganda, in the 1920s.

"Around Manyara Park [in Tanzania] lions have started to add man to their diet," wrote George Schaller in his 1972 monograph, *The Serengeti Lion*. Between 1969 and 1970, a young male lion injured or killed 6 people, both visitors and villagers. An associate wrote to Schaller, "Satima the young male [lion] among the Mahali pa Nyati pride has been shot when he was found eating another killed person near the park headquarters."

In the early 1990s, lions crossing over the Mozambique border into Tanzania's Tundara district killed 30 people in a twelve-month period. The "Man Eater of Mfuwe," a maneless male lion, was shot in 1991 near the South Luangwa National Park in Zambia. Having killed and eaten 6 people or more in 2 months, this lion's body was also given to permanent display at the Field Museum in Chicago.

Asiatic lions once roamed far and wide throughout the Middle East and the Indian subcontinent. They now comprise a remnant population of 250 animals inhabiting the Gir Forest in India, strictly protected by the government in New Delhi. An uneasy truce exists between the human and leonine populations in the area. An intensive investigation by zoologists found that the Gir Forest lions attacked 193 humans in the 13 years between 1978 and 1991. One year there were 40 attacks, in other years there were as few as 7. Not all attacks were lethal, but an average of 2 or more lion-caused human deaths per year occurred during the time period under study.[4]

Tigers, needless to say, rest at the core of man-eating legends. Entire careers of British gentry were based on the removal of man-eating tigers from various Indian states. Jim Corbett, a post–World War I big-game hunter, dispatched the "Champawat Tigress" (436 human casualties—ranked as the premier man-eater in history) and the "Panar Leopard" (400 victims). Corbett subsequently wrote two volumes about his exploits with tigers hooked on human flesh. The books, *Man-Eaters of Kumaon* and *The Temple Tiger and More Man-Eaters of Kumaon,* are chock full of gory deaths and daring exploits. But his respectful admiration for the tiger is also apparent; he was likely one of the first Westerners to realize a need for conservation of Indian wildlife. To give him his due, he also stresses the quiet courage of Indian villagers who lose family and friends to the big cats; by the simple act of looking for a child who has not come home from an errand, a mother risks becoming another meal for a tiger.[5]

Man-eating tigers were rather uncommon in southern India during colonial times but always fairly prevalent in the north. As mentioned in the introductory chapter to this book, the Sundarbans area of India and Bangladesh remains a place where tiger predation is one of life's realities. The mangrove forests of the Sundarbans are also the biggest tiger reserve in the world. Devoid of permanent human habitation, the area still draws transient traffic in the form of honey gatherers, fishermen, and wood collectors. These are the usual victims of the tiger, so creative ways to offset human predation have emerged. One such method involves electrified mannequins artfully placed in boats. These dummies give out a terrific shock when touched. Conservationists hope that negative conditioning from lifelike dummies may be a key to teaching tigers and their offspring avoidance of such prey.[6]

The residents of the Sundarbans, and India in general, seem to be incredibly tolerant of the tiger. John Seidensticker, a Smithsonian Institution cat specialist, was permitted to carry out the non-lethal removal of a young male tiger who had killed a woman in a populated area near the Sundarbans. Local anger was high at the beginning of his project and there was a general call for the destruction of the cat, but publicity generated a dramatic shift toward interest in the fate of the tiger. (Seidensticker collected 81 articles in the English-language Indian newspapers alone.) When the young male tiger died after translocation efforts

These mannequins, which deliver a terrific electric shock when touched, are used to condition tigers to avoid humans in the Sundarbans, India. (Ragui Rai/Magnum)

(due to injuries from a resident male), there was sincere lament at the death of "Sundar."[7]

Despite the fact that this species has been responsible for more human deaths than any other wild cat, tigers actually seem to be less likely to *seek* out human prey than leopards or lions. They seldom penetrate human settlements or move out of their natural habitat to search for human prey. "Rather, humans are attacked on the tiger's own ground; and almost always during daylight. The person is rushed from behind at close quarters following a careful stalk, or they are ambushed at a place of the tiger's own choosing. Occasionally a person squatting or crouching in dense vegetation . . . may be eaten," noted tiger expert Charles McDougal of the Smithsonian Institution.[8]

The smaller leopard takes a toll of human victims far out of proportion to its size. "If the leopard were as big as the lion it would be ten times more dangerous," opined John Taylor, a big-game hunter of great fame. For several years around the turn of the twentieth century, a leopard haunted the Golis Range in Somalia and was reputed to have killed more than 100 people. One of the most notorious wild animals in the annals of world history was a leopard that terrorized pilgrims on their way to a Hindu shrine in the Himalayas in the 1920s. During an eight-year period this particular cat claimed 125 lives. Its exploits were followed with zeal by the British press as the leopard outwitted each plan devised to secure its capture. Finally, the same Jim Corbett of tiger fame dispatched the "best hated and most feared animal in all India." In the mid-1930s another leopard reportedly killed 67 people on the Zambezi River in eastern Zambia. And, a 1961 report told of an African leopard that snatched a baby lying on a rug while its mother was working in the fields; within a short time it had attacked another 5 adults.

Much more recently (1998) saw a front page article in India's *TheWeek* newspaper: "Killers on the prowl—leopards give nightmares to villagers even as authorities ponder how to tackle the menace" was the provocative lead-in. According to forest department officials, leopards killed 95 and wounded another 117 villagers in the Garhwal region of Uttar Pradesh, India, during the period 1988 to 1998. The perceptions of fatalities by villagers were higher; according to the reporter, locals estimated that 17 lives were taken by leopards each year over many decades.[9]

Leopard predilection for human flesh is also a subject worthy of academic study. One researcher stated that leopards continue to provoke predator-avoidance behaviors and to prey on humans in the savannas of eastern Africa and in the Ituri Forest of Central Africa. Research has provided information about the sex of 152 known man-eating leopards. Only 6% were females, but no one knows why males would be more likely to become man-eaters. Another study of 78 man-eating leopards found that the habitual predator on humans is typically a mature male leopard unafflicted by injuries.[10]

In the catalog of large cats, let's not forget the North American wild cat of many names—the cougar, mountain lion, puma, or American panther (the choice of name varies by region, but all refer to the same species, *Felis concolor*)—an animal that also gets into the headlines occasionally. The mountain lion is the single large wild cat that might be encountered in the United States north of the U.S.–Mexican border. As the suburbs encroach on wilderness in states like California and Colorado, mountain lion attacks on people increase. (There have only been 41 fatal attacks nationwide since American records were kept, but 10 of these have been since 1990.)

Of intense fascination to the U.S. media, these somewhat gruesome events are usually given excessive airtime. January 2004 was the latest well-covered mountain lion attack story. Newscasters reported on a cougar that dragged a woman off her bike in a wilderness area of Orange County, south of Los Angeles. National Public Radio, BBC Radio, CNN, and all the major networks and newspapers carried segments on prime-time news. What made this story so unique was the dramatic manner in which the attack and subsequent rescue unfolded. A mountain biker traveling with a companion was pulled from her bike by the big cat; her friend held onto the woman's legs while screaming for help. Another biker arrived at the scene; the new arrival hailed even more bicyclists who threw objects at the mountain lion until it loosened its grip on the woman's head and ran off. The woman who was attacked was critically injured, but a further surprising twist in this drama was an abandoned bicycle found by the side of the trail. It belonged to a man who was found 25 yards away—dead and partially consumed—allegedly the *first* casualty of the cougar.[11]

Hearing the newscasts and interviews, we thought it sounded like an unusually crowded wilderness area, which might somewhat account for the cat's aberrant behavior. Definitely, this cougar was not acting like a normal predator—he was killing and caching but not fully *consuming* prey (the outcome of which would be satiation and a cessation to hunting). Carnivores expend a great deal of energy pursuing prey and finishing it off—the point is to eat the food caught, not stash it away and immediately go out and expend more energy catching additional food. (The earlier report about the leopard in 1961 that devoured a baby and then immediately killed five more people conveys the same illogical behavior.) Was the constant traffic on the trail disrupting enough that the California mountain lion was unable to consume his first victim and got his predatory wires mixed? Were there two mountain lions involved?— highly unlikely in a solitary species, but possible during a mating episode.

We sincerely hope that cougar biologists will be called on to piece together the strange events of this mountain lion attack. Yes, cougars kill humans, but no wild cat kills just for the sake of killing. They kill to feed themselves. Hans Kruuk, the famous carnivore biologist, tackles the subject of surplus killing in his latest book, *Hunter and Hunted: Relationships between Carnivores and People.* Kruuk feels that all carnivores are capable of surplus killing under limited and "abnormal" conditions. Carnivores are hardwired to kill prey when the chance presents itself, and caching (storing food) may be connected to incidents of surplus killing. Most of the time in nature prey do not act passive nor are they confined (such as sheep in a corral), and densities of prey are not high enough for surplus killing.[12]

After two 2001 fatal mountain lion attacks in Montana and Colorado, a Colorado Springs wildlife officer remarked that one of the reasons people move to the Rocky Mountain region is to be near wildlife, but they choose to forget it is also choice habitat for the mountain lion. Seemingly simple things, like children riding bikes or adults jogging, may trigger predatory responses in big cats.[13] Hans Kruuk discusses the complexity of carnivore reactions to prey:

> Hunting itself is far from infallible, and many a time does the prey escape. But overall, the ability of carnivores to penetrate the defences of other animals, of many birds and all other land mammals, and to use them as their main resource is a wonderfully adapted set of behaviour patterns. . . . With the potential of such adaptation, it is not surprising that carnivores have also managed to exploit people as prey, vulnerable as we used to be and often still are.[14]

While modern humans suffer some predation from the remaining populations of the large cats, what the cat family represented to our ancient ancestors must have been another story entirely.

Choose Your Weapon

Scimitars, sabers, daggers, dirks—which will it be? Long, curved, sharp teeth, the fossil cats had all those weapons handily attached to their top jaws.

An incredible array of cats and pre-cats roamed the earth from 10 million years until relatively recently. One wonders how any primate—much less our smallish bipedal hominid—survived the predation of so many large-bodied, large-toothed felines. The figure on p. 65 diagrams

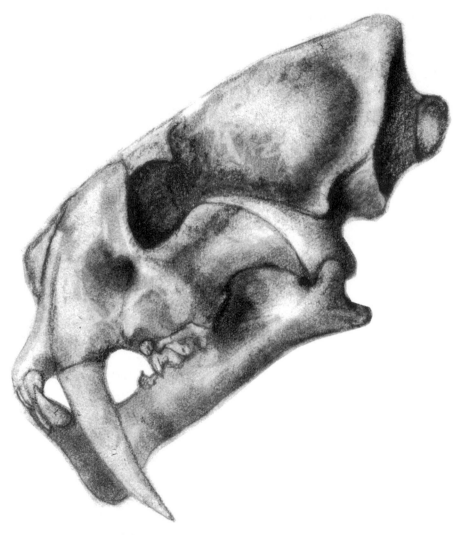

A reconstruction of the skull of *Megantereon*, a fossil saber-toothed cat that roamed Africa when hominids were evolving. (C. Rudloff, redrawn from Hartstone-Rose, et al.)

the *who* and the *when* of all these hungry felines; emphasis is limited to large cats that were present where and when hominids were evolving. The entire felid record stretches back much farther in time and also includes many North and South American mega-predators that were indigenous to those two continents long before human arrival occurred.

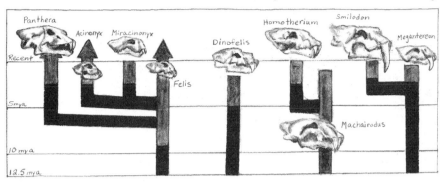

The extensive array of fossil and modern cat species inhabiting Africa from 12.5 million years until the present (light shading denotes fossil record). (C. Rudloff, re-drawn from Hartstone-Rose et al.)

Fossil evidence that will support theories of long-term coevolution (50 million years or more) between the primate order and mammalian predators is uncovered only occasionally. Nevertheless, there are enough of these finds to generate speculation that the very roots of primate origins are buried in episodes of carnivore depredation. For example, *Notharctus* was a prosimian-like primate living in the Eocene epoch 50 million years ago. The death of one such animal was reconstructed based on the size and shape of skull puncture marks matching the teeth of *Vulpavus,* an arboreal predator that looked like a large mongoose and was ancestral to all carnivores.[15] The holes in the skull of the fossil primate are the perfect fit for the fangs of *Vulpavus.*

The creodonts are an extinct group of primitive meat-eating mammals, but these fossil predators behaved very much like big cats of modern times and had several saber-toothed varieties, an adaptation for killing large prey that was to reoccur over and over in successions of later predatory species.[16] Fossil creodonts and their prey have been unearthed in an area called the Fayum, a fossil-hunter's paradise located in Egypt not too far from Cairo. The Fayum contains fossil primates from the Oligocene epoch, dating in age from 25 to 30 million years. When paleontologists measured puncture marks on Fayum Oligocene fossil primates, they found many tooth holes in skulls and long bones, evidence to the paleo-detectives that the primates had died at the hands (or rather teeth) of predators. Due to this simple forensic device, it was concluded that the creodonts preyed and/or scavenged on these primates.

Relative sizes of fossil cats and bears from the time period 8.5 million to 1 million years ago. Each square measures approximately 20 inches on each side; three squares equal 5 feet. From left to right: giant cheetah (*Acinonyx*); saber-toothed cat (*Machairodus*); ancestral leopard (*Paramachairodus*); bear (*Indarctos*); saber-toothed cat (*Homotherium*); saber-toothed cat (*Megantereon*). (C. Rudloff, redrawn from Turner 1997)

We totally agree so far, but this is where we think the detectives lost the trail. Based upon their *assumption* that predation on living primates is a rare event (a paradigm we're trying our best to undermine), the paleo-detectives concluded that it must also have been rare 25–30 million years ago. The case against the creodonts was dismissed on the evidence that only 9–10% of the primate fossils examined showed evidence of death from predation.[17]

Hey, that's no small percentage of predation! A 9–10% predation rate is exactly the impact today's large carnivores inflict on the great herds of grazing animals migrating through the Serengeti in East Africa.[18] And the Serengeti ecosystem, of course, is the quintessential example of predator–prey interrelationships. Twenty-five to 30 million years ago, the creodonts were having exactly the same effect on the demographics of primate prey as lions and hyenas have on wildebeest, zebra, and gazelles today.

As we move closer and closer in the fossil record to the 7-to-10-million-year mark that may pinpoint when apes and hominids split from a common ancestor, we encounter more evidence of predation in the form of those perfect round holes into which predator fangs will fit. To cite one example: standing on the figurative doorstep of the hominid lineage during the Upper Miocene epoch (approximately 7–10 million years ago) is an extinct primate skull evidencing such bitemarks; these holes—once again—fit the canine teeth of a fossil felid the size of a modern leopard.[19]

Saber-toothed cats may have used their teeth to stab prey in much the same downward motion as a person would use a knife. (C. Rudloff, redrawn from Turner 1997)

If we cross that figurative fossil doorstep and enter the time zone of the hominids—the Pliocene and Pleistocene epochs that began 5 million years ago and ran until just 10,000 years past—we find more and more evidence of predation on human and non-human primates. At this point in time there were a lot of cats sporting a lot of very long teeth. You might call it the heyday of cats; in fact we don't have *nearly* the number of cat species in existence today. The large cats that currently exist represent just a few species lucky enough to have survived a dramatic change in world climate about 1.8 million years ago.

Who were the cat predators that lived with, around, and *on* the early hominids? [20] First and foremost, there were the "true" saber-toothed cats. These true sabertooths used their teeth to stab prey in much the same manner that a person would hold a knife in hand and jab with a downward motion. Those long teeth were too delicate to sever spinal cords or inflict other killing bites used by today's robust-toothed wild cats. Instead, the super-sized sabers were used to slice into soft flesh and rip apart prey animals so they would die of massive blood loss.

Machairodus—one of the sabertoothed cats of Africa and Eurasia—had very elongated and stout upper canines with fine serrations. This species was stoutly built and stood about 4 feet tall at the shoulder. Certainly one of the most successful of the saber-toothed lines, individuals in the genus *Machairodus* roamed large areas of the world for an incredibly long stretch of time (earliest fossils are dated at 15 million years and the most recent ones are 2 million years old).

Homotherium, a lion-sized saber-toothed cat with impressive upper canines serrated like a steak knife, is often called the "scimitar-tooth cat" due to its broad saber-canines. It also possessed long, slender legs adapted to the pursuit of prey. Three separate species of a cat smaller than *Homotherium* (but still at 200 pounds, larger than modern leopards) were known as *Megantereons*. The saber-toothed canines of *Megantereons* were long, slender, dagger-shaped, and devoid of crenulations. These cats show a bit of an innovation for protecting those slender daggers—a bony flange right on the chin protruded from *Megantereons'* lower jaw. It was covered with a fleshy pad, and the cat's delicate fangs nested on either side of this protective device. *Megantereons'* limbs were short and robust, and great strength lay in powerful front paws that probably made them quite adept at climbing trees. While *Homotherium* was fleet-footed, *Megantereons* was the sumo wrestler of the ancient cat world.

In North America, *Smilodon* (of Rancho La Brea tar pit fame) was the ultimate in saber-toothedness—its teeth evolved to the maximum size of any known true cat. Just how long were those teeth? Extremely long. To give you a sense of just how long *extremely long* is, African lions have canines that measure 2 and one-half inches; *Smilodons'* were in excess of 6 inches in length. This snow leopard–sized predator was built like a Mack truck; powerful limbs and lower back speak to the fact that it did not chase its prey but waited in ambush for mega-herbivores. The enormous gape allowed it to tear out the throat of its prey with blade-like teeth. Being a North American species, *Smilodon* (sometimes referred to as a dirk-toothed cat) naturally did not interact with the earliest hominids. But it survived until 9,500 years ago, thousands of years after humans advanced into the North and South American continents. As Hans Kruuk commented, "it was around for long enough for it to have seen a good deal of primitive man, and vice versa." (An extinct North American cheetah and lion also survived until between 10,000 and 20,000 years ago.)

Any comparison of saber-toothedness quickly decays to the point of ridiculous relativity: they all had gargantuan teeth! However, another group of felids have been deemed *false* saber-toothed cats. At least four species of *Dinofelis* are called "false" sabertooths because their upper canines were not exaggerated to the degree of the true saber-toothed cats, although both upper and lower canines were still more developed than modern-day lions and tigers. The fangs in the *Dinofelis* group are not as curved as the true saber-toothed cats; they appear to have been more like straight-edged daggers. Size-wise, the false sabertooths were heavily built animals. With heavier front than hind limbs, they may have been midway in size between a modern-day leopard and lion. A particularly fine, intact skull dated at 1.5 million years ago was found at Kromdraai in South Africa, a site also yielding australopithecine remains. Some paleontologists classify one of the false saber-toothed species, *Dinofelis barlowi*, as a potential specialist at baboon and hominid killing.

Starting at about 3.5 million years ago the direct ancestors of today's lions, leopards, and cheetahs (called the conical-tooth cats) existed alongside the saber-toothed varieties. *Panthera* is the taxonomic classification containing all today's modern large cats except the cheetah. The epochs spanning the time between 5 million and 10,000 years ago sported a much wider range of pantherine species than exists today. The oldest fossil record of a lion is dated at 3.5 million years and was found at Laetoli in Tanzania where the famous trail of *Australopithecine afarensis* footprints were discovered. The first record of the extant leopard is also from this same site.

Many species of lions, leopards, and cheetahs did not survive until the present day. One example is the European cave lion. There's a cave by the name of Chauvet in the south of France that contains drawings of 73 cave lions; the drawings can be dated by carbon decay at precisely 32,000 years ago because piles of the charcoal used to make the drawings still lie on the cave floor as if the artist had just stepped away for a moment. The European cave lion was a different species from lions that now roam Africa; it might have been a quarter again larger and heavier than the modern variety. Some of the charcoal drawings at Chauvet are exquisitely accurate in detail and exhibit a fine-tuned knowledge of wildlife behavior, while others are obviously meant to be surreal depictions of a beast that was probably both a dangerous predator and a competitor of human hunters for large herbivores—European bison, mammoths, and giant elk.

THE LONG AND WINDING ROAD FROM
SOUTH AFRICA TO GEORGIA

As we discussed earlier, Man the Hunter as a paradigm for human evolution emerged from the caves of South Africa. Raymond Dart's analysis of over 7,000 fossils led him to the erroneous conclusion that australopithecines killed their huge prey with the bones of former victims, and—due to the high numbers of bashed-in hominid skulls—they also killed each other in callous and brutal fashion. Rigorous scientific examination of fossil evidence has jettisoned Dart's killer ape-man theory. While the killer image lives on in conventional wisdom, we see more and more researchers adopting a different concept of early man, such as this quote from a new volume on primates:

> Ironically, it is now believed that *Australopithecus*, rather than having been a predator himself, was a favorite food for large carnivores. The damage to fossil skulls, which Dart interpreted as evidence for club-wielding man-apes, turns out to be perfectly consistent with predation by leopards and hyenas. In all likelihood, therefore, the beginnings of our lineage were marked more by fear than ferocity.[21]

Eons ago South Africa, needless to say, was not the only location where humans were looked on as tasty meals by the cat family. The famous Olduvai Gorge in Tanzania, home to Louis and Mary Leakey's hominid finds, has been combed for fossils of other species. In the Pleistocene layers, fossilized bones from large carnivores have been plentiful—hyenas, jackals the size of African hunting dogs, saber-toothed cats, and large cats of modern aspect all coexisted with ancient hominids.[22]

This is also the case at other famous fossil hominid sites. Carnivore fossils from the east side of the Lake Rudolf Basin in Kenya and the Omo group formations in southern Ethiopia are abundantly situated in the rock layers with the not-at-all-abundant hominid finds from these areas. Large felines in particular are common and exhibit a wide diversity that has been compiled into the following inventory: true sabertooths *Homotherium* and *Megantereons*, four species of the false saber-toothed *Dinofelis* cats, plus cousins (or perhaps grandfathers) to modern leopards and lions, and—if that wasn't enough cat power—there was even a more massive version of the modern cheetah.[23]

An artist's rendition of the fate of one of our australopithecine ancestors. Fossil leopards, just like modern ones, drag prey into trees to escape competition from lions and hyenas. It is conjectured that bones from carcasses might have fallen into sinkholes; these sinkholes developed over time into caves. (C. Rudloff, redrawn from Turner 1997)

Much the same fossil-cat assemblages are found in South Africa at the famous Sterkfontein, Swartkrans, and Kromdraai cave sites. What makes South Africa so elucidatory for paleo-detectives is that its caves contain not just the perpetrators of annihilation, but also the victims: dozens of australopithecine and hundreds of baboon fossils. The first person to successfully challenge the killer ape-man scenario was C. K. Brain who, just like killer ape-man proponent Raymond Dart, was a South African paleontologist. Brain disagreed with Dart's analysis that australopithecines killed their own kin and their baboon cousins. He felt the fossils might be the discarded food remains of any number of extinct saber-toothed cats, false saber-toothed cats, cursorial hunting hyenas, or the ancestors of leopards and hyenas still found in Africa today. Brain's meticulous comparison of contemporary carnivore remains with the marks and indentations on the hominid and baboon skulls validated his theory and has won over most professional paleontologists.[24]

How did all of these australopithecine and baboon remains get into the caves? The most frequently drawn scenario incorporates the assumption that the caves of South Africa had trees growing near their entrances due to underground water sources and goes like this: Leopards drag their prey into trees to protect it from other predators; skulls and bones fall from the trees as the leopard gnaws on the carcass; skulls and bones end up in the cave. Brain suggested that another explanation might be that baboons and early hominids slept in the caves; leopards or other cats devoured them in the caves and the remains of the repasts piled up.[25] Thinking outside the box, Brain tried an experiment to see how a troop of baboons that used a cave as a sleeping site might react to a predator in their midst. He acted the part of the threat himself, hiding in the cave and appearing after the primates had settled down for the night. True to form for baboon behavior, even the intrusion of a danger such as a human being—while causing complete and utter pandemonium—did not force the baboons to leave the cave in the dark. It seems logical to assume that a predator hiding inside the cave would have easy access to baboon meals.

Earlier, we briefly mentioned the existence of caves located in modern-day Kenya that seem to replicate what may have been going on in South Africa millions of years ago.[26] The Mt. Suswa caves are havens for baboons, but not necessarily *safe* havens. The primates use the caves as night refuges—places to gather in large groups and sleep—as opposed to the usual baboon preference for cliffs or trees. But, the leopard population in the Mt. Suswa area knows the baboon sleeping site provides easy pickings, and generations of leopards have subsisted off the Mt. Suswa cave baboons. We are conjecturing here, but it makes sense that the leopards handle the particulars of cave predation with extreme subtlety. Rushing into an underground chamber and causing utter pandemonium in the hopes of catching a primate meal would probably culminate in the eventual abandonment of the caves by the baboons. If, however, the leopards finessed this situation (in just the way they prey on sleepy baboons ensconced in trees), they would carry out a stealthy approach with a quick swipe at an individual on the edge of the troop and then retreat with the victim into a deeper subterranean passage. That would cause havoc, but no more than baboons (or early hominids) have always tolerated from leopards. This careful "harvesting" of prey concurs with the alternate hypotheses posed by Brain to explain the hominid and baboon remains in South African caves.

We must add that even with all this evidence pointing to long ago carnivore activity in South African caves, there was still a bit of reticence to accept how amply primates figure in the diet of carnivores. When Brain formulated his hypotheses about predators of australopithecines and baboons at Swartkrans, he found it a strange and noteworthy state of affairs that over 50% of all the animals in one of the vertebrate fossil assemblages were hominids or baboons. He was amazed that fossil leopards may have concentrated so intensively on this kind of prey when no studies of contemporary primates suggested they played a major part in leopard diets.

Brain's conclusion that predation on living primates probably provides an accurate reflection of predation on early hominids serves our theory of Man the Hunted well. Three of the large Old World cats are now known to prey on apes: lions on chimpanzees, leopards on chimps and gorillas, and tigers on orangutans.[27]

Leaving South Africa, we turn to Eastern Europe. *Dmanisi* was not a name on the tip of every paleoanthropologist's tongue until very recently. But this village in the Republic of Georgia has shaken up the most entrenched theories regarding what our human ancestors were doing, and when and where they were doing it. Dmanisi, in the foothills of the Caucasus Mountains, lies close to the famous Silk Road of Marco Polo fame. It is a site worked by David Lordkipanidze, a Georgian scientist, and his team of paleontologists. And the fossils this team has found at

Dmanisi are revamping the reputation of one of our closest ancient relatives—*Homo erectus*—the long-legged and big-brained hominid who has
been acclaimed as the first to colonize terra firma outside the continent
of Africa. Lordkipanidze has found relatively primitive hominid skulls securely dated between 1.7 and ·1.8 million years in age—skulls that are
unlike any other *H. erectus* fossils found so far.[28] The Dmanisi specimens
look in many ways like an earlier twig on the hominid bush—*Homo habilis*. Could it be that a small-brained, long-armed, and short-legged *H.
habilis* was the first hominid to suffer from wanderlust? What a revision
in current theory is necessary if it *didn't* take a striding gait, or a fairly big
brain, or sophisticated stone tools to leave Africa and invade Eurasia!
Another explanation for the strangely primitive fossils is that the
Dmanisi hominids are a new species somewhere in the evolutionary
space between *H. habilis* and *H. erectus*. We'll have to wait for the discovery of the leg bones that go with the skulls to find out more about this
human relative who moved to Georgia so long ago.

One of the few crystal-clear things that can be stated about Dmanisi
is that—whomever they might be—the wandering hominids were
preyed on by many large carnivores. Here's a roster of fossil carnivores
that share the site with the mysterious hominid: Eurasian wolves, two
saber-toothed cat species, one bear species, and one leopard species.
From this lineup of the usual suspects, one of the perpetrators that
preyed on Dmanisi hominids has been disclosed in the customary forensic manner—a Dmanisi skull bears the signature set of holes into which
saber-toothed fangs fit with perfection. In addition gnaw marks on one
of the hominid lower jaws "reveal that some of the hominids at Dmanisi
ended up as cat food."[29]

The Dmanisi collection of carnivore and hominid fossils, accompanied by simple chopping and scraping tools, has evoked speculation that
early humans might have been at risk from big cats (and wolves and bears)
while at the same time benefiting from the ready food supply they could
scavenge from the predators. The theory that early hominids were primarily scavenging species does not, in our opinion, fit the evidence of the
fossil record nor the living primate paradigms. Nonetheless, there are no
lack of distinguished proponents who advance this scenario.[30] The scavenging theory, unlike Man the Hunter, does not discount the fact that
hominids were prey to many large and dangerous prehistoric animals.

One of the champions of a scavenging design for early hominid lifestyle is Curtis Marean, an anthropologist who has given a great deal of weight to the relevance of saber-toothed cats on hominid evolution. It is Marean's theory that hominids scavenged off the massive herbivores (such as elephants) that saber-toothed cats killed in a densely wooded habitat. This "close" environment made the stealing of carnivore food fairly safe (run quickly, steal part of carcass, dive back into dense forest, shinny up tree). Then at the pivotal 1.8-million-years-ago mark, a climate change began. The world got colder and dried out. . . . the dense woods disappeared, and with the habitat so went the giant sabertooths and their giant herbivorous prey. By 1.6 million years ago Africa was a different environment entirely. The large carnivores who survived the climatic shift were the ones that had lived on the grassland plains eating so-called medium-sized herbivores, like buffalo, gazelle, and zebra, so they were unaffected by the drying up of the wetter forests. They had been savanna predators and they remained savanna predators, and it was not nearly as easy for hominids to get away with stealing their suppers! As the climate morphed, our smallish bipedal ancestors had to confront big cats that had killed medium-sized prey in open areas. With this scenario, *becoming* the prey was just as likely as *stealing* the prey.[31]

What happens when the environment changes, the rules change, and a species is challenged? Adapt or die out are the only two options. Marean proposes that the need to confront large cats in open habitat spurred adaptations in the hominid line. Confrontation with cats may have forced a growth spurt—not just in behavioral adaptations, but also in anatomical ones. *Homo erectus* was on the scene by 1.6 million years ago and *H. habilis* seems to have departed from the landscape. According to Marean, the evolutionary consequences of predation by big cats might underlie a growth in height, bulk, and length in lower limbs, and the substitution of a striding gait for tree-climbing ability—all characteristics of *H. erectus*. Fossils of *H. erectus* also manifest a significant increase in cranial capacity with the development of a whole new tool-kit containing sophisticated stone gadgets. Under Marean's scenario, noticeable brain size increase from 650 cc in *H. habilis* to 1,000–1,100 cc in *H. erectus* might be part of the morphological changes brought about by a combination of climate change and predation by big cats.

KILLING MACHINES

Nearly every feature of a cat's body is related to its ability to detect and catch prey, including adaptations such as camouflaging patterns of fur, heightened senses of sight and hearing, skeletal design to enhance speed and power, and specialization of teeth and jaws. Olfaction—the keen sense of smell found in many mammals—is surprisingly less important to cats for prey location than it is for other carnivores, such as members of the dog family.

Size is also a less important limiting factor with felids than with many other predators. The maximum size prey many wild cats are able to kill is exponentially related to their own body mass. A small wild cat such as an ocelot weighs an average of 30 pounds and preys on animals weighing up to 25 pounds. However, the African caracal, weighing approximately 40 pounds, preys on animals twice its own mass, and tigers are able to kill animals four times their own weight. Lions, on the other hand, have the added advantage of a permanent social group, and the size of prey will increase with the number of lions present at a hunt.[32]

All of the carnivores—cats, wild dogs, hyenas—use a slow and partly concealed approach to their intended prey in the initial stage of predation. Their bodies are held lower than the normal position when stalking. Making considerable use of cover, the stalk is facilitated in the cat family by the sleek feline body shape and camouflaged coloration. Felids stalk their prey in elaborate fashion before rushing; they crouch down for periods from just a few minutes up to as long as an hour. For cats, a minimal distance covered in the final charge is strongly correlated with a successful kill. The closer they can get while stalking, the shorter the rush at the end and the less time the prey has to react and get away.

The basic sequence of cat predation is search, stalk, immobilize. Once potential prey have been observed, most cat species approach through a series of crouched stalks or slinking runs between available cover. Cats possess adaptations for leaping and grasping prey with their sharp, retractile claws.[33] A single, well-directed neck bite (which severs the prey's spinal cord) is the lethal specialty of all cat species, allowing them to kill prey larger than themselves. As if that weren't enough, the feline repertoire includes three other killing bites (one to the neck that can choke prey to death; another that clamps onto the nose and mouth of prey to suffocate it; and yet another that can crush the victim's skull).

BEFORE THE AGE OF ULCERS

What would it feel like if all these tremendously powerful wild cats—lords of all they surveyed—were out there stalking us with their teeth and claws? How did our ancestors deal with so many predators casting around for their next meal? One of us (DH) experienced an hour or two that might have supplied the tiniest fraction of those ancient hominid feelings.

"What if they weren't satiated and sleeping?" popped into my mind as I was sitting under an acacia tree in Mikumi National Park, Tanzania, with two park rangers. The tree was decorated with a dozen sleepy lions draped over branches like huge tawny tinsel on a Christmas tree. It was a favorite after-feeding hangout of the lions (who don't ordinarily take to trees for siestas). My official government hosts had the requisite rifle—just in case—but no one felt anything like danger. This must be how prey animals feel when predators are obviously not on the hunt, I mused. I couldn't even conjure up the panic that 12 lions would have aroused if I hadn't been so assured by their full stomachs and heavy-lidded eyes. Later, after we began writing this book, I realized I had had an experience not unlike a far-distant hominid relative. Obviously, prey species cannot live in a state of terrified panic all the time—the stress would kill them before the predators did! There has to be a certain sense of safety between infrequent moments of all-out terror. Weren't my colleagues and I under the acacia tree experiencing the same placidity that impala exhibit when they calmly graze in the presence of resting lions? Yes, there was a weapon someone could grab; but to tell the truth, if a lion had jumped or fallen out of the tree, no human possesses the reaction time necessary to assess the situation, aim a gun, and pull the trigger before a lion leaped onto . . . me? (Well, in retrospect, maybe these little excursions aren't such a bright idea. Maybe I was falling into the "stupid Yellowstone tourist" trap. . . . you know, the guy who places his little boy next to a bear so he can get a really cute picture of their vacation.)

Recalling and discussing this experience brought up some colossal questions:

1. What is the physiological basis for fear?

2. Why are people who do not experience the impact of predation still so afraid of predators?

3. How could early hominids (or any preyed-upon species for that matter) withstand the psychological pressure of predation?

Question number 1 is probably the most straightforward to answer.[34] The anatomy of fear includes dilation of pupils (to increase visual cues to danger), dilation of bronchioles in the lungs (to increase oxygen uptake), a spike in blood pressure and heart rate (to provide the brain and muscles with more fuel), breakdown of glycogen in the liver (to provide instant energy), flooding of the bloodstream with adrenalin (to guarantee a strong defense), contraction of the spleen (to pump out white blood cells just in case they are needed), preparation to void the bladder and colon (in anticipation of violent action), constriction of capillaries in the stomach and gastrointestinal tract (to divert blood to the muscles), and piloerection of hair (the strange phenomenon of body hair "standing on end"—perhaps to enhance size). All of these are accomplished through the work of a primitive part of the brain called the amygdala. The amygdala sends an all-out systems alert to the central and autonomic nervous systems that gets these physiological responses up and running.

Question number 2 (why would humans retain such an undiluted fear of predators without personal experiences?) is also answerable, but only because of 25 years of research by Joseph LeDoux of New York University. The amygdala also stores memories of fear, danger, or threat. It can be a totally unconscious memory that is retained and kicks in only when sight, sound, or touch prompts it. "Conditioned fear" is the amygdala's specialty. This is what makes you freeze before you have time to process in your cerebral cortex whatever it was that scared you. The amygdala portion of the brain is found in the brains of many vertebrate species and functions in the same way—it's natural selection's best shot at giving organisms an edge in a dangerous environment. But "conditioned fear" doesn't mean that you have, for instance, survived a mauling by a wild lion so that the next time you see a lion all the fear responses kick in. It *does* mean that large, predatory animals that pop out of nowhere (and scary stories told or read about the same) have been parked in the amygdala and underlined as *extremely* important. One way to explain this adaptation is that

> Our brains seem to have been designed to allow the fear system to take control in threatening situations and prevent our conscious awareness from reigning. This may have been an optimal design from predator-rich environments in which survival was a minute-by-minute question. . . . The fact that the amygdala's basic architecture reappears in so many species is testimony to its evolutionary importance: Natural selection doesn't tinker with components that have proved essential to basic survival. Of course, the persistence of the low road [the non-cortex reaction] in a world where predators are largely nonexistent may no longer be adaptive, but that's the trade-off of human culture.[35]

The answer to our final colossal question (how can the threat of impending predation be tolerated psychologically?) is speculative since scientists do not know all of the neural pathways that maintain mental equilibrium in the presence of extreme but intermittent stress. War zones provide some clues since posttraumatic stress disorders ("shell shock") are now accepted as a common aftermath of combat experiences even though the soldiers may seem to relax and behave normally for short periods between battles. We suggest that the only possible answer to this question lies with continued observation of prey species. We must refer to other species for information on how it is possible to graze happily (if you are an impala) while in the presence of lions. As primatologists we firmly believe—based on observation of wild primates—that prey go on with the minutiae of their lives between instances of predator activity. Under normal ecological conditions, the adrenaline rushes subside after the predator attacks, and hormones revert to neutral gear—except for the unlucky individual who became the predator's meal. Did our ancestors have respite from constant psychological terror produced by the presence of large cat predators? A resounding "yes." We primates are amazingly resilient. There is a threat of attack by a predator and all hell breaks loose. The predator leaves the area (with or without a meal) and the primates soon resume their lives of foraging and social interactions. Wild primate lives are not constant battles to stay alive, nor was there a continuous state of terror for Man the Hunted.

Perfect Primate Predators

None of the discussion above obviates the fact that primates are a frequent prey item for many species of wild cats. (The frequency in which primates occur in leopard diets ranges as high as 80%.)[36] And, as we've said before, if we want to project what might have happened to our early ancestors, we can look at modern non-human primates that end up as prey for the big cats. Normally opportunistic hunters, the availability of prey or total prey numbers are the important criteria for food selection by cats. In other words, most cats are not searching out a specific kind of food. They hunt and kill what they encounter, and the more prey of one species in their neighborhood, the more likely the cats are to encounter an individual of that species.[37]

Leopards have a wide geographic range over much of Africa and southern Asia. Particularly flexible in their environmental needs, they are able to exist in almost any habitat, from arid grassland to semi-desert to dense rain forest, and from mountainous foothills to riverine habitat. The hunting strategy of the leopard is largely a matter of lurking in likely places (water holes are always good) and approaching its prey in a stealthy manner, followed by a quick spring and swipe with the paw. (It has been noted that when capturing primates a leopard will grab ahold wherever possible rather than grabbing only for the neck as it would if capturing a herbivore; primates are obviously a little more agile than a buffalo.) The use of stealth by hunting leopards cannot be overstated. Leopards are adept at silently creeping up on sleeping animals; baboons asleep in rocks are a frequent prize of nocturnal hunting. So ghostly silent is the hunting leopard that humans and dogs have been killed in their beds without waking others in the house. The famous naturalist, Jonathan Kingdon, wrote about one specific case in which a human baby was taken off the breast of its sleeping mother by a leopard.[38]

Leopards feed on relatively small prey, such as primates, because they hunt alone and need to carry carcasses into trees to keep their kills from being pirated away by larger cats or pack-hunting dogs and hyenas. Leopards also have a much wider prey base than other large cat species,

Leopards typically rely on primates as food throughout their range. (Peggy and Erwin Bauer)

which enables them to utilize primates of all sizes in their diets. Consequently, the range of non-human primate species in the diet of leopards is rather extensive. In Africa they are known to prey on bonobos (pygmy chimpanzees), common chimpanzees, western lowland gorillas, many species of rain-forest guenons, vervets, and species of savanna and forest baboons. In Asia leopards prey on langurs, golden snub-nosed monkeys, a range of macaque species, and gibbons.[39]

The proportion of primate prey in the diet differs greatly among species of cats, but leopards *commonly* consume primates throughout their extensive range. During a classic study of leopard ecology in Côte d'Ivoire, Bernard Hoppe-Dominik discovered that seven different species of primates accounted for about 16% of the prey in the diet of leopards. Based on analysis of leopard feces, George Schaller found that Hanuman langurs composed almost one-third of leopard diets at a site in India. Researchers reported one of the highest frequencies of primates in a leopard diet (about 82%) at another research site in India. Primatologist Lynne Isbell found that an influx of leopards caused such an escalation in vervet deaths at Amboseli National Park, Kenya, that nearly half the vervet population she was studying was killed during a 1-year period. One last example—an absence of deer and antelope (possibly due to poaching) in Indonesia's Meru-Betiri Park converted both tigers and leopards to reliance on primates as their primary prey. John Seidensticker of the Smithsonian Institution, along with Ir. Suyono of the Indonesian government, estimated that the percentages of primates in tiger and leopard diets totaled 33% and 57%, respectively.[40]

The clouded leopard of Southeast Asia (a separate species that is different in its anatomy and is much smaller than the true leopard) is one of the most arboreal of the cat family. It is intermediate in appearance between the large cats of the genus *Panthera* (leopards, lions, tigers) and the small cats of the genus *Felis* (ocelots, caracals, bobcats). With a relatively small head and yet with large canines and muzzle, the clouded leopard is supremely efficient in the capture of primates. Clouded leopards have been known to prey on large primates such as juvenile orangutans and proboscis monkeys.[41]

One species of wild cat, the cheetah, might be considered an implausible predator in comparison to other members of its family. Of all cats only the cheetah has no sheath into which its claws can retract. (Precisely speaking, it is not that they are unable to retract their claws, there is simply no skin into which the claws can be drawn.) The cheetah also exhibits smaller canines and larger nostrils than other large-cat species, and they differ radically from other cats in their hunting techniques as well. Unlike the other cats, cheetah bodies are geared for high-speed pursuit of prey and not for stealthy ambush. Cheetah prey are smaller in size than that of lions or leopards, and their unusual claws make them completely terrestrial. Compared to the other large cats, few records exist of cheetah predation on primates.[42]

Tigers are solitary, territorial hunters that thrive in dense vegetation where their camouflage stripes almost totally hide them from prey. Stripes serve to break up the tiger's silhouette in long grass, thus giving the species a great advantage during the stalking phase of the hunt. Tigers are usually assumed to take only huge prey (for example, water buffalo that weigh in excess of 800 pounds), but tigers—like all cats—are opportunists, and a smallish primate is often a quick and satisfying meal. Tigers have been identified as predators of Hanuman langurs, orangutans, and many of the Asian macaque species.

Leaf-eating langurs are one of the major prey species of tigers in the forest of Ranthambhore, India, where tigers catch these partly terrestrial monkeys when they descend to the ground. Although langurs are a regular part of the tigers' diets in the Ranthambhore study, finding a langur carcass is rare because a 25-to-40-pound monkey is consumed completely by a tiger at one feeding. Fecal samples gathered in Royal Chitwan National Park, Nepal, confirmed the inclusion of langurs in the tiger diet there, and at Kanha, India, langurs and rhesus monkeys are commonly captured by tigers.[43]

All cats are solitary hunters except lions. In his monograph on Serengeti lions, zoologist George Schaller calculated that lions paired up with at least one other pride member in slightly over half of their hunts. However, the number of prey killed per lion per hunt actually *decreases* when more than two lions are hunting together. Benefits of group living must accrue to female lions through the maintenance of territories and protection of young, because the foraging benefits of social hunting for lions are not sufficient to account for the formation of groups.

Lions begin their hunt by randomly searching their environment for prey. Once prey has been sighted, the stalk phase of the hunt can be of varying length, alternating between crouched movements and frozen stillness. If the prey animal remains unaware of the stalking lion, the predator will make a final, fast, and deadly dash. At several African sites, fecal analyses showed a low range of primate prey in lion diets (near zero to 6%).[44] However, we know from personal experience that some lions actually may come to prefer primates.

We had the opportunity to observe two lions that were practically baboon connoisseurs. Todd Wilkinson, guide at Rukimechi Reserve near Mana Pools National Park, Zimbabwe, had told us of two lionesses whose favorite prey was baboons. Todd was so familiar with the wildlife of the private reserve that he found the two lionesses lying in a dry riverbank within an hour. They were the only two in the pride who had a predilection for primate prey. Todd had witnessed two kills himself and explained that the "girls" had started preferring baboons at an early age and kept up the habit as they grew older.[45] Six sightings of baboon kills by the two lionesses were recorded in a four-year period. Given the rarity of seeing a lion kill, this was an impressive number.

GIVE US THE BEAR FACTS

Where do bears fit into the Man the Hunted scenario? The clear-cut relationship between fossil cats and fossil hominids does not exist for the bear family, but present-day situations lead us to a supposition that ancient bears were unlikely to pass up a hominid meal when it presented itself. Large and clever predators, bears deserve a discussion.

The bear family evolved about 30 to 40 million years ago.[46] The bears are more closely related to dogs than to cats, so why are we talking about them along with lions and tigers? We decided to discuss cats and bears together because they usually live solitary adult lives hunting by ambush or opportunism. Wild dogs and hyenas, alternatively, normally hunt in packs and run down (in other words, exhaust) their prey.

The most majestic sight imaginable is a polar bear in the wild. While in Nunavut (the Inuit territory of the Canadian Arctic), one of us (DH) witnessed the world's largest terrestrial carnivore in the act of predation. The sun was breathtakingly bright, the water an icy blue sheet, and as the small outboard motorboat rounded a rocky outcropping in Wager Bay—so tiny it didn't qualify as an island—there stood a large male polar bear dragging a recently killed bearded seal out of the water. The bear's muzzle was stained red with blood as he started eating. He stared at us humans nonchalantly—an insignificant intrusion on his dining pleasure. Deciding a drink would be in order, he lumbered down the rocks to the water's edge. Male polar bears reach a length of nearly 10 feet and weigh about 1,400 pounds (without winter fat) to 1 ton (with stored fat).[47]

Their power is awesome. I was shown a small plane, the roof of which looked as if it had been opened with a dull can opener. A female polar bear and her cubs had "investigated" the interior of the plane to see if food was available. Sadly, word reached camp the same day as our encounter with the large male that an Inuit grandmother had been killed by a polar bear as she tried to protect her grandchild from an attack.

Deaths from polar bears have always been a part of Inuit life. Even today, with polar bear populations declining due to global warming and other human-related environmental offenses, there are often several incidents every year. These tend to occur most often under certain circumstances—females with cubs to feed or inexperienced and hungry subadults—and in certain locations, such as sites of human habitation, hunting camps, or weather stations. Polar bears, unlike the other living species in the bear family, seem to mentally catalog all mammals—*Homo sapiens* included—as prey items. They are much more willing to consider humans as food, and an attack from an animal the size of a polar bear almost always ends in death.[48]

Bears are carnivores by ancestry and anatomy. Modern bears, except for the polar species, have nevertheless evolved over time into omnivores in a functional sense, quite happy to eat vegetation and berries, but never passing up the occasional warm-blooded opportunity that wanders into their path.[49] Bears, as we know them—huge animals—appeared about 6 million years ago. The first large bears were contemporaneous with hominids in time but whether they lived in the same places as hominids is quite fuzzy. There were gigantic bear-like predecessors in Africa around 7 million years ago and these lasted until 2–3 million years ago, but it is possible that no ursids (true bears) were residents of Africa except in the Atlas Mountains of Morocco. There is a clearer record of the bear–human relationship after hominid migration from Africa to Asia. Three lines of bear ancestors are traceable: two of these occurred in Asia and one only in Europe.

An extinct European fossil ursid, commonly called the cave bear, spanned the time period of 10,000 to 50,000 years ago. The extinction of cave bears is cloaked in mystery. Investigation of several caves in the heart of Europe unearthed skeletal remains of these bears numbering in the tens of thousands, as if the remains were piled up by human hands. Did the early Europeans hunt the bears? Did they kill them for ritual purposes? Or—and this is a legitimate theory because there is a heavily disproportionate number of old individuals—did the subterranean caches represent natural graveyards for elderly bears? Or, was hibernation during the Ice Age a sometimes-fatal *in*activity? The cave bear disappeared at the close of the Ice Age concurrently with many of the large European mammal species, which may point to climatic reasons for their extinction rather than human intervention.[50]

The current speciation of bears is fairly simple: the northern bears (polar, Asian black, American black, and brown or grizzly) are large enough to be human predators. The southern bear species (sloth, sun, and spectacled) are smaller, less common, and are not known to prey on humans. The polar bear, as described earlier in this section, is definitely a predator with our species on the menu. As top gun in their white and icy world, they are probably behaving as bears did throughout time past. This species has not been exposed to humans, guns, and organized hunting for long enough to have evolved a gene pool that is extremely wary of people.

According to Stephen Herrero, naturalist and bear expert, this is exactly what has happened to black bears and grizzly bears. He estimates a North American population of 600,000 black bears and 60,000 grizzlies, so there are countless times when the bears and humans are in proximity *without* the occurrence of predation. In U.S. and Canadian police and park warden records there are only 23 human fatalities from black bears and twice as many grizzly bear–caused deaths from 1900 to 1980. But in the 1990s an upsurge occurred: there were 11 human deaths from black bears and 18 from grizzly bears. As with the mountain lion, this seeming increase may have more to do with the increasing tendency for people to encroach on bear habitat than with an increase in the ferocity of bears. Unfortunately, the new millennium started off with the killing and consumption of an Alaskan camper by a grizzly bear who had become accustomed to the garbage that wilderness visitors produce.[51]

Herrero has written a book entitled *Bear Attacks: Their Causes and Avoidance*. He divided all bear attacks into two categories: defensive and predatory. Defensive attacks comprise mother–cub protection, food protection, or just a startled bear that feels it is cornered and must react aggressively. For these kinds of attacks, Herrero gives advice on how to avoid, minimize, or escape the danger. It is possible, if a person curls up and plays dead, that the bear will inflict some bites and then leave the scene. The trick is to know the defensive bear from the predatory bear because the aforementioned "play dead" behavior will possibly only make you "real dead" more quickly if the bear views you as prey. *Bear Attacks* contains Herrero's analyses of 414 bear–human interactions. He found that of the fatal attacks in the 1900–1980 period, black bears (the smaller of the two species) were most likely to have killed a human for predatory reasons. Counterintuitively, the black bear is more likely to view people as prey than the larger, more feared, grizzly bear. In fact 90% of the black bear attacks with fatal results were in the predation category. More statistics make this an even clearer picture—half of the black-bear human victims were aged 18 or younger and one-quarter were younger than 10 years old. There is no question in an investigator's mind when predation is the motive for a bear kill: the victims are eaten in the same way that a deer would be consumed—torso and innards first, followed by fleshy parts such as the upper legs. While the size of children fits the black bear's mental image of prey, they will also attack a full-grown man with impunity.[52]

One of the most horrifying predation attacks by a black bear did not result in a fatality. A geologist working for the state of Alaska, Cynthia Dusel-Bacon, was dropped off by Ed, her helicopter pilot, about 60 miles south of Fairbanks one August morning in 1977. Cynthia was out to obtain rock samples in an uninhabited area, but she was wilderness savvy and practiced good bear keep-away behavior, including yelling every so often to let bears know they should clear out of her space. One black bear didn't see the yelling as anything but a come-and-get-me invitation. The geologist could tell a bear was stalking her and no amount of aggressive action on her part seemed a deterrent. When the bear circled around and finally attacked, she was dragged by the arm into thick underbrush. She then tried the play-dead advice; the bear started to eat her right arm and the flesh under it. "I was completely conscious of feeling my flesh torn, teeth against bone, but the sensation was more of numb horror at what was happening to me than of specific reaction to each bite."[53]

The narrative gets pretty powerful when she relates the sensation of the bear biting her head and tearing at her scalp, hearing the crunching sound of the bear's teeth cracking into her skull. Whew! And yet she survived. She managed to keep her cool through all of this and get a radio out of her backpack with her uneaten arm while the bear was taking a break from its meal. She activated the transmitter and holding it close to her mouth, said as loudly as she could, "Ed, this is Cynthia. Come quick,

I'm being eaten by a bear." Cynthia explained later that "I said 'eaten' be-cause I was convinced that the bear wasn't just mauling me or playing with me. I was its prey, and it had no intention of letting me escape."[54]

Cynthia's is a long narrative, and we wish we could say that Ed and the rescuers arrived quickly. They didn't. Her good arm was also eaten by the bear before noise from a helicopter scared the bear away from its prize. Cynthia lost both arms, but her head wounds healed and she con-tinued her life in Alaska.

Some say that the Asian black, or moon bear (named for the large white crescent on its chest), is more irritable and less intimidated by hu-mans than the North American black bear. Locals can attest to a nasty disposition in these 400-to-500-pound ursids. The moon bear is the most carnivorous of all the Asian bears, and individuals of the species are known to kill animals as large as adult water buffaloes by breaking their necks. This species has a long and violent history with humans. Each year in Japan 2–6 people are killed and 10–25 injured in bear attacks; most of the encounters are in warm weather when people tend to gather bamboo shoots in the wild. However, the species hardly matches the car-nage that *humans* have inflicted on the moon bears. Thousands are hunted every year in Japan, and the Chinese have made an industry of killing moon bears for their paws and gall bladders. There's not much hope for the continuation of wild populations of this species.

The brown bear of Asia is the same species as the North American grizzly. One of the many races of brown bears dwells in Tibet and several provinces of western China. Known as the horse bear because of a yellow, saddle-shaped cape on its shoulders, it is still fairly common in these ar-eas. Chinese biologists contend that 1,500 people are killed annually by horse bears—most of the attacks are on farmers who are newly cultivat-ing the Tibetan Plateau. Firearms are not allowed in China so contact or conflict with these huge bears almost always ends up with the bears as the winners. No records exist for bear predation on humans in Russia, al-though a Japanese wildlife photographer of great renown was killed by a Russian brown bear in 1995.[55]

So, we have now scrutinized the type of hominid predators that slowly and carefully stalk and ambush their prey. What about the other kind of carnivore—the packs of fast dogs and hyenas? They aren't often implicated in hominid predation. . . . or are they?

5

COURSING HYENAS AND HUNGRY DOGS

It's surprising how many times university professors hear a comment from an undergraduate student and it begins a whole new train of thought. Since both of us are in the classroom, we often mention our predation research to students as it relates to course subject matter. One of us (DH) brought up predation as an analogy to another anthropology topic and received a remarkable insight through the comments of a young lady who had visited relatives in Croatia over the summer of 2002. Her relations had talked a lot about wolves, and a lot about their fear of wolves, and a lot about wolves *literally* at their door. Sometimes you find students will innocently repeat old wives' tales, and you just shrug your shoulders at the silly things people will believe—in this case, especially about predators—even in the twenty-first century, and in Europe no less. I am afraid I mentally put her comments into this category. I am now offering my *mea culpa*: Dear student, you were not duped; your relatives were not pulling your leg; you were simply far ahead of us in our research.

The student's comment about a fear of wolves especially bothered us because it dealt with two unresolvable sets of facts, both from unimpeachable sources. L. David Mech is undoubtedly the world's authority on wolf behavior and ecology. He's been the acknowledged expert on wolves since the first of his landmark studies was published thirty-five years ago.[1] Mech carefully studied all records of alleged wolf attacks in North America. His findings support the fact that no (non-rabid) wild wolf has ever attacked a human in North America during historical times.

Yet, Hans Kruuk, also a world-renowned zoologist who specializes in carnivore behavior, has investigated tales of wolf predation on humans in Europe. It's as if the records deal with two different species. North American wolves are wary and avoid human contact (except their penchant for eating tied-up sled dogs in Alaskan hamlets), while European wolves have a recorded history, from before medieval times up to the present, that is quite the opposite.

WOLVES AT THE DOOR

European wolves prey on humans, especially in the summer when females are on the lookout for extra food to feed their cubs.[2] We realize this is a bold statement that deserves to be supported with facts. A patient reading of the next few pages will provide the rationale for our contention that humans, especially small humans, might have been one of the most available and appropriate prey for wolves in the past. But to get there from here we need to tell a fascinating story.

Hans Kruuk, the zoologist mentioned above, was studying mink populations during the 1990s in Belarus, a republic that borders Russia and that was formerly included in the Soviet Union. When he arrived at his study site, he was immediately immersed in wolf predation events. The first incident involved a local man who was walking home on a cart track through a forest (the only motorized vehicles owned in the outlying villages of Belarus are tractors—cars are practically nonexistent). He never arrived at his destination. There wasn't much debate about what had happened to him or why he had disappeared—in this small Eastern European village wolves eat people; it's as simple as that. Two months earlier a woodcutter had vanished—a few bits of the man were found along with wolf tracks. Just a week or two before *that* incident a little girl who had been kept late after school as punishment never made it home. Her father found her head and some blood in the snow, along with wolf tracks. (The father subsequently shot the schoolmaster. In the parent's eyes, the teacher had meted out a virtual death sentence through his disciplinary action, placing the child in the dangerous position of walking home alone after nightfall.)

What was going on in this out-of-the-way part of Europe? Kruuk pursued the topic and unearthed archival information that surprised him greatly. Something—wolf predation—had been going on for centuries and not just in out-of-the-way parts of Eastern Europe. His native area of southern Holland had been the scene of heavy wolf predation on children in the nineteenth century. A wave of wolf attacks took place between 1810 and 1811 in the Netherlands that resulted in the deaths of twelve children and attacks on five others (all the fatalities were children between the ages of 3 and 10 years).

Just as the student who visited relatives in Croatia had implied when relating her comments, there is a constancy of wolf predation on humans throughout European history. North Americans are surprised by the incidents; we have no awareness regarding the extent of deaths attributable to hungry wolves. Kruuk mused on the same subject:

> These events happened recently near a village and in an area that I happened to visit. No one there collects the statistics, and the authorities have other things to do. But I could not help wondering how much more of this would be going on there in the endless wilds of Belarus and Russia, never reported except in the odd newspaper article. . . . [A] scientist with vast experience in the area informed me that wolf attacks are not at all uncommon. There are many wolves, and people are surprised that anyone in the west should doubt that wolves kill people.[3]

We find this quote thoroughly compelling. Westerners may be able to fathom that far away in the wilds of Africa or somewhere in India there are human populations presently subjected to predation from large, fierce animals. But what a shocking wake-up call (like a bucket of cold water overturned on our collective heads) that people in modern-day Europe can declare "wolf predation just happens; it is a fact of life."[4]

Predictably, Kruuk found much the same situation when he expanded his research. He happened to travel to the Baltic nation of Estonia, and while Kruuk's decision to investigate Estonia was entirely random, it ended up providing the first factual basis for the Eastern European perception of wolves as a never-ending danger. In Estonia he encountered a cultural anomaly: precise records. They were in the form of meticulous registries kept by Lutheran churches for many centuries, notations that included information on each parishioner's cause of death. What's more, these parish records had been carefully scrutinized by a local historian. Reliable data were available for this rather small nation, and if Estonia could serve as a microcosm of present–day Eastern Europe, it would allow for extrapolation of the entire phenomenon. Here's a small amount of the data gleaned:

Never a crowded place, Estonia's population in the nineteenth century hardly totaled more than a few hundred thousand people. Out of this demographic entirety, 111 people had been killed by wolves between 1804 and 1853; 108 of them were children (average age 7 years).

There were waves of wolf attacks rather than a steady annual rate. Seventy-five percent of the attacks and/or fatalities in Estonia occurred in the northern district of Tartuma. (Was it the least human-populated district, or was it the most heavily wolf-populated district? Was there some correlation with an ecological situation—such as a reduced deer population in that area? Good questions, but we'll probably never know the answers to them.)

There was a definite seasonality in the casualties. The months of January through June averaged 10.7 human fatalities per month; in July through August the average jumped to 25 deaths per month; from September through December the average dropped to 5 per month. Kruuk, as a carnivore biologist, recognized the significance of that spike in the summer months. Wolf pups are born in early spring and are wholly dependent on mother's milk for the first few months; at about 4 months old, they will begin to need solid food as a supplement to nursing. Most recorded kills were by lone wolves, rather than packs, which is another logical correlation to the hypothesis that female wolves were feeding their growing offspring.[5] This pressure for female wolves to bring home extra food to pups probably translates into hunting forays seeking small, weak prey. The descriptions of several deaths support this; children were *selectively* taken by the wolves. For example, in entries it was noted that a child herding cattle would be killed, but the cattle would be left alone.

When Kruuk looked at the Dutch records he found much the same situation—a spike in the number of children eaten by wolves in the summer months. And, 30 years previous to Kruuk's study, historian and naturalist C. D. Clarke, who had reviewed the records on human deaths by wolves in central Europe, also found that most victims were children. Clarke was specifically looking at the three-year period (1764–1767) in the Gévedaun area of France. During this time 100 people (almost all children) in a relatively small portion of central France were attacked and consumed by wolves. The wolves (eventually killed and examined) were a male and female alleged to be much larger than the average European subspecies. Clarke postulated they may have been first-generation wolf–dog crosses exhibiting excessive hybrid vigor.

Back in Chapter 3 we brought up a 1996 headline ("India Fighting Plague of Man-Eating Wolves") found on the normally sedate front page of the *New York Times*. The edition carried the story of villagers in Uttar Pradesh, a state in northern India, who were experiencing assaults by a wolf pack.

> The wolf pounced while Urmila Devi and three of her eight children were in a grassy clearing at the edge of the village, using the open ground for a toilet. The animal, about 100 pounds of coiled sinew and muscle, seized the smallest child, a 4-year-old boy. . . . and carried him by the neck into the luxuriant stands of corn and elephant grass that stretch to a nearby riverbank. When a police search party found the boy three days later, half a mile away, all that remained was his head. From the claw and tooth marks, pathologists confirmed he had been killed by a wolf—probably one of a pack that conservationists believe has been roaming this area, driven to killing small children by hunger or by something else that has upset the natural instinct of wolves to avoid humans, like thrill-seeking villagers stealing cubs from a lair.[6]

Seventy-six children in all—under the age of 10—disappeared over a six-month period in 1996–1997 from that area; all deaths were attributed to wolves. (In this same locale, in 1878, British officials recorded 624 humans killed by wolves.) The reference to the villagers stealing pups in the quote above prompted an Indian conservation organization to explain that most of the remaining wolves in India live outside wildlife reserves where they easily come into conflict with poor farmers. Poisoning of wolves and killing of pups is illegal but routine.[7] Despite the allegation in the *New York Times*, it's almost ludicrous to propose that wolves would be eating human children as a direct result of their own pups being killed. Revenge is hardly as adequate an explanation for predation as hunger.

Over and over we kept returning to the unresolved question of why predation by a single species should be diametrically different on one continent than it was on others. Hans Kruuk wrestled with it, too:

The almost complete absence of wolf attacks on people in North America is confirmed by several . . . authorities, and it must be genuine, not just resting on a lack of information. It is in striking contrast to recent history in Europe, where stood the cradle of Little Red Riding Hood. That fairy tale is based on actual horrendous incidents, which were not that rare either. Why wolves in Europe (and Asia as well) should behave so differently from those in North America is still quite unknown—but the data show indisputably that wolves were (and still are) regular predators on humans, often on children.[8]

Here's a theory we'll throw out on the table to account for the conflicting data summed up as zero wolf attacks in North America versus untold numbers of wolf attacks in Eurasia. Our theory is based on simple logic and new paleontological evidence:

- No hominids originated in North America; humans first colonized the New World perhaps 20,000 years ago at most.

- When humans did arrive in North America 20,000 years before the present, they already possessed fire, weapons, speech, and large-scale hunting capabilities.

- Thus, from their first contact with humans, North American wolves were introduced to a dangerous competitor for herd animals and, in some unknown number of generations, they passed on the genetic information that it was wise to stay as far away from these new upright beings as possible.

- The historical record of wolf–human interactions in North America encompasses only 500 years since European exploration and colonization, but involved the use of firearms, confirming the wolves' view that it was best to avoid humans.

- But we know that in Eurasia wolves have spent a minimum of 1.7 million years in a relationship with hominids because we have the fossil proof from the Dmanisi site in the Republic of Georgia, showing that wolves and hominids were coexisting in time and space.

That the relationship of wolves and hominids was totally different in the Republic of Georgia from the North American experience is undeniable. Specifically, the "pea-brained"[9] hominid who lived at Dmanisi 1.7 million years ago wasn't a powerful hunter, and wasn't a competitor with the indigenous wolves for grazing animals. We don't think there is evidence that little Mr. or Ms. Dmanisi Hominid even stole scraps from the wolf kills. The little Dmanisi hominid acted like prey and was viewed as such. Wolves were *predators* of Man the Hunted 1.7 million years ago in Eurasia, and we see the evidence in the predatory attempts of the few remaining wolf populations today. And, unlike the short time span wolves and humans have both inhabited North America, the power of life and death was on the wolves' side for most of the evolutionary expanse of wolf–human interactions in Eurasia.

No Laughing Matter

Hyenas are scorned by indigenous cultures wherever they occur, often representing despicable characters in myth and folklore. Yet, they aren't weak, silly, or base creatures—and, just like wolves, hyenas have the strength and predatory instinct to attack people. After the work of field researchers in the 1970s and 1980s (notably Hans Kruuk, who wrote a seminal monograph entitled *The Spotted Hyena*, and Hugo van Lawick and Jane Goodall's *Innocent Killers*), the old myths of cowardly, skulking hyenas waiting to steal kills from noble predators, hopefully, have been vanquished. Hyenas are efficient hunters of large animals. Unlike popular misconceptions of hyenas as primarily scavengers, it turns out that three-quarters of their food intake is obtained by hunting and only one-quarter by feeding on the carrion of other predators. With their whopper-sized teeth operating much like hammers, their gigantic jaws are capable of both killing prey and crushing most of the bones. Here's a statistic that'll blow the average trivia collector's mind—the teeth of a spotted hyena can exert a pressure of 11,400 pounds (that's over 5 and one-half tons!) per square inch.

Spotted hyenas, the largest of the three living species, group in social clans of up to 80 members. Their tendency to yelp and chortle serves the same purpose as our human conversations—it gives important information to other hyenas. Their large vocabulary of calls, as Hans Kruuk has noted, make a hyena kill an especially noisy affair. Plenty of the noise is in the category of squabbling over who gets how much food. Hyenas are nocturnal hunters whose prey are usually fast and large—zebras, wildebeest, or antelope—but anything is on the hyena bill of fare, including human corpses. A Masai traditional "burial" involves laying a dead loved one out in the bush for hyenas to dispose of—not a bad idea, since it precludes the need to bury in dry, hard earth and neatly recycles deceased individuals back into their native ecosystem.

Tribal peoples are not the only ones to employ hyenas as a cleanup crew. Prior to World War I, hordes of hyenas lived in the vicinity of Nairobi slaughterhouses, tidying up viscera and bones and any other unwanted leftovers. When the slaughterhouses closed, the hyenas began eating everything that wasn't permanently attached to the buildings—brooms, bicycle seats, leather goods—and several women who were farming in the nearby fields.[10]

Actually, many accounts exist of spotted hyena attacks on living humans.[11] For no discernible reason, the southern African nation of Malawi seems to be the scene of quite a number of these reported incidents. In 1955 three separate deaths were attributed to spotted hyenas. In each case, the sleeping adult or child was dragged from a hut and devoured. These three deaths may have been just the beginning of the five-year rampage by Malawi hyenas in the late 1950s. Twenty-seven people (many of them children) were eaten, all under similar circumstances: People prefer to sleep on their verandas in the hot, dry season; hyenas quietly grabbed a child or adult off the porch and dragged them away to be devoured in the bush. Historical records in Malawi showed that similar bouts of hyena fixation on human prey have occurred many times before.

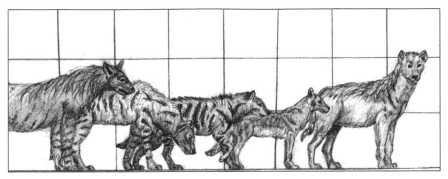

Relative sizes of fossil hyenas and dogs from the time period 8.5 to 1 million years ago. Each square measures approximately 20 inches on each side; three squares equal 5 feet. From left to right: ancestral hyena (*Pliocrocuta*); hunting hyena (*Chasmaporthetes*); dog-like hyena (*Hyaenotherium*); ancestral wolf (*Canis*); bone-crunching hyena (*Adcrocuta*). (C. Rudloff, redrawn from Turner 1997)

A little farther north in Africa, Tanzanian newspapers reported that hyenas were terrorizing an area near the city of Arusha in 1968, actually entering houses occasionally to obtain women or children. Neighboring Kenya's *The Nation* newspaper carried a story headlined "Girl Eaten Alive by Hyena." A young camel shepherd, stealing a daytime nap, was awakened by a hungry hyena ripping flesh from her face. Fellow shepherds responded to the girl's screams, saving her before she really was eaten. Near the Serengeti, a similar assault occurred in 1995; a spotted hyena dragged an American tourist from her tent and began mauling her face and arm. The Masai guide for the tourists saved the girl's life by spearing the hyena.[12]

HOWLS IN THE PREHISTORIC NIGHT

Ten million years ago—perhaps the earliest time at which our hominid line might have been diverging from a common ancestor with chimpanzees, big mammalian predators were the order of the day. Big saber-toothed cats were on the rise (as we talked about in the last chapter), and giant hyenas and dogs roamed singly and in packs. While the hyenas and dogs were not as agile as the previously cited fossil cats (much the way domestic dogs are not able to contort themselves into the yoga-like positions of the average pet kitty), these predators had three assets for successful predation not found in the felids: (1) tremendous and massive jaws, (2) long legs for running prey to exhaustion, and (3) cooperative group hunting by a pack of related individuals.

Let's discuss the hyenas first. There are only three species of hyenas that still roam Africa and Asia, but paleontologists have identified over 100 *extinct* species of this carnivorous family.[13] The first true hyenas appeared about 17 million years ago, and they did well. We could even expand on that quite a bit and say they did *very* well. We could take this tribute one step further and admit they were the premier carnivores during their reign. Is that clear enough? Want more hyperbole? Then we could up it to this little sketch: If Gary Larson had created a "Far Side" cartoon about that particular period of time, we'd probably see a hip hominid asserting, "Yeah, dude, HYENAS RULE!"

With more than 100 extinct species, we won't be doing a roll call of all the hyenas that might have eaten smallish bipedal hominids. We'll just draft the major trends and deal with a few species that have relevance to hominid fossil records. First of all, there was such a wealth of hyenas that they diverged in two different evolutionary directions. One arm of hyena adaptation seemed to produce fast animals—the coursing type. Some of the high spots from this line included the cursorial hunting hyena, *Euryboas.* This was a long-legged, cheetah version of your basic hyena model. *Euryboas* was so successful that it eventually populated a vast range covering Europe and stretching all the way down to the Sterkfontein and Swartkrans caves of South Africa where these hyena fossils are found with australopithecine remains. Another South African hunting hyena was named *Hyaenictis;* it was a species that was likewise fast and long-limbed, and that ran down its prey, but it appears to have been more wolf-like than *Euryboas.* Due to the wealth of hominid remains that ended up in the South African caves, these two cursorial hyenas are assumed to have preyed upon australopithecines, as did saber-toothed cats, false sabertooths, ancestral leopards, and the ancestors of modern hyenas. Quite an array of carnivore culprits!

The second direction that hyenas took is quite apparent when studying today's surviving members of the family. This second line evolved larger and heavier teeth that were locked into massive jaws until they became the bone-crushing carnivores clearly visible in the three modern species. One giant version of this mega-jawed line has been termed the cave hyena. It inhabited Europe and used caves as denning sites.

Artist's depiction of fossil hyenas catching sight of their *Homo erectus* prey. (C. Rudloff, redrawn from Boaz and Ciochon 2001)

Denning sites are also food-eating sites, and we shall see that caves can tell many stories about a time when lots of whopper-chopper hyenas were bringing home bipedal hominids for dinner—not as guests but as the main course.

We want to give special attention to another of the big cave-dwelling hyena species called *Pachycrocuta*, the "short-faced" hyena. There was nothing short about this predator except that its face did not have the slender tapered snout of the previously described fast and wolfish line of hyenas. *Pachycrocuta* was the size of a lion, probably weighing about 440 pounds. It was, in fact, the largest hyena that has ever existed.

Fossils of *Pachycrocuta* have been unearthed in Hadar, Ethiopia. (These have been dated at approximately 3.5 million years, placing them in the same place and time as the famous Lucy and her kin.) Evidently,

Pachycrocuta individuals resided over much of East Africa during the time when australopithecines lived; recently, giant hyena fossils have also been identified at South Turkwel hominid site in northern Kenya. Moreover, the range of this mega-predator extended to southern Africa and far and wide all over Eurasia. It used caves as denning and dining sites; it probably hunted in packs very much like the modern spotted hyena. We know it was a formidable predator of large prey such as giant elk and woolly rhinoceros in China because its long-abandoned dens contain the aftermath of many feasts—the fossilized bones that were *not* crushed to smithereens by *Pachycrocuta* molars. Oh, and other clues to the relaxing atmosphere of hyena banquets are present in abundance— they are called coprolites (fossil feces). These hyenas, just like their modern relatives, installed latrines conveniently close to home base.

As if a 440-pound bulk were not enough, added weaponry in the *Pachycrocuta* arsenal included immense teeth and tremendous jaws (for perspective, visualize an open mouth able to almost totally envelop a human head). Those huge teeth and jaws, in fact, are key facets in solving one of paleoanthropology's greatest fossil mysteries.[14]

The story begins in China during the 1920s in an area a little south of Beijing. Entrepreneurs in the area sold "dragon bones" dug up from a local hill for use as medicine. Chinese and European paleontologists identified some of the bones as coming from hominids, and the saga of the Zhoukoudian cave began. Eventually, remains of 45 *Homo erectus* individuals were discovered in the cave, the name "Peking Man" being used at that time to identify them. Analysis of the fossils by the most famous paleontologists of the day came up with theories that early humans used the cave as a home and hunting base, and also presided over barbaric practices there, such as cannibalism and, specifically, the eating of fellow hominids' brains.

By this time World War II was on the horizon, and when Japan invaded China, the precious Peking Man fossils were hidden from the enemy. They were hidden so well, in truth, that no one ever saw them again. Luckily, casts had been made prior to the fossils being spirited away, but the combination of losing the original fossils, the victory of Chairman Mao Zedong over General Chiang Kai-shek and his Nationalist Army, and the subsequent isolation of the People's Republic of China, kept the rest of the anthropological world from further work at the Zhoukoudian site for many decades. The theory of savagery and cannibalism practiced by early humans took on the mantle of indisputable fact to the point that several generations of American college textbooks touted the Zhoukoudian cave as the best citation for the bestial derivation of human nature.

What was the evidence that spoke of cannibalism and violence? It consisted of a preponderance of skulls in the *H. erectus* remains that had been found, rather than equal numbers of bones from all parts of the body. Besides the skulls, there were no hominid appendages in the cave except for a few large leg-bone pieces. A heavily skewed ratio of skulls to other hominid skeletal parts were present, and all of the crania were "modified" in the same way.

Admittedly, the manner in which the skulls had been manipulated was grotesque and spoke of some malevolent operation. The facial bones were gone and the opening at the base of the skull had been broken into and enlarged. Cannibalism—and a particular appetite for the fatty tissue of the brain—seemed the only plausible explanation. Granted, compared to the number of fossils of other creatures found at Zhoukoudian, the hominid remains weren't all that numerous. But the conventional story that early man had hunted from the cave both for other species and his own kind seemed logical given the killer-ape scenario rampant in academics and popular literature. It was especially logical since the experts claimed that no animal could have battered and crushed those skulls—that kind of destruction could only have been the work of men with stone tools.

Well, you see where we're headed. Chinese academics worked the site and eventually Western scientists also returned. In the space between the end of World War II and the reunification of Chinese and American anthropologists, much research had been carried out on australopithecine activities in the caves of South Africa. The venal atrocities misapplied to South African hominids were deconstructed through analyses of leopard predation carried out by C. K. Brain and others, and it was also finally accepted that hyenas had more than enough power to crush human bones. Observation of living hyenas even led to the knowledge that hyenas would eat prey crania in exactly the way the Zhoukoudian fossils demonstrated—face gone and base of skull enlarged. Eventually an analysis of the extreme size of *Pachycrocuta* fossils showed that hominid cranium-crushing and brain-eating would have been a simple task—a piece of cake, so to speak.

Noel Boaz and Russ Ciochon were American scientists on the team that cracked the case. They proposed that the Zhoukoudian *H. erectus*

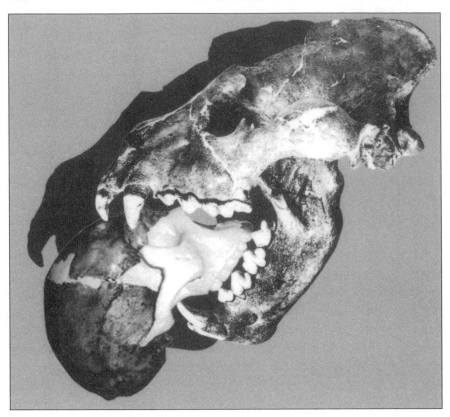

Drastically "modified" *Homo erectus* skulls unearthed at Zhoukoudian cave in China indicate that giant hyenas preyed upon these early hominids. (Copyright Russell L. Ciochon and Noel T. Boaz 2000)

crania showed all the signs of biting, chewing, and skeletal manipulation by a huge hyena. The steps to achieve the exact state of the Zhoukoudian crania could be reconstructed in a sequence that corresponded to the biting, chewing, and manipulation observed in modern-day hyena dining habits. First step: strip off the edible facial muscles causing subsequent damage to cheek bones and upper jaw. Second step: crack the center of the jaw open to reach the tongue. Third step: crush the facial skeleton to obtain marrow. Fourth step: break open the cranial vault to expose the brain, an organ that is prized by hyenas for its plentiful lipid content.

Pachycrocuta preyed on hominids in the area, and then brought pieces of their prey home to the cave. There they chewed up the facial skeleton to obtain marrow and broke open the skull vault to get at the fatty brain tissue. Mystery solved.

Obviously the hyenas were having a grand old time during the period of hominid evolution, but what was the dog family up to? Answer: some *really* unusual-looking characters. Like a fashion designer plagiarizing from this year's Parisian styles, the dogs tried on other species' wardrobes to see what would fit. How about hyenas? Yes, there was a group of hyena-like dogs with swollen foreheads called *Osteoborus*. Cats? Definitely. There was the dog family's version of a big cat, a jaguar-like creature called *Enhydrocyon*. Super size? Of course! Just like the cats and hyenas, the dog family also tried out extra, extra large species, such as *Aelurodon*, the bone-crushing dog. A huge member of the ancient dog family, *Aelurodon*, is predicted to have weighed more than 250 pounds. As the name implies, this particular carnivore had such massive jaws that paleontologists applied the descriptive appellation *bone-crusher* to its fossil remains. Combined with its mass and strength, these animals were probably similar to today's wild dogs—fast and powerful, and augmented in their capacity to kill by hunting in packs.[15]

There was even an extinct family of bear-dogs (not related to bears at all except that their size was that of a modern-day grizzly bear). The massive and carnivorous bear-dogs lived from 25 million years until nearly 5 million years ago. Reconstruction of a fossil bear-dog found in France indicates that it was an active predator, combining the powerful forelimbs of a bear with the hindlimb musculature of a large cat. What made it so effective in the context of predation was the bounding activity associated with felids, added to teeth much like the wolf. Its diet is conjectured to have been similar to present-day wolves.[16]

Our earliest ancestors coincided in time with the era of the bone-crushing dogs and bear-dogs, but those dog ancestors originated and proliferated throughout Eurasia and North America. Presently, there is no indication that the mega-dogs ever lived in Africa. The members of the dog family that did finally emigrate to Africa were wee versions of the giants found on other continents. It isn't even clear if a good-sized wolf was dispersed into sub-Saharan Africa, although a large *Canis* specimen has been found at Kromdraai in South Africa. Most of the canids that shared the countryside and knew australopithecine hominids were probably similar to the African hunting dogs and jackals found on the continent today. Hominid digs in Kenya and Ethiopia have uncovered fossil canids of precisely these dimensions.[17]

Unlike the cat and hyena families, so far there is no fossil evidence that incontrovertibly *proves* that wild dogs preyed on our early hominid ancestors, but emerging data on wolf predation, added to our study of predation by jackals, dholes, and the Arabian subspecies of wolves on non-human primates, leads us to the conclusion that the earliest hominids would have been at high risk of losing juveniles to the wild-dog family. Then, as hominids dispersed from Africa, they would have encountered larger wolfish canids that were truly formidable predators. These would have been true cursorial animals, coursers in the most exact sense of the word, able to run fast and rely on pack-hunting strategies. We don't think they can be discounted as marauders. Just around the corner, perhaps at the Dmanisi site, for example, there may be the fossil evidence that provides rock-solid evidence that dogs, before being man's *best* friend, might have been—to put it delicately—less than friendly.

LEADERS OF THE PACK

During our study of predation on non-human primates, we considered the wild dogs and hyenas together due to similarities in their ecological niches and social behavior (although, taxonomically speaking, hyenas are more closely related to the cat family than to dogs). Both dogs and hyenas have completely terrestrial lifestyles, and most of them employ cooperative (pack) hunting strategies, allowing for the killing of very large prey. The efficiency of cooperative hunting by spotted hyenas and African wild dogs is reflected in capture rates. A species' capture rate is estimated by calculating the number of successful kills divided by *all* attempts to kill prey. Most predators don't have very high capture rates, but researchers calculate a 35% success rate for spotted hyenas (for wildebeest calves it can rise to 74%) and an astounding 50–70% for African hunting dogs.[18]

Wild dogs and the spotted hyena also can be defined by their habits of trailing, chasing down, and attacking prey from the rear. They lack the claws and powerful clutching forelimbs of cats but compensate with heightened olfactory powers along with long legs and deep chests that give them superior endurance to run down their prey. Some of the top speeds for these carnivores are impressive: spotted hyenas have been clocked at 40 miles per hour; African wild dogs can maintain speeds of 44 mph; even the pint-sized jackals move out at 37.5 mph. Primate prey (except for those unique sprinters of the African savanna, the patas monkeys) are usually not chased over long distances and may be killed by individual dogs or hyenas if they are come upon by chance.[19]

African Hunting Dogs

The African hunting dog is a daytime predator that relies heavily on sight. There's not much sense in staging an elaborate concealed stalk when wary prey can easily see every move in the short-grass savanna habitat of this dog-family member. It wouldn't do any good to slowly approach potential victims, so they shun artifice and go from a state of not hunting to a full-barreled chase with no middle ground. Hunting dogs are spectacular specialists in what they do best—running high-speed "relays" that eventually culminate in total exhaustion for a wildebeest or zebra they have marked as their target. Relay should be interpreted as the outcome rather than the intent of the pack. The dominant dogs in the pack try to stay in front for the entire chase, but the veering diversionary tactics of the animal being pursued often means that the trailing pack members sometimes suddenly find themselves closer than the leaders to the prey.

The social organization of African hunting dogs is, well, very sociable. All adults share in a kill with a minimum of fighting over fair shares. In a further display of gracious manners, pups are allowed to eat first while the adult animals patiently wait until the youngsters have had their fill.

Hunting dogs are the least common of the African predators and are becoming more and more endangered in their entire range. Luckily, since much of their natural habitat—the short-grass savanna—has been converted to agriculture, hunting dogs are able to exist in other environments as extreme as deserts or swamps. They probably take primate prey on occasion when a single dog is hunting on its own, but only anecdotal accounts exist of suspicious situations—combinations such as unusual primate disappearances while hunting dogs are in the area.[20]

Dholes

Dholes are the beautiful russet and yellow wild dogs of Asia. About
the size of a medium-to-large breed of domestic canine, the dholes
have a lifestyle much like African hunting dogs. They are diurnal
hunters that live in extended family units—the families of approximately four to ten animals compose individual packs. Although it had
been assumed that dholes, as pack hunters, concentrate on large Asian
deer (such as the sambar), almost half of the dhole kills in the
Bandipur Tiger Reserve, India, were animals under 50 pounds. Dholes
are so rare currently throughout their historic habitat (the Indian subcontinent, east through China, north to Russia, and south to
Indonesia) that there's no truly comprehensive picture of their diet
composition. Nevertheless, two studies in India and one in Indonesia
found primate remains in dhole scats.[21] Notes from a naturalist in the
1930s concur (in rather stylish language) with the concept of dholes as
primate predators:

> The extraordinary habit of monkeys leaving trees when attacked by
> [dholes] . . . is common also in the case of the Nilgiri Black Langur . . .
> and a good account of this curious trait will be found . . . published in
> 1876; no explanation is however offered for such peculiar behaviour.
> That wild dogs profit by this failing is evident from the fact that I have
> on more than one occasion in the Kundahs found black monkey fur in
> wild dog droppings.[22]

Dholes have been accused (as have most other wild dogs and hyenas)
of being wanton and cruel murderers because they kill by disembowelment. Any animal the pack brings down is literally torn apart while alive.
But authorities contend that shock sets in rapidly due to immense loss of
blood when carnivores rip open the underbelly, and the time from initial
capture to official death is probably no longer—despite the seemingly
chaotic attack by a pack of wild dogs—than that from a swift bite by a
big cat. Dholes, as a species, possess one behavioral trait that lessens any
suffering by a downed victim: their competition at a kill is manifested
through accelerated eating speeds rather than fighting among themselves.
A sambar fawn, for instance, might be dismembered and consumed
within seconds after the kill.

Jackals

The small wild dogs of Africa and Asia, the jackals, live in close family units where parents and helpers of both sexes will tenderly care for pups. All four species of jackals pick up scents and pounce on their prey rather than run it down in packs. Zoologists hypothesize that in areas without a full complement of larger carnivores, jackals often become major predators of animals the size of primates by hunting cooperatively in twos and threes. Calculations have been worked out showing that the rate of capture efficiency is tripled when a pair of jackals hunts together compared to when one solitary jackal pursues prey on its own.

Published data support the position that jackals are predators on primates.[23] In Asia golden jackals, hunting in pairs, successfully captured arboreal leaf monkeys and semi-terrestrial Hanuman langurs while researchers watched. One primatologist, Craig Stanford, recorded two sequences of golden jackals hunting langurs in Bangladesh. In the first case two jackals were patiently waiting for a displaced infant to cross 15 feet of forest floor in order to rejoin its mother. When the infant finally made the dash of its life, the jackals simultaneously broke from different hiding places, but were unsuccessful in capturing the infant. In the second case an old female, who habitually foraged close to the forest floor, was attacked and killed by three jackals.

Capturing very old or very young langurs is one thing, but going after baboons is quite another. Jackals weigh about 24 pounds, but adult male hamadryas baboons weigh in at 40–45 pounds. Not exactly the best match-up for small wild dogs, even if they are hunting in pairs. Probably the jackals choose their baboon prey quite carefully to avoid tangling with "the big guy," the dominant male. Hans Kummer has studied hamadryas baboons for over 4 decades. He once witnessed a pair of jackals harassing a sick female baboon who was lagging behind the rest of her troop. When the adult male hamadryas returned to check on the female, the jackals departed in great haste.

A smaller savanna primate—the patas monkey—uses diversion rather than sheer bulk to outsmart predators. The male patas runs in the opposite direction from where females and young are hiding in order to draw predators away from the troop. Evidently, jackals are quite prone to stalk this primate species since all observed encounters between jackals and patas monkeys in West Africa were aggressive in nature.

Hyenas

There are, oddly enough, great differences in looks and lifestyles between the remaining trio of this ancient family. All three hyena species sport well-muscled forequarters and sloping backs, they all have manes around their necks, they all have anal pouches for scent marking. But after those basic morphological items, the similarities cease.

Spotted hyenas have been the subjects of a great deal more research than the brown or striped hyenas. The spotted ones exhibit a rarity in the mammalian world—large, dominant females. The label of sexual dimorphism in a mammal species usually denotes that males are much larger than females. Spotted hyenas are sexually dimorphic, but the females are 4–12% heavier than the males. In addition, the female spotted hyena is socially dominant, and also possesses an enlarged clitoris that mimics the male penis. (Obviously this has lent itself to the hyena mystique.) Females of the same clan will den their cubs together, although each female cares for her own biological offspring. Because young hyenas do not have preferred status at a kill, and may be totally excluded at the dinner table, cubs are nursed for up to 18 months.

Our review of present-day spotted hyena predation on baboons and other savanna-dwelling primates indicates that hyenas are opportunists who will sometimes hunt singly for prey of smaller size, such as primates. Due to the relatively small size of monkeys in relation to their typical prey—large African ungulates (hoofed animals such as antelopes, zebras, and gazelles)—packs of hyenas cannot depend on primate-sized animals as staple food. Instead, primates appeal to the solitary forager, such as the single spotted hyena looking for a quick meal. There are records of primates in the diets of all three species of hyenas—spotted, striped, and brown—but instances of observed predation events on primates by hyenas are rare. Nevertheless, researchers witnessed the capture and killing of an adult male yellow baboon by a spotted hyena in Amboseli National Park, Kenya, and zoo hyenas were observed catching a red colobus monkey that entered their enclosure at Abuko Reserve, The Gambia.

Brown and striped hyenas have been less studied in the wild than the spotted hyena. As with all of the surviving forms, these species are committed to bone crunching. But in several ways the brown and striped hyenas are similar to each other and dissimilar to their spotted relative. For one thing there is a size bias toward the male rather than the female in brown and striped hyena species. For another, both brown and striped hyenas hunt by lowering their noses to the ground and picking up scents. It's just a roll of the dice regarding what will be the next meal, and it is in opportunistic situations like these that they are known to consume primates.

Brown hyenas are currently found only in southern Africa. This species (an animal that looks as if it is having a perpetual bad hair day) lives in clans that share large territories and exhibit much the same social organization as the spotted hyena. However, spotted hyenas routinely hunt in packs, whereas brown hyenas are solitary foragers. And, because they do not hunt in groups, the browns scavenge on the carrion of other predators more than the spotted hyena. The propensity of brown hyenas to hunt individually may mean that they are likely to prey on primates. This has been substantiated in analyses of the bone accumulations at brown hyena breeding lairs. Predation on baboons seems to be especially common, particularly when cubs are being raised. (There are also numerous unauthenticated reports that brown hyenas have captured small human children.)[24]

Domestic Dogs

When discussing the canid family's predation on living primate species, we can't forget the large numbers of feral and semi-feral dogs throughout continental Africa and on the island of Madagascar and in Asia and the Neotropics. The damaging effects inflicted by feral dogs on wild-animal populations should never be underestimated. An evaluation of wildlife predators found records of domestic dogs killing seven different species of primates in south Asia. In populated parts of India and Sri Lanka, feral dogs more frequently attack and kill langurs than do any other carnivore.[25]

Just as an aside, in the United States pet dogs inflict injuries on 200,000 people each year, but not for predatory reasons. Most likely the dogs that injure family members or neighbors view the people in their lives as fellow pack members and are displaying aggression either out of fear or an assertion of dominance.[26]

Wild dogs chasing ancestral hominids—their hot breath palpable as they draw nearer and nearer. Scary stuff, but it's very hard to look at our beloved pet dogs and visualize them as the savage predators of long ago. In the next chapter, though, it may not be so difficult to make a direct and instantaneous connection between living pythons, crocodiles, or Komodo dragons and the cold-blooded reptilian predators that hominids faced in the past. Funny, isn't it, that almost any large or slithering reptile will cause that primitive part of our brain to shriek, "Danger! Keep away!"

6

MISSIONARY POSITION

We have now trekked through scenarios of saber-toothed cats and giant hyenas preying on our ancestral line. We've also delved into
modern-day attacks by carnivores of many species. The group of vertebrates
that most consistently assault humans, however, are reptiles. Julian White,
an Australian toxicologist, estimated that venomous snake bites to humans
number in excess of 3 million per year, resulting in 150,000 deaths worldwide annually.[1] Snake bites can be fatal, but seldom have any connection
whatsoever to predatory behavior—in fact, quite the opposite, since most
snakes fear humans and react defensively to protect *themselves* from perceived predation by humans.[2]

The six species of so-called giant snakes, nonetheless, may constitute
anomalies.

There is no dearth of stories about man-eating giant snakes. So, to begin
this chapter, we present the beautifully understated, but entirely serious, instructions from an early magazine published for missionaries working in
Africa. These are the directions to follow when encountering an African
python:

> Remember not to run away, the python can run faster. The thing to do is to
> lie flat on the ground on your back with your feet together, arms to the

sides and head well down. The python will then try to push its head under you, experimenting at every possible point.

[Authors' note: At this point almost every human will conclude that bipedalism as an adaptive trait evolved *expressly* to cover the possibility of running away from giant snakes.] Okay, returning to the instructions . . .

Keep calm, one wiggle and he will get under you, wrap his coils round you and crush you to death. After a time the python will get tired of this and will probably decide to swallow you without the usual preliminaries. He will very likely begin with one of your feet. *Keep calm.* You must let him swallow your foot. It is quite painless and will take a long time.

[Authors' note: Hmmm . . . "quite painless?" . . . simply a tad irritating because it will take a long time? It's very "likely" he will begin the painless swallowing process with one of your feet? What if the python wants to start his painless swallowing from the other end of his immobile meal—the head?] But, there's more. . . .

If you lose your head and struggle he will quickly whip his coils around you. If you *keep calm*, he will go on swallowing. Wait patiently until he has swallowed about up to your knee. Then carefully take out your knife and insert it into the distended side of his mouth and with a quick rip slit him up.[3]

How many missionaries took this advice is open to question. How many survived after taking this advice is even more speculative. Nevertheless, any missionary who managed to carefully follow those directions—*keep calm while the python swallows you!*—definitely possessed faith far beyond the norm. Who actually wrote the directions or had the personal experiences upon which the instructions were based remains, sadly, a mystery.

THE SERPENTINE ROUTE

To say that primates in general—including humans—are fearful of snakes is a generalization that just might be provable through statistical analysis. Avoidance of snakes is a well-documented behavior in non-human primates, although, in seemingly perverse behavior, primates sometimes approach snakes out of sheer curiosity.[4] Innate avoidance of snakes by primates would presuppose some evolutionary relationship with snakes, either as predators or as dangerous co-inhabitants of tropical and temperate territories.

Experiences of a personal nature always hit home more than any number of descriptions, and any up-close-and-personal encounters with large and dangerous snakes in the wild are especially memorable. While studying primates in the forest, you spend most of the time looking into trees and not watching where you put your feet. You get used to stepping on or tripping over exposed roots of large trees, fallen branches, rocks, and so on. One of us (RWS), while studying lemurs in Madagascar, had the shock that often lurks just around the corner for all field researchers. Stepping on a large branch, I felt it begin to move. Letting out a scream, I nearly jumped out of my shoes. I had stepped not on a branch, obviously, but on an extremely large Malagasy boa. Knowing the snake was not poisonous (there are no venomous snakes in Madagascar) was comforting, but it's still a major shock when the ground moves under your feet and you look down on a truly massive snake.

It's possibly even more shocking to inadvertently encounter a deadly snake, such as a viper, as it lies in ambush. When doing primate research in most forests of Africa, Asia, and the New World, where poisonous snakes are common, one must constantly be aware of their presence and be prepared to avoid attack. It's also necessary to have a precautionary plan in case someone is bitten. In most regions where primates are studied, poisonous snakes are the most dangerous things one is likely to encounter during research.

While doing a census of primates at the Costa Rican forest reserve of La Selva, a student and I were walking on one of the trails when we came face to face with a 10-foot-long fer-de-lance. These are among the most feared and dangerous snakes of the Neotropics and are much more inclined to bite than any other large viper. From a Western perspective, compared to other snakes, they also are extremely frightening looking. (While hating to fall into the anthropomorphic trap, it's hard to describe these flat-headed, snub-nosed snakes as anything but downright ugly.) The snake was coming toward us on the path. Needing to get past the snake and continue in the same direction, we finally decided that I would try going into the forest and walking around the fer-de-lance while the student monitored the snake's movements. After entering the dense underbrush and starting to make some progress around the snake, I heard shouting that the snake was moving. Luckily, after an initial adrenaline rush, the student added that the snake was moving *away* from me into the forest on the other side of the path. The incident was so disturbing that no one on the research team returned to the forest for the rest of the day.

The little vignette above could be interpreted in a couple of different ways: (1) those were truly timorous researchers to shut down operations for the rest of the day because of an encounter with a snake, or (2) we have stumbled onto a fascinating topic—is there an instinctive and/or learned fear of snakes in human and non-human primates?

There's scientific support for theories that avoidance of snakes is instinctive behavior in primates based upon studies of chacma baboons, squirrel monkeys, and several species of tamarins and marmosets. But, there's also research that supports the theory that fear and avoidance of snakes are learned behaviors; this side of the debate is based upon studies of squirrel monkeys, macaques, and lemurs. So far, neither side has proven their point conclusively.[5]

The controlled study of *human* fear or avoidance of snakes has not been a prolific area of research. In 1928 two psychologists, Harold and Mary Jones, published their research entitled "Maturation and Emotion: Fear of Snakes," in the journal *Childhood Education*. They found that children up to the age of 2 years had no fear of a harmless 6-foot-long North American snake nor of a small boa constrictor, but by the age of 3, children showed caution around the snakes, and definite fear was apparent after the age of 4. Another study in the 1960s asked children to identify their own fears. Fifty percent of the 467 children aged 5–12 years in this study picked animals as the most feared objects, and the most frequently cited animals were snakes.[6] From this small sampling, we must conclude that no definitive answer regarding "nature versus nurture" is available in regard to human or non-human primate avoidance of snakes, but the very fact that any evidence exists for a comfortable curiosity in very young children exposed to large snakes makes a hardwired primate fear response highly implausible.

Indian pythons are one of the six species of giant snakes. (Mark O'Shea/Krieger Publishing Company)

With or without innate fear . . . with or without learned fear . . . the relevant question we want to address remains: Does any evidence exist that snakes were predators on early hominids?

Because snakes swallow their prey whole, we need only consider snakes that are large enough (that is, with a large enough jaw gape) to accommodate a meal the size of one of our ancestral hominids. Clifford Pope, one of the first herpetologists to write factually about the giant snakes for the general public, described the prey of the pythons and boas: "Almost any not too formidable creature weighing less than 125 pounds is a potential victim, horns, armor, and spines notwithstanding."[7] An extinct hominid the size of "Lucy," the famous australopithecine fossil—estimated when alive to have stood 3 and one-half feet tall and to have weighed approximately 60 pounds—would have posed no problem for the ancient relatives of today's so-called giant snakes to consume.

Six species, to be exact, earn the *gigantic* designation: the African python, the Indian python, the Asian reticulated python, the amethystine python of Australia, the South American boa constrictor, and the South American anaconda. These are labeled "giant snakes" for obvious

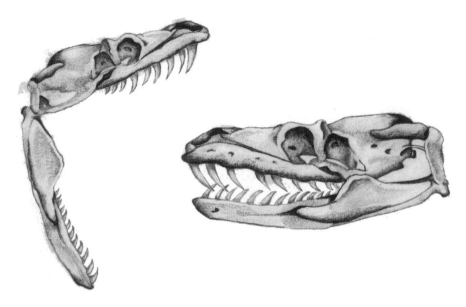

The gape of a python or boa allows prey much larger than the snake's head to be swallowed whole. (C. Rudloff, redrawn from Whitfield 1978)

reasons. Measuring a maximum of 18.5 feet, the boa constrictor is the peewee of the group. The other five species are *truly* large—up to a maximum of 33 feet—the longest terrestrial animals alive today.

The weights of giant snakes are less known than their lengths due to the logistical challenge of getting an extremely long snake to cooperate by lying coiled on a scale. (This is why photographs you see of mammoth anacondas or pythons are posed with five or six people holding up different sections of the snake.) Two dependable estimated weights found in the published literature are pretty impressive—200 pounds for a 19-foot Indian python and 305 pounds for a 25-foot reticulated python.[8]

Depending on their sense of smell and, to some degree, heat sensitivity, the giant snakes are able to hunt prey both nocturnally and during the day. They are also just as at home in water as they are on land. They seek mammalian food, and they are able to swallow prey as large as their own weight (one huge meal may equal 400 times their daily energy needs). One of the most common misunderstandings is that giant snakes *crush* their victims. Not true! Clifford Pope explained: "After seizing its prey in vise-like jaws, the serpent coils its body about its opponent and squeezes. The muscular pressure is sufficient to keep the chest [of the prey] from expanding and thus halt the ability to breathe. Bone-breaking exertion, therefore, is unnecessary."[9] The mouth—indeed, the whole digestive system—of a giant snake is intricately modified to facilitate consumption of colossal food items. Approximately 50 needle-sharp curved teeth flare backward on both the upper and lower jaws, and curved teeth even appear on the palate. A well-aimed strike is as hard as a blow from a hammer; the force of the strike allows the curved teeth to penetrate deeply, resulting in attenuated, jagged lacerations.[10] A python or boa's jaw hinge is situated at the farthest point on the back of the skull ,which allows immense flexibility for its gigantic gape; a gape that allows prey much larger than the snake's head to be swallowed whole. Once swallowed, an extendible, spacious gut receives the huge meal.

Pythons, boas, and anacondas rely on a combination of sensory inputs to locate their food. These include vision, vibration, heat, and odor.[11] Many other reptilian predators hunt by speculation, wandering around until they come within range of suitable prey; but among snakes, in particular, success in catching prey involves inconspicuously lying in wait for it to approach.[12]

Because they eat mostly active animals, giant snakes hunt mainly by sit-and-wait ambush, although at night reticulated pythons will search actively for prey. One boa constrictor under study in Panama entered a different medium-sized mammal burrow every 3 or 4 days, waiting up to 96 hours for prey to approach within striking distance. When prey is encountered, these snakes will usually retract their head and neck, then rapidly strike, immediately immobilizing the victim by constriction, followed by swallowing. Giant snakes eat a wide variety of vertebrates and, generally, this leads them to be very opportunistic in their choice of prey, taking advantage of almost any potential prey species of an appropriate size. Adult Asian, African, and Australian pythons, and anacondas and boas of the Neotropics, are restricted to terrestrial or aquatic habitats because their heavy weight precludes arboreality.[13]

All of the giant snakes have an especially frightening mystique, and all are reputed to be possibly dangerous, but better documentation concerning current and historical human predation exists for the super-sized reticulated python found in Southeast Asia, a giant snake that most authorities credit with being the longest and either the heaviest or at least the second-heaviest in the world. This species in adulthood reaches lengths exceeding 25–30 feet (females are larger than males, and adults continue to grow throughout their lives), and a 15-foot python is considered small.[14]

During the early twentieth century, on the Moluccan Islands off Indonesia, a 14-year-old boy was killed and swallowed by one of the smaller reticulated pythons. In the same area, in 1926, an adult man was seized by a python and squeezed to death. The snake was killed while still coiled around its meal, although it had not yet ingested the man. On the island of Sumatra, again in 1926, a 15-foot python dragged its victim— an adult man—into the forest by keeping its tail wrapped firmly around the reputedly shattered skull. And in Singapore, in 1937, 15 men were required to release a man from the clutches of a python measuring 22.5 feet in length.[15]

More recent reports tend to smack of tabloid sensationalism—as, of course, might the stories above. Two internet websites—*Man-Eating Snakes I* and *Man-Eating Snakes II*—actually exist to *dis*credit tabloid stories by debunking doctored photographs, such as one showing a super-tremendous bulge in a snake's middle (a very obese human?), and another showing a human corpse supposedly liberated from a snake's stomach (still wearing—considering the situation—relatively unwrinkled clothing). Another "new" photo that hit the front pages in newspapers all over the world showed a "recent" incident of a man swallowed by a python; the photo had actually been snapped when Japanese soldiers were invading Southeast Asia during WWII.[16]

Man-Eating Snakes I website does document eight confirmed cases of human deaths in recent years caused by African, Burmese, and reticulated pythons in captivity. In none of these cases did the snake attempt to eat the human it had smothered by constriction.

Also substantiated are several incidents that occurred in the past two decades, incidents investigated by credible sources who collected copious details. On Thursday, 22 November 1979, in Northern Transvaal, South Africa, a teenage cattle herder was grabbed and killed by an African python lying in ambush in long grass. The snake was entwined around the corpse when a hail of stones from tribal elders caused the python to release the body. Dr. Bill Branch, one of South Africa's most respected herpetologists, determined the following about this attack:

The case reported here . . . is almost certainly a true feeding attack, and indeed there is every indication that the snake would have continued swallowing the boy had it not been disturbed. Pythons are known to catch antelope, etc., by lying in ambush by the sides of game paths. The close proximity of the cattle being herded by the victim, and his sudden arrival as he ran along the path, probably initiated an instinctive feeding reflex in the python.[17]

Dr. Branch and his associates reviewed several other events that seemed to constitute human predation by African pythons. One occurred in 1973 in Angola; a photograph documents the human body encased in the digestive tract of a python. There is no doubt that ingestion occurred, but whether the adult male human was alive or dead at the time his body was swallowed remains in question, since there was a bloody civil war going on and a battle casualty might have been scavenged by a hungry snake.[18]

So far we've been discussing giant-snake predation on adult humans, but as one university professor from Brazil reminded us, there are frequent stories about anacondas taking human babies from hammocks in rural areas.[19] An incident reported from northern Australia involved a traumatizing event; a mother reached into the crib for her baby and found a python (likely amethystine) beginning to encase the infant's head with its jaws.[20] Stories of reticulated pythons in Southeast Asia consuming infants and children are almost too numerous to recount individually. Suffice it to say that "giant snake eats baby" is either true or one of the most frequent urban (in this case substitute *rural*) myths throughout the tropics.

The fossil record for snakes is scarce and, unfortunately, there's not much that can be inferred from it about the relationship between any of the large snakes as predators and early hominids as prey. One related fact we can state unequivocally is that snakes—the latest of the reptilian groups—began radiating into many ecological niches at the same time that mammals diversified. The evolution of snakes is seen by paleontologists as closely tied to a predator–prey relationship with mammals. Early members of the suborder Serpentes were relatively large terrestrial carnivores in the process of evolving the present adaptation of jaw mobility that enables them to swallow their prey whole.[21]

While snakes are the most recent of the reptilian groups to evolve, the boid family—the pythons, boas, and anacondas—are most similar to the primitive snakes. The oldest known snakes are from the Eocene epoch (approximately 35–55 million years ago). These early specimens were large and stout; boas and pythons seem to be their little-modified descendants.[22]

John Murphy and Robert Henderson in *Tales of Giant Snakes* discuss the tantalizing and oft-touted idea of ancient "supersnakes," but they conclude that if prehistoric supersnakes existed, paleontologists have yet to find any evidence. In reality the long and bulky ancient snakes that have been found in the fossil record from the Paleocene to the Pleistocene epochs are smaller (measuring a maximum of 27 feet) than some living giant snakes of today!

Another window to the relationship between giant snakes and early hominids is the predator–prey relationship between these reptiles and living non-human primates. Our research into predation on primates found that reptiles are recorded in low numbers of unsuccessful attacks (2.5% of the total), verified predations (4%), and suspected predations (about 13%). It's our opinion, nonetheless, based on discussions with herpetologists, that these low percentages are more attributable to a lack of fieldwork on snakes in Africa, Madagascar, Asia, and the Neotropics than on any tendency for snakes to avoid consuming primates. Despite the paucity of research, we could still identify both the African python and the reticulated python as "primate specialists," meaning these two giant-snake species appeared repeatedly in our data sets when we looked at both anecdotal evidence and quantitative data.[23]

While the field studies on all tropical snakes are few and far between, making for sparse data on the interactions between primates and these predators, nevertheless, the record of snake predation is replete with descriptive anecdotes. If we start at the beginning of the written accounts of primates as prey to snakes, we must go back to the late nineteenth century for the first published record. A short report by Mr. O. Channer, entitled "The Food of the Python," appeared in the *Journal of Bombay Natural History Society* in 1895. Illustrated by a masterful woodcut, the entry briefly describes the capture and strangulation of a Hanuman langur (the sacred monkey of India) by an Indian python.

This woodcut of an Indian python coiled around a Hanuman langur appeared in a natural history journal published in 1895.

Baboons captured by African pythons were also observed and re-ported.[24] One field naturalist in the 1960s recorded the entire sequence of just such a dramatic life and death struggle:

> I witnessed a python catching a half-grown baboon. I was attracted to the scene by the noise of the baboon troop and arrived shortly after the snake had wrapped its coils round its prey. The other members of the troop crowded round the scene of the tragedy, the more adventurous amongst them occasionally darting forward and nipping the coils of the snake in a hopeless effort to frighten it and make it discard its catch.[25]

A 5-year study of red colobus monkeys in Abuko Nature Reserve, The Gambia, carried out by Erica Starin, revealed that predation by rep-tiles (African pythons and Nile crocodiles) was a major cause of mortality in adult monkeys. Based on her direct observation of kills and the examination of carcasses, 40% of known deaths were attributable to pythons and crocodiles. Subsequently, she suspected an additional 13 red colobus in the study group that had disappeared without a trace were also python victims—snake predation leaves no evidence unless the event is witnessed or the snake's stomach contents are examined. Pythons were surprisingly ubiquitous in the Abuko Nature Reserve—entering tourist photohides, eating captive primates in the reserve's zoo, and allowing close approaches by humans. Starin and an associate found that the population density of pythons over 6 feet long (considered adult at this length) was approximately 20–25 snakes in an 83-acre area. The researchers surmised that pythons at this density have considerable impact on small- and medium-sized mammals, such as primates.[26]

Giant snakes also consume small, nocturnal, arboreal primates as two German scientists found out in Indonesia a few years ago.[27] During a study of slow loris (a nocturnal prosimian of unhurried, deliberate movements), weak signals from a radio-collared loris were traced to a patch of dense ferns on the forest floor. When these signals continued over a 3-day period from such an unlikely location for an arboreal primate, the field researchers investigated and found a reticulated python. They confirmed that the signals were being emitted from the interior of the python that had, undoubtedly, swallowed the slow loris. Using this unexpected opportunity, they radio-tracked the python for a week longer until it excreted the radio collar. However, there was no trace of the slow loris in the feces. There's a certain whimsical lesson involved in this exercise: primate researchers must be patient—it's not exactly like waiting around for paint to dry, but waiting for a python to defecate can be a leisurely operation. The other revelation is that snake predation involving small primates is nearly impossible to observe even indirectly. The predator–prey connection is revealed only if researchers are on the scene.

Being on the scene is mostly just plain luck—a case of being in the right place at the right time. Researchers in the Tampolo forest of Madagascar were alerted to an incident of snake predation by the calls of birds and lemurs. They found a bamboo lemur in the coils of a large Malagasy tree boa. The process of suffocation through constriction took 60 minutes.[28]

The first quantitative study of large tropical snake diets was not published until 1998. Giant snakes may not have attracted much scientific attention, but they have been, and continue to be, exploited in huge numbers by the exotic leather industry. Wild and captive pythons are routinely slaughtered at factories where their skins are tanned into leather. After the pythons were gutted in factories in the city of Palembang in southern Sumatra, Indonesia, Australian herpetologist Rick Shine examined the contents of stomachs and intestines for recognizable prey items. Of the

417 identifiable remains of food in the python alimentary tracts, less than 4% consisted of primates (11-pound long-tailed macaques and two species of leaf monkeys that weigh approximately 15 pounds).[29]

Any relationship between ancestral hominids and giant snakes would by virtue of geographic origin involve the Asian and African pythons rather than the New World boa constrictors and anacondas. Even today's Old World pythons have a wider variety of large terrestrial mammals—such as primates—to choose from than do anacondas and boas, since fewer large, ground-dwelling mammalian species have evolved in the Neotropics.[30] Thus, the range of species and absolute numbers of primates and other medium to large mammals in the diets of Asian and African pythons can be expected to be greater than those found in the diets of the Neotropical giant snakes.

Given that fact, there are still quite a few instances of snake predation on New World primates witnessed by field personnel. Eckhard Heymann of the Deutsches Primatenzentrum in Germany witnessed an anaconda capture a moustached tamarin in northeastern Peru.[31] The tamarin family under study by Heymann regularly used fallen tree trunks to cross a narrow lake. On one of these excursions the adult female was seized by the giant snake, and three coils were instantaneously thrown around the monkey. Heymann conjectured that the anaconda must have hidden directly beneath the water surface and was further obscured by aquatic vegetation. Boa constrictors are one of the predators of capuchin monkeys,[32] but these active, tool-using little Neotropical monkeys have plenty of anti-predator behaviors up their sleeves to foil snakes. They mob boas quite viciously, and one monkey was observed clubbing a venomous snake with a branch.[33]

We feel compelled to say just a few words, before we leave the subject of snakes, about other serpents besides the six giant species. Vipers and pit vipers, cobras and mambas, mussuranas and rat snakes have different feeding patterns than the giant constricting boid snakes. Many inject venom, an adaptive strategy that allows them to subdue and ingest very large prey.[34] After cobras strike, for example, they retain an initial grip until struggling ceases; most vipers, however, bite rapidly, then release their prey, and relocate the prey after it has died. Poisonous snakes were a significant source of mortality to sleeping rhesus macaques at a research site in India.[35] Again, there is a striking similarity to our primate cousins since modern humans experience 3 million snake bites each year. Snakes

and primates; snakes and hominid ancestors; snakes and humans—a
long-term relationship.

BREATHING FIRE: THE KOMODO DRAGON

We have to state at the beginning that neither one of us has ever had the
pleasure of personally meeting a wild Komodo dragon, the largest of the
monitor lizard family and feared denizen of several small Indonesian islands. But, being hominids, we succumb to the fear they may have
generated within the primate brain for millions of years. For worst nightmares there is really nothing comparable to the thought of a gray,
slobbery, 9-inch-long forked tongue picking up your scent and tracking
you to an inevitable death by disembowelment. The creature possessing
the forked tongue is the largest predatory lizard now extant—a rapid and
ravenous carnivore who easily reaches 9 feet in length from snout to
tail.[36] And on top of that, it is capable of taking down a half-ton water
buffalo by an efficient two-step process: first step, immobilize large prey
by severing tendons in hind legs; second step, administer a *coup de grace*
by ripping out the intestines.

Komodo dragons are terrestrial and feed mostly on mammals, including monkeys. Initially, explorers reported an exaggerated,
almost-mythical beast 30 feet in length (hence the dragon appelation).
It was not until 1912 that scientists recognized the species officially.
Actually, the reality is impressive enough without any embellishment:
Komodo dragons average 9 feet in length for males (some full-grown
adult males may reach 10 feet in length, but this is a maximum) and 6
feet for females. Weight of a 9-foot specimen has been estimated at as
much as 550 pounds, but some experts speculate there may be a difference of hundreds of pounds between a Komodo dragon with a full
stomach versus the same animal without a recent meal. Regardless of
length or weight, no exaggeration was involved when early naturalists
reported that the bites of Komodo dragons were lethal, and they were
"occasionally man-eating."[37]

The range of this species is restricted in modern times to a group of
islands called the Sundas, part of Indonesia. The best known of the islands is the volcanic dome of Komodo where seasonal temperatures can
reach 120 degrees Fahrenheit. The Komodo dragons are not particularly

active during the heat of the day. They are, however, very agile creatures, and the giant monitors are considered terrestrial, aquatic (they've been seen swimming to smaller islets where sheep are pastured in order to prey on them), and even arboreal when they are young.

The hunting strategy of all monitor lizards is relatively active in comparison to other reptiles that prey on primates. Formidable predators, Komodo dragons hunt much like the big cats. They hide by the side of game trails and strike swiftly with a sudden lunge at large mammals as they pass by, grabbing at the leg or throat and throwing the hapless victim to the ground. Like many reptiles, Komodo dragons share the trait of swallowing large prey whole. (A small Komodo, weighing just 101 pounds, managed to swallow a 90-pound wild pig.) The jaws are very strong and the teeth are shark-like, able to rip and shred as well as bite. Evisceration of prey is quickly accomplished—15 minutes from attack to scraps in the case of one 40-pound pig. Besides the ambush strategy, monitor lizards pick up scent trails with their long forked tongues and follow them to prey. Their tongues are highly specialized—a bifurcated, highly sensory tip connected to a resilient base. The tongue, in essence, looks like a huge, gray, wet rubber strap, extending and retracting with elastic snaps.[38]

Walter Auffenberg (the American herpetologist acknowledged as a world expert on monitor lizards), launched a 13-month study on Komodo dragons in the late 1970s for his doctoral dissertation, the most comprehensive field research so far on the species. Auffenberg contended that the Komodo dragons attack humans without provocation. This makes sense since a rapacious carnivore that can attack, kill, and eat a 1,000-pound buffalo, and is known to devour monkeys, surely would find humans an appropriate prey item. Auffenberg reported that native workers on his project were injured both while working in the bush and sleeping. Members of the expedition were attacked while in their tents and even while located in blinds trying to observe the animals. One of Auffenberg's men was killed by a Komodo dragon instantly; other fatalities were from infection. Virulent infection, because their mouths are loaded with bacteria, and hemorrhage are eventualities if humans are wounded by a lizard.[39]

The aggressiveness of the Komodo dragon has been attributed to its position as the only large carnivore on the islands where it occurs. Komodo dragons are also scavengers and one popular conception is that they will unearth and eat human corpses—bodies left from warfare or buried in shallow graves. Such a ghoulish vision is likely based on the attraction of monitors to carrion; groups of them tend to congregate and gulp down hunks of dead animals.[40]

A television documentary about the Komodo dragons, aired on the Discovery Channel,[41] emphasized that local people have learned to coexist with the huge reptiles, respecting them by taking precautions but not living in terror or, alternatively, calling for elimination of the predators. Only nine island residents have been killed by the lizards. Most of the human victims have been visitors, one casualty being Baron Rudolf Von Reding Biberegg, who earned the dubious distinction of being the first European victim of a Komodo dragon. A camera, hat, and one bloodstained shoe were the only remains of the baron after he mysteriously disappeared on the island of Komodo in 1974. The baron was touring with a group but lagged behind after an arduous climb. One moment he was in view of the rest of his party and vice versa; the next moment he was gone.[42]

Despite all the emphasis on the aggressive nature of the Komodo lizards, there is mention more than once of the intelligence and variation in individual animals' behaviors. A photograph even survives from 1929 showing an infant playing with an unrestrained adult Komodo dragon at the London Zoo.[43]

So few studies have dealt with predator–prey interactions of monitor lizards that it is impossible to assess what impact they may have on primates in general and on our hominid ancestors in particular. The fossil record of this family—the varanids—begins earlier than the snakes, sometime between 65 and 100 million years ago.[44] The close relationship of monitors with snakes is a point of general agreement with those who study reptile evolution and is based on the presence of similar forked and retractable tongues in both groups.[45]

The largest fossil member of the monitor group has been named *Megalania*. It reached lengths of 20 feet and roamed Asia and Australia. Fossil evidence supports *Megalania*'s existence in Australia until less than one million years ago.[46]

While we have focused on just one species of the monitors—the Komodo dragon—the monitor lizard family is quite varied. Asian water monitors are large predatory reptiles inhabiting Sri Lanka, India, the extreme south of China, and eastward to the Philippines and Indonesia.

Nile crocodiles have a well-deserved reputation for dining on non-human and human primates. (S. C. Bisserot/Nature Photographers)

They measure approximately 4.5–6 feet in length and weigh about 100 pounds, although in 1983 a 7.5-foot water monitor was observed in Malaysia.[47] Water monitors have formidable claws and sharp teeth, along with a well-developed sense of smell and keen eyesight (but they do not have the bulk of the Komodo dragons). In addition they are good swimmers, run at high speed on land (they are said to be able to outrun a man), and are agile arboreally. One can speculate that water monitors, along with their bulkier Komodo cousins, might qualify as potential hominid predators in the distant past.

MY, WHAT BIG TEETH YOU HAVE!

Snakes and lizards are not the only reptilian predators the human lineage has faced. The large saltwater and freshwater crocodiles have garnered a well-deserved reputation for dining on primates of many species in general, and hominids in particular.

To say that a headline in the 24 March 1993 edition of the *St. Louis Post-Dispatch* caught our attention does not fully convey the impact of seeing "Woman Loses Arm to African Crocodile" in 1-inch-high type.

We were already deep into our research on primate predation, so the story had strong intellectual interest. The fact that one of us (DH) had met the woman in question just a few months prior to the headline, and personally heard about her intention to move to Zaire, added a personal and emotional facet. Ms. Sandra Rossi had just finished a stint as campaign coordinator for Geri Rothman-Serot, a candidate running for the U.S. Senate from Missouri. After the exciting but unsuccessful campaign, on election night Rossi told me of her plans to be in Africa by January and start an entirely new life as a tutor for the children of a couple engaged in wildlife research deep in the interior of Zaire (now Democratic Republic of the Congo). Two months into her job, a near-fatal incident occurred; she was attacked by a crocodile while wading in a river with the 8-year-old girl who was her pupil. Doctors in Zaire were forced to amputate Rossi's arm to the elbow after the croc mangled the limb beyond repair. A man nearby rescued Rossi by yanking her from the clutch of the crocodile's powerful jaw (packed with about 80 sharp teeth). The man suffered cuts and abrasions. The little girl escaped injury completely.[48]

Rossi proved to be optimistic and indomitable. When she returned home for surgery, her continuing good humor earned her the admiration of local television and print reporters who followed the story. In subsequent newspaper interviews she showed only enthusiasm for her new state-of-the-art prosthesis. Perhaps she realized just how lucky she was. Of 43 investigated crocodile attacks on humans in northern Zululand and southern Mozambique, 23 were fatal. The crocodiles were aggressive and ferocious; after grabbing their victim, not sticks or knives or stones or spears could make them give up their prey. (An unknown factor is how victims fare *after* a crocodile attack is aborted. Death may frequently follow because of infection. Often subsequent to an attack and rescue, septicemia is likely; the sharp, pointed teeth of the crocodile can introduce pathogenic bacteria deep within the victim's muscles.)[49]

Researchers often encounter the respect and terror inspired by crocs in human populations who live in proximity to the reptiles. During research in southwestern Madagascar along the Mongoky River, one of the authors (RWS) had a fantastic Malagasy guide and assistant, Folo Emanuel. Folo was born and grew up in a small village on the eastern rain-forest coast of the island. In these rain forests, there are many crocodiles in the rivers, and the reptiles are known to attack and kill people on a regular basis. However, I was told that crocodiles had been eliminated from the region along the Mongoky River long ago and that there was nothing to fear, at least where I was doing my study. Once while surveying by boat along the river, Folo heard a large splash; from that time on the guide was convinced that crocodiles were still around. When I took a swim near the campsite, Folo would sit on the bank nearby, shaking his head and exclaiming, "Crocs! Die soon sure!"

That fatalistic acceptance of crocodiles as a predator on humans is widespread throughout the tropics. And with good reason. This ancient group of reptiles is still having an incredible impact on the human species today. A case in point—twelve fatalities were attributed to saltwater crocodiles in northern Australia in the 13 years between 1975 and 1988. And the large and aggressive Nile crocodiles, found over much of Africa, are estimated to kill thousands of people per year, throughout the sub-Saharan portion of the continent.[50]

> It is impossible to estimate the numbers of people who fall victim to crocodile attacks each year. Indeed, in some cases, there is simply no obvious trace left of the person, and their disappearance may remain a mystery. People who live along side crocodilians, using the lakes and rivers for everyday activities such as washing, often turn to various charms and incantations for protection. But the risk is still present, and perhaps 3,000 people are seized, mutilated and, in most cases, eaten by crocodiles annually.[50]

Many tales of crocodile predation on humans come from the Indo-Pacific. One documented report is particularly grisly. When the British campaign to retake Burma during World War II forced the retreat of about a thousand Japanese soldiers, they entered a mangrove swamp between Burma and Ramree Island, seeking evacuation ships sent by their navy. A British blockade prevented the Japanese naval vessels from arriving, and the soldiers were trapped in the swamp during one entire night. The crocodiles moved in. British troops in the blockade could hear the screams of wounded men as they were crushed in the jaws of crocodiles. One wrote that "the blurred worrying sound of spinning crocodiles [crocs rapidly twist in the water to break up prey into edible chunks]

Crocodile warning signs are found throughout the Northern Territory of Australia, yet fatalities are still common. (C. Rudloff, redrawn from Conservation Commission, Northern Territory, Australia)

made a cacophony of hell that has rarely been duplicated on earth."[51] By the light of day, only 20 Japanese soldiers were left alive to describe the night of horror. The survivors thought the vast majority of their comrades were killed by crocodiles, although some drowned and some might have been shot.

For crocodilians, there is a direct relationship between the size of the individual crocodile and the size of the prey taken. Over 60% of the diet of large crocodiles consists of mammals; mature crocs do not expend energy on very small prey even if it is available.[52] As is the case with the other large reptiles, little comprehensive research on the diet of African crocodiles has been published. The one published study of the stomach contents of Nile crocodiles took place in the 1950s; the overall incidence of human prey in 444 specimens was small—only 1% of the crocs had human remains in their stomachs.[53]

The fossil record for crocodiles and alligators is much more complete than for snakes or monitors. They are an evolutionary success in the strictest definition. Any group that has changed only a few structural details over a period comprising hundreds of millions of years must have hit on a pattern that works. Since the Jurassic period—the heyday of the dinosaurs nearly 200 million years ago—crocs have hardly changed. ("Least progressive" is one compliment to their staying power; "only members of this ancient stock which survived beyond the Age of Reptiles" is another.) *Prior* to that time eons ago, crocodile ancestors underwent the adaptation of longer legs that elevated them off the ground and allowed them to breathe more easily when on land. This increased their ability to be fearsome predators since the longer-legged crocs actually *sprinted* over land to run down prey. They can legitimately be termed "cursorial," just like the wild dogs that run their prey to death. These ancestors were also more terrestrial than the modern crocodiles; today's modern crocodiles have returned to the water and rarely trek overland.[54]

Crocodiles have undergone at least three major episodes of adaptive radiation and are presently master predators on a wide tropical food base. Crocodilians are aquatic in lifestyle, which helps them excel in the attack stage of predation. They cannot pursue prey very far on land and must take advantage of their prey species' dependence on water for drinking. For mammalian prey as large as primates, adult crocodiles will lurk offshore near game trails and watering places. Upon sighting the prey, the crocodile quietly submerges, using stealth, surprise, and a sudden fatal upward rush. Modern-day crocs are probably mistakenly characterized as sluggish; one has only to see a crocodile explode at its prey to realize the speed bursts of which they are capable.[55]

Besides the strength of a lone individual croc—which can reach up to 21 feet in the Nile species—Nile crocodiles often hunt cooperatively and may even divide prey among group members. These "sluggish" animals are also capable of chasing prey on land at a speed of 10 miles per hour for short stretches.[56, 57]

This may be why lowland gorillas and other non-human primates are so cautious when at river edges. On two occasions crocodiles seemed to be stalking silverback western lowland gorillas in Democratic Republic of Congo.[58] In both cases, the male gorillas hastily left the area after becoming aware of the crocodile's presence.

Erica Starin, who we mentioned earlier, observed two juvenile and one adult monkey being captured by crocodiles while she studied red colobus in The Gambia. When crossing the river at the Abuko Nature Reserve, the monkeys frequently used a narrow land bridge where camouflaged crocodiles would lie in the grasses. During another study of predator diets in southern Africa, remains of baboons and macaques were found in Nile crocodile stomachs. In Indonesia, false gharials—a long-snouted crocodile—previously assumed to eat only fish, have been observed preying on crab-eating macaques and proboscis monkeys as the primates swim across rivers.[59]

In an ironic scenario that played one species off against the other, knowledge of the crocodilian penchant for primates became an unusual stratagem to foil a man-eating terror. In 1933 several residents of Java fell victim to an Indopacific crocodile. The local government administrator wrote to Jakarta, the capital city, requesting permission to trap eight proboscis monkeys as bait to capture the man-eater, based on the Javan belief that these primates were the crocodiles' most favored prey.[60]

There is no direct proof implicating crocodiles as predators of ancient hominids. Yet, it would suggest scientific hubris to ignore all the circumstantial evidence leading to a conclusion that early hominids contended with crocodiles as predators. Let's lay out the facts: Early hominids lived in woodlands near lakes or rivers; later hominids on the savanna also were tied to water holes. Crocodiles wait for prey at just such locations. Hominids are the right size for crocodile meals. (Actually, almost anything is the right size for mature and subadult crocodiles except small items.) A large adult Nile crocodile may outweigh a human by a factor of 14.[61] And, finally, here is a fatalistic acknowledgment still today throughout tribal cultures in Africa and Southeast Asia that crocodile predation is a reality.

On Top of Everything Else, Sharks, Too?

A discussion of shark attacks is included in this chapter because they, like the reptiles, are cold-blooded vertebrates that will attack and eat humans. They also attack and eat other primates besides humans. And they, undoubtedly, given an opportunity, attacked and ate our ancestors.

Both shark attacks and the crocodile massacre of Japanese soldiers certainly fall into the category of predation on humans, but these two cases probably constitute aberrant examples. Sharks, it is often noted, mistake swimming humans for seals or sea lions. Saltwater crocodiles, one might assume, will seize any large mammal (humans included) unfortunate enough to be huddled in the shallow waters of a mangrove swamp for long periods of time. Regardless, in both cases, the prey (that is, the humans) were in the decidedly non-primate element of the ocean. There are several species of primates that swim and take advantage of riverine and coastal habitat—including humans—but the ocean is outside the normal range of primate habitat and certainly not a milieu in which primates evolved.

It is most unlikely that our distant hominid ancestors had access or inclination to enter the ocean. More recently in our lineage, some populations of the first anatomically modern *Homo sapiens* may have exploited the seaside niches foraging for shellfish and, thereby, encountered sharks. Also, in their diaspora out of Africa, modern humans may have rafted across straits and fell prey to sharks.

Likewise, populations of rhesus macaques—a colonizing species of diverse habitats, like modern humans—exploit the mangrove swamps of the Sundarbans, India, and fall prey to sharks. Besides Indian pythons and estuarine crocodiles, wolf sharks (also known as common thresher sharks) and requiem sharks prey on macaques when the monkeys swim across estuaries at ebb tide. Wolf sharks are approximately 18 feet in length, half of which is an elongated tail used to stun prey. Wolf sharks are usually found offshore but not in exceedingly deep waters. Requiem sharks are found in tropical and temperate seas and reach a maximum length of 12 feet, but little is known of their natural history.[62]

Shark deaths are not a major mortality factor for humans or other primates, but shark attacks are among the most feared events that occur in the ocean. And, no shark attack story can quite rival the survivor tale of Rodney Fox, an Australian spearfisherman.[63] Fox was diving in a competition off the coast of South Australia in 1963. After a dive in 50 feet of water, he suddenly sensed a stillness; a few seconds later a huge force hit his left side, knocking off his face mask and causing his speargun to fly from his hand. His arm was serrated to the bone as he withdrew it from a shark's mouth and kicked to the surface for air. Attempting to avoid being bitten again, he grabbed the shark's back with his legs and ended up being pulled down to the ocean floor, rodeo-style, where the shark proceeded to try to scrape him off. Struggling back to the surface, Fox was grabbed again, but for a third time managed to kick to the surface. By sheer luck a boat was only a few yards away and he was pulled out of the water. His injuries were terrible—rib cage bared open, lungs and stomach exposed, legs and arms shredded. In fact, his wet suit was left on because it was thought the suit was the only thing keeping him intact. After a 4-hour operation, and 462 stitches, he was out of danger. He survived because he was in superb physical condition, did not go into shock, and, most importantly, the shark had not tried to eat him.

We've now considered the predators of land and sea. Lest we feel we are now mindful of all perils faced by our hominid predecessors, let us not forget another dimension from which danger can issue—the air.

Terror from the Sky

7

There aren't many birds of prey, either in far distant times or right now, that reach a size large enough to attack and kill a hominid. There aren't *many*, but there are a few.

Several years ago we interviewed a U.S.-government researcher about his stint in the forests of Uganda. One of his objectives was a study of a very unique raptor, the crowned hawk-eagle. This research brought him in contact with local people who told stories of harrowing encounters with the great forest eagle. There was even a survivor with only one arm—an eagle allegedly ripped the limb from his body when he was a young boy. Healthy skepticism of such stories slowly turned to astonished conviction on the part of the scientist. He came back from his field site with the opinion that many of the stories concerning attacks and injuries from crowned hawk-eagles were *not* fabrications.

After talking to him we uttered a collective "wow," and agreed we'd just received some pretty provocative information. Crowned hawk-eagles have been known to prey successfully on large primates such as adolescent mandrills (adult members of this forest baboon species reach 60 pounds) and young bonobos (adult males weigh nearly 100 pounds), and one primate probably looks just like another from an eagle's perspective. So—next step—could we find any corroboration of the Ugandan lore regarding this bird of prey as a predator of small, or young, humans?

Eagles and hawks are the major and most competent predators on non-human primates. African crowned hawk-eagles (metaphorically called "leopards with wings") have even been known to attack children. (Used by permission of Zoological Society of San Diego)

We made a decision to follow this lead with copious literature searches, internet quests, and calls to ornithologists.

The last option does not turn out to be one of our greatest ideas. "Eagles do not kill people!" is enunciated with heat and not a little exasperation from the bird experts. "We know that," we say "and, of course, we don't think eagles are a threat to humanity. But we're looking for the possibility of eagle predation on early hominids. You know, 60-pound australopithecines?" After we assure the raptor connoisseurs of our purely academic interest, they relent enough to admit that the crowned hawk-eagle seems to be in a class by itself as far as predation is concerned. Yes, rumors of human predation by crowned hawk-eagles do circulate. But rumors of eagles flying off with babies are the fodder of many folktales—all of which have served in the past to help justify a slaughter of eagles that took place in the Western world up until the late twentieth century. It was only in the last thirty years or so that conservationists engendered an appreciation for endangered raptors in the public mind and heart.

Next step in our quest: the ubiquitous internet concordance, google.com, is consulted. It furnishes little assistance, although the photos of crowned hawk-eagles are magnificent. Steely eyed raptors with an attitude, they won't be the ones to blink in any staring contest!

Literature searches hit pay dirt. A classic 1983 volume, entitled *Birds of Prey of Southern Africa* by Peter Steyn, contains the following passage:

> One grisly item found on a nest in Zimbabwe by the famous wildlife artist D. M. Henry was part of the skull of a young African. That preying on young humans may very occasionally occur is borne out by a carefully authenticated incident in Zambia where an immature crowned eagle attacked a . . . [44-pound] seven-year-old schoolboy as he went to school. It savagely clawed him on head, arms and chest. . . . the boy was nowhere near a nest, so the attack can only have been an attempt at predation.[1]

Steyn, the author of this passage, is a well-known eagle authority and the citations he provides in his bibliography are faultless. Further delving unearths the full story of the unfortunate schoolboy from the primary source, a senior biologist with the Zambian Department of Veterinary and Tsetse Control Services. The story: Young Damas Kambole was walking to school, as his older brother bicycled, when an eagle swooped down from a tree onto him, ripping open gashes in his head, arms, and chest (he was wearing a khaki school uniform that probably saved him from fatal injuries). The boy grabbed at the eagle; a woman walking the same road to her fields ran to help the child. She was carrying a sharp garden hoe and killed the eagle with it. The boy was taken to a local hospital and received urgent care from the mission sisters in residence. The eagle was a subadult with a wingspan of over 6 feet, the eagle's foot measured 7.5 inches in width, and one claw measured 2.5 inches in length. The biologist investigating the attack surmised that the bird mistook the child for prey since the method of attack was standard crowned hawk-eagle hunting behavior. After 3 months the child's wounds had healed, but his father's fearful interpretation of the incident had not. Damas' father perceived the attack as a bad omen and moved the boy to another location.[2]

FEATHERWEIGHTS AND TALON TIPS

We knew from our data collection and quantitative analysis of predation on non-human primates that eagles and hawks are the major and
most competent predators on primates worldwide.[3] Our research
found that 46% of published eyewitness accounts of primate predation relate to raptor kills. And a good portion of these primate kills
were the work of crowned hawk-eagles. In what seems, from our study
at least, to be a fairly "typical" attack by a crowned hawk-eagle, the
bird initially launched itself into flight approximately 500 feet away
from feeding vervet monkeys. Using tree cover to make an undetected
approach, it suddenly burst skyward from the canopy with a monkey
grasped in its talons. In another instance, a crowned hawk-eagle
snatched a colobus monkey from a tree less than 5 feet above an ob-
server's head, driving its talons straight through the monkey's cranium
in the process.[4]

   We found that 81 species of raptors in all are known or alleged to
prey on primates. The raptor category, we should add, includes diurnal
species of hawks, eagles, and falcons, plus owls (the nocturnal equivalent
of the daylight-hunting birds of prey) and other miscellaneous carnivorous birds (crows, toucans, and shrikes).

   The most singular feature of birds is their feathers. Many members of
the animal kingdom fly—bats, butterflies, mosquitos—but only birds
have feathers; parenthetically, many birds do not fly—penguins, ostriches, kiwis—but they all possess feathers. Many birds of prey are to a
large degree "all feathers"; efficient killing machines that weigh little and,
with very few exceptions, take prey that is half or less than the bird's own
weight.[5] The crowned hawk-eagle (and certain other large raptors) represents an exception to this rule—it kills extremely large prey for a raptor,
even forest antelopes and adult male colobus monkeys. Eagles support
the large loads they must carry back to a nest through the unequaled
structure of their feathers. Feathers—an aerodynamic marvel—prevent
any "stalling" or sudden breakdown in the lifting power of the wings by
securing smooth airflow onto the wing's top surface.[6] Most raptors have
ten primary feathers (located farthest from the body on each wing) and
twelve secondary feathers (those closest to the body). The responsibility
of the primaries is to propel the bird through the air with each beat of the

wing. The secondary feathers create lift, allowing a bird to maintain altitude during flight as the wings beat.[7]

Nocturnal raptors (the owls) usually hunt from perches and at fairly close quarters, without the impressive variety of adaptations found in diurnal raptors.[8] Nevertheless, one hallmark adaptation of the owl is as impressive as it is understated. Wing feathers of diurnal birds are sharp and well defined, but owl feathers have soft, fringed edges to cut down on noise. The result is silent flight that surprises prey as the owl swoops through the night air.[9] Herein may lie the perception of owls as bad omens found in many African cultures. As one famous ornithologist noted: "Man fears the night for, like a baboon, he is then at a disadvantage; and as a result the creatures of the night tend to be disliked and feared."[10]

For the diurnal birds of prey, sight is the most important of all the senses. Great speed, high visual acuity, and deadly accuracy make them astonishing predators. They possess full-color vision and the ability to rapidly adjust the focus of their eyes while moving at tremendous speeds. What is truly remarkable is the "resolving power" of the raptor eye—what can only be described, in essence, as a hyper-resolution of an image that the lens casts on the retinal surface of the eye.[11] The raptor eye possesses a resolving power four to eight times greater than the human eye. Using the lower of these estimates means that a soaring eagle can see a rabbit at a distance of 2 miles. The late Leslie Brown, a Kenyan ornithologist who literally wrote the book on large raptors, gave a real-life example of raptor optics in one of his numerous volumes: If a grasshopper is placed on a contrasting background, the human who placed it (and therefore, knows its location) cannot see the insect at greater than 35 yards; a bird of prey, on the other hand, can detect a green grasshopper in green grass at greater than 110 yards when it has no knowledge that there may be an insect in that spot.[12]

Strong legs and powerful feet equipped with sharp curved talons, in conjunction with a hooked bill, define all birds of prey. The upper bill, especially of an eagle, can be 4 inches in length, with a menacing pointed hook overlapping the flattened lower bill. Hooked, curved beaks are not tailored for obtaining prey but, instead, are universally used by hawks, eagles, and even vultures to tear apart the flesh of prey already killed or scavenged.[13] Again, the crowned hawk-eagle exceeds the norm. When

scientists saw a dramatic crowned hawk-eagle attack on a subadult mandrill, they were amazed that the eagle had the baboon on the ground,
holding onto its prey with its talons, and striking repeated blows at the
mandrill's head with its beak.[14]

Raptor feet, however, are the actual killing apparatus. A raptor's feet
are dangerous weapons, and their power is exceptional. Upon impact,
the talons are performing three functions simultaneously: (1) they
drive into the body of the prey, (2) they contract and close, and (3)
they exert a crushing pressure. All of these actions work in concert; but
the blow, or force of impact, delivered by the feet in a strike is at least
as important as the piercing, gripping, or crushing force of the talons.
And it is the relative size, curvature, and thickness of talons—along
with the length of the toes—that will vary among birds of prey with
the type of food consumed.[15]

Raptors that prey on good-sized mammals have thick toes, well-
curved talons, and large *tarsi* (a raptor tarsus is the anatomical equivalent
to a human ankle). It is this combination that gives the legs of a raptor
such strength. Raptor talons probably serve as much to provide anchor-
age for the powerful grip as to be used as daggers for incapacitating prey.
The inner and hind toes are the most powerful and work in opposition
to each other, applying the main grip to prey. Crowned hawk-eagles have
exceptionally thick, powerful legs and short thick toes that end in very
strong rigid talons. Their talons can wrap around the top of a branch that
is as thick as a man's thigh, and their "killer" hind claw is the diameter of
a man's little finger.[16]

Tom Struhsaker, a primatologist who has consistently incorporated
predation into his ecological studies of African forest monkeys, commented about the extreme precision of a crowned hawk-eagle attack.
Picture this: The crowned hawk-eagle not only has the power and the
momentum, the surprise and the speed, but those great talons are used
with such exactitude that the *heart* of the prey is the target. When freshly
killed monkeys were examined by Struhsaker and his colleagues, the
heart was pierced in three out of three examinations. In one juvenile
monkey the heart was triple-pierced from a single deathblow; the talon
went in one side of the heart, came out the other side, and—achievable
only because of the camber of the eagle's talon—curved back and reen-
tered the heart once again.[17]

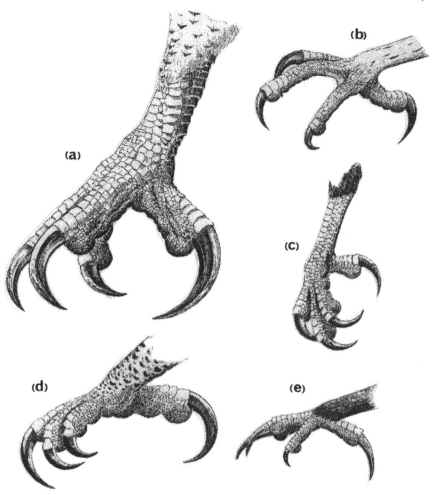

Feet and talons are the raptor's killing devices. This illustrates the massive legs, feet, and talons of harpy eagles and crowned hawk-eagles in comparison to other large eagles: (a) harpy eagle; (b) Bonelli's eagle; (c) African fish eagle; (d) crowned hawk-eagle; (e) Asian black eagle. (Redrawn from Brown 1977)

CRESTED VIRAGOS

Raptor derives from a Latin word meaning "plunderer." Etymologists studying the origins of language might contend that the word *raptor* illustrates a fusion of fear and awe that birds of prey have always inspired in the human mind. Historically, three massive raptors are acclaimed as fiercest of the fierce (we list them in descending size, but not necessarily in decreasing ferocity): The harpy eagle of the Neotropics, the Philippine eagle found only on the island of Mindanao, and the crowned hawk-eagle of Central, East, and Southern Africa. The harpy eagle has been described as a "flying wolf." (*Webster's New Collegiate Dictionary*'s definition of the word *harpy*, however, sounds unremittingly misogynistic; the nicest part reads: "A foul, malign creature of Greek mythology that is part woman and part bird.") Crowned hawk-eagles were labeled "leopards of the air" by the European explorers of Africa, and the Usambara people of the former Belgian Congo called the crowned hawk-eagle *kumbakima*, "the monkey beater."[18] In all three of these species the female is the larger of the sexes, and each species sports a signature crest of feathers on their heads that rises and collapses with the fire of their temperament. We began calling them the "fearsome threesome," but then decided "viragos"—defined by *Webster's* as overbearing women (and in the case of these eagles, the males qualify also) of great stature, strength, and courage—was by far the best collective label.

Heavy eagles that prey on primates within the forest canopy, such as the harpy, Philippine, and crowned hawk-eagles, have short, broad wings and relatively long, graduated tails. This silhouette is not the common one we visualize when thinking of a soaring eagle; we tend to envision a powerful bird of prey with a huge wingspan and a tail that is relatively short. That combination of long wing and short tail works well for *soaring* eagles hunting in open country. Unlike the soaring eagles, though, our viragos hunt within dense rain forests and they have, accordingly, evolved the apparatus to give them maximum proficiency in their ecological niche. A long tail is a crucial trait; the ratio of tail length to wingspan can predict the maneuverability of eagles. The tail of a raptor, then, is quite as important as its wings when the bird lives in a rain forest. The length of a virago tail is up to 85% of its wingspan.[19] When you see a raptor with this ratio in the flesh, it registers as a notably *robust* bird.

Wingloading—the ratio of body weight to surface area of wings—has great effect on the flight performance of birds of prey. It is also a subject best left to experts in aerodynamics to discuss. We can only make the simple statement that the weight, wingspan, and tail length of a harpy eagle, a crowned hawk-eagle, or a Philippine eagle occur in serendipitous combination. Their wing–tail adaptations allow the eagles to maneuver

The harpy eagle is the premier raptor of the Neotropics. (R. W. Sussman)

better in the air and dodge dexterously around trees and other obstacles in thick forest as they target their prey. Crowned hawk-eagles, in some cases, are able to do the seemingly impossible and lift off almost vertically from the forest floor while clutching their dead prey.[20]

Scientific research has upheld and, for the harpy and crowned hawk-eagle, even expanded upon their reputations as rapacious non-human primate predators. The harpy eagle—nearly the largest and undoubtedly the most powerful eagle in the world—is the premier predator of many Neotropical monkeys. Harpy eagles weigh 15–20 pounds and have a wingspan of approximately 8 feet. The harpy eagle exhibits the same classic characteristics as the crowned hawk-eagle. A harpy eagle possesses a tarsus as thick as a child's wrist; its feet span 9–10 inches; and the massive dagger-like talons are nearly 3.5 inches long.[21]

People who have worked with captive harpies report that a fully grown man must brace himself securely to prepare for the landing of one of these eagles on his arm. Not a surprising observation since harpy eagles attain speeds of 40–50 miles per hour and can exert 13,500 foot-pounds upon impact with their prey: that's nearly three times the muzzle energy of a bullet from a heavy rifle. The harpy soars low and missile-like over the rain-forest canopy and hits its victim from the back with powerful talons, catching the monkey totally unawares. After the harpy eagle's initial impact with its prey, momentum allows it to continue in flight and carry its victim to a nesting or feeding tree. Either the talons are driven through the body of a monkey to kill it instantly, or the monkey may be struck with such force that it dies by falling to the ground.[22]

Those lucky enough to have beheld the elusive and endangered harpy in action wax poetic in their descriptions of its magnificence as a predator: "King of the raptorine birds . . . [f]rom the topmost branch of some dead forest giant it surveys the forest below for signs of movement. Then, like a bolt from the blue, it swoops with unerring accuracy upon a sleeping sloth or a leaping monkey and bears off its prey in triumph."[23]

Another species of colossal, primate-eating raptor, the Philippine eagle, has a huge, narrow bill (which may be an adaptation to enhance its binocular field of vision) and tarsi almost as heavy as the harpy eagle. The Philippine eagle's scientific nomenclature, *Pithecophaga jefferyi*, emphasizes predation on monkeys—*Pithecophaga* is derived from the Greek words *pithekos,* meaning monkey, and *phagein,* eater. Its common name was officially changed from "monkey-eating eagle" to "Philippine eagle" in 1978 by President Ferdinand Marcos as a public relations move, since the monkey-eating appellation was seen as a denigration of this noble bird and the nation it represents.[24]

Of course, names may not always be entirely accurate. While data on the frequency of primates in the diet of Philippine eagles are sparse, three studies have estimated only 3–6% of their diet consists of macaque monkeys. This range is considerably lower than the level of primates found in the diets of harpy or crowned hawk-eagles. Pairs of Philippine eagles have been observed hunting together, and estimates for successful capture of monkeys were significantly higher when two mated birds combined their efforts. But actually, it appears that the Philippine eagle relies more on a diet of colugos—squirrel-sized, gliding mammals sometimes called flying lemurs—as the staple of its diet, rather than primates.[25]

Of the three viragos, the crowned hawk-eagle is the smallest in size. Female crowned hawk-eagles—the larger of the sexes—have wingspans of just under 6 feet and weigh in at 8–9 pounds, about 50% lighter in mass than the harpy eagle.[26] Yet a combination of stout tarsi with exceptionally strong talons has given the crowned hawk-eagle a reputation as a metaphorical "leopard with wings." (Not a bad metaphor at all, since the leopard is a relatively lightweight member of the big-cat family, yet has the strength and boldness to assail a gorilla. And, like the leopard, the crowned hawk-eagle is a primate specialist; studies of this raptor in the Kibale Forest of Uganda found that approximately 85% of its prey were monkeys of three types—colobus, mangabeys, and guenons. At another research site in the Kiwengoma Forest Reserve, Tanzania, a species of guenon, the blue monkey, composed nearly 90% of the prey remains at a crowned hawk-eagle roost.)[27]

The crowned hawk-eagle is the second largest of all African eagles (second in size only to the martial eagle), but it is without a doubt the most powerful raptor on the continent and is able to kill the largest prey. While its average weight is 8–9 pounds, it routinely kills antelope weighing 40–44 pounds—nearly five times its own weight. The largest recorded kill by a crowned hawk-eagle was a 66-pound subadult bushbuck ram.[28] It's a feeble understatement, but these are incredible birds.

The crowned hawk-eagle's geographic range extends across the width of sub-Saharan Africa in dense tropical rain forest. Their hunting strategy consists of long periods of silent watchfulness from a perch within the forest, culminating in a swift and deadly accurate drop onto the unfortunate prey. Most kills are made on the ground where the carcass is dismembered and partially consumed. Such is the strength of the crowned hawk-eagle that, if a monkey is killed on the forest floor, the eagle will fly almost vertically upward with the whole carcass.[29] Here's another firsthand description regarding their power and maneuverability:

> It was not long before there were some astonishing events. The male [crowned hawk-] eagle suddenly, and in a shower of green leaves, burst through the canopy where the monkeys were feeding, upside down with wings closed, and with a monkey firmly grasped in both sets of talons. In other words he must have approached and taken his prey at high speed from below and his momentum was such that it carried him a full 15 feet upwards above the tree tops before he opened his wings, rolled over, and flew heavily back carrying his prey to his cliffside perch.[30]

The crowned hawk-eagle's unremitting reliance on intelligent primates has been credited with the evolution of several predatory behaviors, such as coordinated hunting of monkeys by breeding eagle pairs. Team hunting by a mated pair seems to be a tactic often employed by crowned hawk-eagles. One of the pair may swoop low over the trees; as it flies away a monkey may climb out of the foliage to watch the departure of its feared enemy. At that point a second eagle will take off from its perch and dive at the monkey from behind. Other observers have detected soft whistling on the part of the hunting eagle to attract naturally curious monkeys.[31]

A protracted 2-year breeding cycle on the part of the eagles has been documented. This adaptation—biennial rather than annual breeding—is also found in the harpy eagle and may indicate specific coevolution with their primate prey. The pressure on prey species (in the eagles' case, slow breeding primates) is doubled when a pair of harpy or crowned hawk-eagles are feeding a fledgling in the nest. (Nests, by the way, are massive—6 feet deep and 6 feet wide.) Economical utilization of prey has very wisely evolved; spacing the extra food requirements of a nestling out to every other year gives prey a respite to recover their numbers before the next breeding cycle of the eagles.[32]

Coevolution between raptors and their primate prey is patently visible in primate polyspecific associations, when two or more different monkey species feed, travel, or rest together. What may have provided a strong incentive for these multi-species aggregations? The evidence points to birds of prey since polyspecific associations of many New World and African monkeys are limited to geographic regions inhabited by harpy eagles of the Neotropics and crowned hawk-eagles of Central Africa.[33]

Harpy eagles probably have exerted such strong selective pressure on many Neotropical primate species that predation is manifested not only in group living and polyspecific associations but also in the evolution of increased size. Neotropical primatologist John Terborgh discussed the relation between size and escape from predation for the primates at Cocha Cashu, Peru. Escape through an increase in size was identified as a distinct evolutionary strategy of Neotropical primates to thwart predation. The smallest primates, tamarins and marmosets (weighing 1–3 pounds), spend many hours per day in safe hiding places. Slightly larger species, such as capuchin and squirrel monkeys, seek protection in groups. The strategy of escape through size increase applies to adults of the largest species (spider, woolly, and howler monkeys). These primates are often found at rest in conspicuous exposed perches in the canopy. From such vantage points, the larger primates scan for harpy and other big eagles, species in which a few birds are highly dispersed over huge territories. Increased size, combined with group-living and agility, may render the larger Neotropical primates very difficult prey even for the harpy eagle. Howler monkeys were observed to evade and chase a harpy eagle that attacked one of their group, but the successful capture of a fully grown adult male howler by a harpy eagle was witnessed, even though smaller individuals were in the same group and available as prey. Medium-sized monkeys in the range of 4–8 pounds, such as capuchin monkeys, sakis, or bearded sakis, constitute the most regular prey for harpy eagles.[34]

While the medium-sized monkeys of the rain forest are the most commonly recorded primate prey for crowned hawk-eagles also, a wide range of larger species are within the potential of this bird. The geographic range of the crowned hawk-eagle extends into huge areas of the eastern and southern African savanna, where it depends heavily on various species of antelope and the occasional baboon.

AN ALFRED HITCHCOCK MOMENT

The office of a colleague, paleontologist Tab Rasmussen at Washington University in St. Louis, houses an awesome, frightening treasure. It's the talon of an extinct raptor that once lived in Madagascar. The raptor has no common name. Like many fossil species, it is known only by its scientific name, *Stephanoaetus mahery*.

Recently, we had the opportunity to examine this talon. It came from a large eagle that became extinct 1,500–2,000 years ago. The talon was from the front of the raptor foot. Measuring over 1.5 inches, it is robust and *very* impressive. Those talons could have done major damage to any prey species. The long *hind* talons of the fossil eagle are equal in size and massiveness (and the tarsometatarsus is actually larger) than modern specimens of crowned hawk-eagles. *Stephanoaetus* is also the genus in which the modern crowned hawk-eagle of today resides. The fossil and today's crowned hawk-eagle are relatives—the crowned hawk-eagle being the only surviving member of the genus. "Exceptionally robust" in size and proportions—along with "exceptionally prominent" muscle attachment surfaces—were mentioned in the first published description of the extinct eagle by Steve Goodman, an ornithologist at Chicago's Field

Museum. He credits the long hind talon of the crowned hawk-eagle with its ability to subdue very large prey. Since the hind talons of *S. mahery* and its modern cousin are similar in massive length and girth, he assumes that *S. mahery* would have been a formidable predator of lemurs, just as the crowned hawk-eagle is the premier threat to African forest monkeys today.[35]

We started putting ourselves in the place of prey to that fossil eagle. We know it was as large or larger than the extant crowned hawk-eagles of Africa, which have a wingspan of 6 feet. Primatologists Lysa Leland and Tom Struhsaker wrote that seeing crowned hawk-eagles swooping low in the forest—when you are standing under them in the shadows of their outstretched wings—is like being back in the age of the pterodactyls.[36]

One of us (RWS) had the experience of being the target of a pair of hawks that decided to dive at an offending human. I recalled that while following one of my groups of brown lemurs under the trees in a deciduous forest in southwestern Madagascar, I disturbed a pair of small hawks, probably Henst's goshawks. They must have just built a nest or hatched a brood of nestlings, because I had been in this portion of the lemurs' range many times before without incident. Both of the birds began diving at me and coming so close that I could feel the wind as they flew past. They continued to do this for a few weeks, becoming ever more intimidating. I would try to stay clear of the area, but when I had to follow the lemurs into their range, I'd take a stick to wave at the hawks in an attempt to discourage their rambunctious attempts to take my head off. Once one of them actually glanced off my forehead as it flew by. The fossil *S. mahery* would have been more than three times larger than the hawks that dived at my head. I wouldn't have wanted that large extinct eagle to be the bird diving at me in a Madagascar forest!

This is virtually what *did* happen to the late Leslie Brown, who was the world's authority on the crowned hawk-eagle. Brown included an impressive photograph in one of his books that speaks louder than any words about the pain elicited by an attack from a large eagle. Three half-inch-wide ropey scars spread about 8 inches apart on his back are testimony to the power of crowned hawk-eagle talons. A female eagle had acted aggressively toward him over a period of several years when he was monitoring her nests. Finally, one nesting season she had enough of this human intruder and launched a full attack. The eagle flew directly at him from 300 yards away at high speed and delivered a violent downward impact with one open foot. He declared it felt like a crushing blow from a heavy stick; if he had not been wearing a shirt, which was mostly what her talons grasped, he would have sustained even more serious damage. (Reminiscent of the Zambian schoolboy whose khaki uniform saved him!) Needless to say, Brown opted for discretion over valor and kept away from her nest after the incident.[37]

THE RECORD OF GIANT RAPTORS

The talon from *S. mahery* was found in Madagascar. So far, no fossils of great antiquity have been found on that island, so it is more accurate to designate this eagle as a *subfossil* since it is only a few thousand years old. In that period 1,500–2,000 years ago there was a varied, now-extinct mega-fauna (including pygmy hippos, giant elephant birds, and large lemurs) on the island of Madagascar. The arrival of humans at this point began a wave of extinctions—at least 17 species of lemurs disappeared soon after the human ingress.[38] Many of the subfossil species were quite unlike surviving lemurs and filled ecological niches that have now been left unfilled. The largest lemurs were the size of a chimpanzee or even heftier and were probably too large for the eagle to take. However, many were the size of small baboons, and others were about as large or larger than living forms. This immensely powerful raptor must have specialized in capturing large, daylight-loving lemurs.[39]

The now-extinct eagle left its imprint on the behavior of present-day lemurs in Madagascar. Today there are strong stereotypic responses to birds of prey given by ringtailed lemurs and sifakas,[40] but the diurnal hawks currently inhabiting Madagascar that evoke this anti-predation behavior are black kites, Madagascar harrier hawks, and Madagascar buzzards. They are relatively small compared to the subfossil eagle and would have extreme difficulty in subduing and killing an adult lemur.

Just how *many* extinct relatives the crowned hawk-eagle may have had is unknown. The origin of the *Rokh* (or Roc) myth—a huge bird discussed in the Second Voyage of Sindbad "that feedeth its young on elephants" and "as it flew through the air, veiled the sun and hid it from the island"[41]—may be an outgrowth of tales based on *S. mahery* or other extinct birds like it. Steve Goodman, the ornithologist who identifed the extinct subfossil eagle, thinks references to the *Rokh* could be based on an extinct bird of Madagascar, perhaps this very eagle.[42]

Another extinct raptor—known from paleontological digs in New Zealand—is called Haast's eagle. Its fossilized skull measures 6.5 inches from back to front—several inches longer than contemporary eagles. It inhabited New Zealand from at least 30,000 until about 1,000 years ago and may have preyed on a wealth of indigenous large flightless birds that populated New Zealand until the islands were colonized by humans. Because the eagle's head is so big, it is fair to speculate that it was larger than any living eagle; the size of the skull, combined with other fossil parts—robust legs and talons that rival tiger claws—speak to yet another fearsome extinct eagle.[43] Haast's eagle and *S. mahery* both became extinct in recent times, shortly after the arrival of humans to a large island ecosystem—New Zealand and Madagascar. Their similarity as top predators and their extinction speaks to a correlation that cannot be entirely coincidental.

Truly ancient raptor fossils are abundant, representing species that lived from 30 to 50 million years ago up through more recent times. Since raptor-like birds are found in the 30-to-50-million-year range, paleontologists estimate that raptors must be an ancient group that evolved early in the bird radiation. Despite abundant fossils of 62 different extinct species, there is not a clear relationship or descent discernible in the raptor family tree. The first morphologically modern raptor was discovered in European rock formations dated to approximately 13 million years ago. The only living raptor it resembles is the secretary bird of Africa, which is a turkey-sized raptor with a very distinct appearance, reminding one of an ancient bird just shedding some of its more reptilian features.[44]

Lots of unusually large, unusually terrifying raptors have been found in the fossil record. The teratorns were the ancestral cousins of condors and survived until 1.8 million years ago. They were stork-like in appearance, but at that point any similarity to the passive storks of today ended. Their wingspans were 23 feet and they weighed about 260 pounds! One ornithologist commented that "they led the lives of active and awesome predators."[45] The teratorns first appear in the fossil record of South America; caution must be used, however, when attempting to understand the geographic origins of raptors. This cautionary note is evidenced in the case of condor-like fossils known from excavations in France laid down some 35–40 million years ago, even though currently, all condors are found only in the New World.[46]

Another geographic mystery involves *Phorusrhacus*, one of a group of mammoth, flightless predatory birds. These birds stood anywhere from 4 and one-half to 9 feet in height. Some of them possessed 20-inch skulls topped off with wicked hooked beaks. The whole group had been categorized as South American in origin and radiation, yet French paleontologists found fossil evidence that one of this group had existed in France during the period between 22 and 55 million years ago. One additional huge, non-flying predatory bird called *Diatryma* existed 55–65 million years ago in Asia and Europe. *Diatryma* and its relatives were 6 feet tall, had enormous skulls ,and robust legs tapering to feet with immense claws.[47] These fossil finds of giant flightless predatory birds pose interesting—but as yet unanswerable—questions: How long did these creatures exist in the Old World? Were they limited to Asia and Europe or did they occur elsewhere? Specifically, did they occur in Africa also? And, were they still around when hominids were evolving?

THE TAUNG CHILD TELLS ITS TALE

It's time to leave theoretical discussions and talk about the specifics of raptor predation on ancestral hominids. The first evidence that eagles preyed on the human line appears, coincidentally, as part of the same fossil evidence that humans evolved in Africa. The very same child's fossilized skull and brain that Raymond Dart carefully removed from its mineralized crust in 1924 holds the clues to raptor predation on hominids.

After much scientific debate and investigation during the past decade, it is now considered likely that this first South African hominid fossil found by Raymond Dart—the Taung child, which he named *Australopithecus africanus*—was the consequence of predation by a raptor at least the size and strength of a crowned hawk-eagle.[48]

A three-person University of Michigan team composed of a primatologist, paleontologist, and geologist reviewed the bone assemblages found under the nests of modern crowned hawk-eagles and then applied the information and identification marks to the Taung child fossil. Certain indicators of crowned hawk-eagle predation are routinely found on non-human primate remains: these include nicks, punctures, and "can opener" perforations on thin bones such as the skull and pelvis, plus

"Can opener" perforations on the skull of the Taung child indicate that this fossil hominid was the victim of predation by a raptor much like the modern crowned hawk-eagle. (C. Rudloff, redrawn from Zihlman 2000)

heavy raking and shattering of shoulder blades. Similarly, distinct patterns of bone damage can also identify the "signatures" of large-raptor predation on fossils. The Taung child fossil that Dart freed from its breccia husk exhibits these marks of raptor talons.[49]

Despite their impressive weaponry in the form of talons and beak, the crowned hawk-eagles are quite fastidious in their dining habits. Compared to the bone crunching of modern or fossil carnivorous mammals, raptors tend to dismember the trunk of the prey delicately and consume the organ contents of the body cavity with the precision of a well-mannered diner. Crania are usually left intact, but intense manipulation is exhibited by visible nicks, perforations, and lacerations inflicted during the eagles' efforts to get at the brain through thin facial bones. The great pressure of the talons probably leave the signature marks—the sharp talons can move through some thin bones just as a can opener slices through steel. A small bone flap is created with each turn of the can-opener talons.

Phillip Tobias, a paleontologist of great repute who was Raymond Dart's successor at the University of Witwatersrand, hypothesized that the eagle responsible for the Taung child predation must have had a hind talon length of over 5.5 inches.[50] The crowned hawk-eagle surfaces as the best extant representative of the type of bird that lived approximately 2.5 million years ago and could inflict the marks found on the Taung child cranium.[51]

The Taung child is the only hominid fossil found at this paleontological site so far, but over 33 baboon skulls were present and, as we predicted earlier, one primate probably looks just like another to a raptor. What might have been the circumstances that surrounded the death of the Taung youngster? Was it wrested away from its mother's arms? Did she lay the child down on the ground for a moment and turn away for a few fateful seconds? Were the mother and child so far away from their social group that no others were around to prevent the abduction?

We will never know the exact story, but there are a few details that might help us put the puzzle together. First, the Taung child was most likely between the ages of 3 and 4 years and weighed about 20–24 pounds. This is deduced from the dimensions of its skull which correlate to a modern juvenile chimpanzee in size.[52] A 3- or 4-year-old child would have been at that developmental transition point where constant

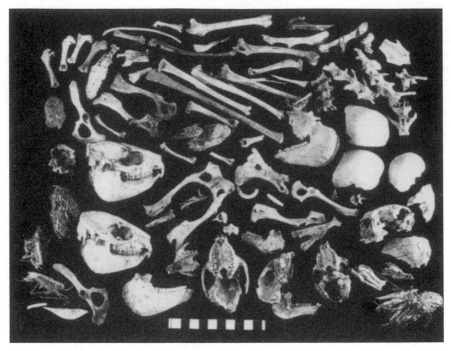

Bones collected from beneath a black eagle nest in southern Africa. The collection includes remains of hyrax, hare, birds, and baboon. Note the skulls with attached lower jaws—one of the signatures of eagle predation. (Berger and Clarke 1995, by permission of L. Berger)

carrying by an adult was not a necessity. If raptor predation was a fact of life for young hominids, then natural selection would have opted for parents who invested protracted intensive care in their youngsters. A type of social organization that promoted group investment in each child might also have been an adaptation resulting from predation directed at offspring. Or both of these assets might have been selected for, which is the case in many hunter-and-gatherer societies that exist today.

We must explain, too, how the head of the youngster might have gotten into the quarry at Taung. That may be the easiest part of this puzzle to match. Much work has been done to analyze the non-hominid relics found in the Taung quarry area. Small- to medium-sized animal remains discovered at Taung correspond to what is found under living crowned hawk-eagle nests. Intact mandibles (lower jaws)—as found on the Taung child—are a rarity in hominid fossils. The only time intact mandibles seem to be usual in prey remains is when raptor predation is involved.

Because the eagle is fastidiously removing the base of the cranium or the facial bones of prey to get at brain matter, rather than crunching up the whole head, the lower jaw is not removed from the skull.[53]

We may have fit a few puzzle pieces together, but many niggling questions linger. Because these early hominids were not living in deep forest with thick, obscuring foliage, were large fierce hawk-eagle predecessors still able to swoop down unnoticed? With all the large terrestrial predators around, were raptors the least of the hominid worries?

One can look at the Taung child as an unusual accident or it can be considered a representative sample of widespread predation by birds of prey. The latter opinion opens up the question of the evolutionary effects of raptor predation on young hominids. For example, did this type of predation stimulate adaptations in infant care?

RUNNING HAWKS, HUNGRY TOUCANS, AND GIANT OWLS

Based on all that we have presented in this chapter, we came to the conclusion that very few raptor species were large or powerful enough to have influenced the evolution of hominids through predation. Until more paleontological discoveries are made, we have only the Taung child and current anecdotal observations to go on when we try to envision the effects of predation by a massive primate specialist—analogous to the crowned hawk-eagle—on early hominids. Fortunately, as with so many other aspects of human evolution, we can look at our relatives—the primates that endure intense predation from raptors—for clues. Any or all of their experiences may shed light on our past and what it meant to exist in the presence of raptor predation on our young. From our own research on non-human primates, we could see what the cumulative behaviors induced by raptors might be. For example, diving to the ground from a tree was a reaction directed only at raptors. Monkeys feeding in trees, immediately upon seeing an eagle, dropped out of the canopy and plunged earthwards to thwart predation. Additionally, about 75% of the time that primates fled through the canopy to a tree trunk, it was because raptors were present.

Intense predation has been speculated to be the cause of many behavior patterns observed in lion tamarins, a New World monkey weighing only 1 pound. Their constant state of alertness, readiness for swift flight,

and descent to lower strata in the forest when sensing danger may be indicative of the large number of diurnal raptors that prey on tamarins.
Early retirement to night shelters and the small diameter of shelter open-
ings suggest that nocturnal raptors, such as the great horned owl, also put
lion tamarins at risk.[54]

There is a proliferation of small hawks that live in Central and South
American forests. Neotropical hawk species are twice as numerous as Old
World species mainly because of the ubiquitous small-sized forest falcons
of the genus *Micrastur*. The same pattern of long tail–short wing proportions found in crowned hawk-eagles and harpy eagles is repeated in
smaller genera of forest–hunting New World raptors. These include, to
name a few, bicolored hawks, grey hawks, roadside hawks, black hawk-
eagles, ornate hawk-eagles, Isidor's hawk-eagles, barred forest falcons,
slaty-backed forest falcons, and collared forest falcons. The hunting technique of small rain-forest hawks combines an interesting mix of active
and inactive behaviors: they sit motionless and inconspicuous, but inter-
sperse the inactivity with occasional swift and soundless flights from tree
to tree. Some species pursue active hunting, such as the collared forest
falcon, which actually *runs* along branches, through thickets, and even
on the ground in pursuit of prey![55]

Field researcher Sue Boinski saw this species make 29 predation attempts on newborn squirrel monkeys at Corcovado, Costa Rica. Squirrel
monkeys live in large social groups averaging 20–75 individuals, although groups of more than 300 have been reported. Pregnant females
give birth in synchrony, perhaps as an adaptation to the heavy predation
by raptors. Predatory birds swoop through and around the groups of new
mothers, trying to pluck newborn infants off the females' body. At the
same time the collared forest falcons were preying on newborns, Boinski
also saw grey hawks and roadside hawks make attempts. Additionally,
chestnut-mandibled toucans joined in the melee and tried to scoop newborn squirrel monkeys up with their larger-than-life beaks. (Boinski
reported that *successful* attacks on newborns were accomplished by the
toucans and an ornate hawk-eagle, while a collared forest falcon killed
one of the adult female monkeys.)[56]

This high level of predation pressure by raptors on small Neotropical
primates is supported by other studies. John Terborgh of Duke
University recorded one or more raptor attacks at Manu National Park in

Peru in almost all 3-week periods into which his study was divided. The attacks were more frequent against squirrel monkeys and tamarins than against larger primates, such as capuchin monkeys. In another study, also at Manu, tamarin groups underwent attacks by raptors about once every 1 or 2 weeks. In Brazilian Amazonia, raptors attacked a mixed group of two species of tamarins at the rate of about once every 9 days. Other researchers calculated that diurnal raptors attacked squirrel monkeys at Corcovado and at Manu at the rate of one attack every 6 or 7 days.[57]

Since ornithologists estimate that as a general rule birds of prey launch more *successful* than *un*successful attacks[58] (although, of course, researchers cannot always see the outcome of the event), based on the sightings of attacks listed above, it is our assumption that predation pressure on Neotropical primates from predatory birds may be even higher than field records indicate.

Besides the crowned hawk-eagle and the harpy eagle, which are able to navigate so elegantly through thick forest, there are many large eagles that hunt primates by scanning for prey on the ground from a perch or while soaring. In South Africa black eagles are known to prey on baboons and vervets, but it was unclear whether the capture of an animal as large as a baboon was just an anomaly. That question was answered when documentation was published of this same huge eagle attacking hamadryas baboons in the Eritrean highlands four times in 4 days.[59]

Madagascar harrier hawks have special morphological adaptations of the legs that enhance their ability to hunt primates. The bones in their legs are articulated in a fashion that allows them to bend and probe into narrow tree cavities and behind tree bark to find resting mouse lemurs during the day.[60]

Barn owls, along with the Madagascar red owl and the Madagascar long-eared owl, are also predators of small, nocturnal prosimians, especially the mouse lemur. Until research carried out by Steve Goodman, at Chicago's Field Museum of Natural History, no one guessed that the geographically widespread barn owl was such a major predator on primates. Goodman's breakthrough field study has been especially instrumental in defining the scope of owl predation on lemurs. The barn owl is the most common and widely distributed nocturnal raptor in Madagascar. It has unparalleled acoustic ability and is able to detect, locate, and catch prey in utter darkness. Mouse lemurs are small, solitary, nocturnal foragers that are particularly vulnerable to barn owl predation.

How do you tell exactly what an owl has eaten? Well, they provide a very reliable tool to ascertain the composition of their diet. At regular periods (for example, every 2 or 3 days) owls regurgitate a pellet that is a compacted accumulation of undigested bones, hair, or fur. Because they swallow their prey whole (rather than tearing it apart as do the diurnal raptors), the pellets of owls are particularly handy for the identification of prey. At one nest of Madagascar long-eared owls, 50% of the prey identified from pellets were sportive lemurs. Mouse lemurs constituted a range of 17–44% of the prey killed by pairs of Madagascar long-eared owls when four other nests were evaluated. Goodman's conservative calculation, when the combined predation pressure on mouse lemurs at Beza Mahafaly Reserve by barn owls and long-eared owls was considered, estimated a removal rate of one-quarter of the mouse lemur population each year.[61]

What about large-owl species that might be able to prey on small or young hominids? Verreaux's eagle owl, a huge nocturnal African bird, has two hunting strategies that depend on the age of the individual owl. Adults sit singly on an elevated perch with a wide field of vision over open ground. Subadults, however, roam more than adults, actively seeking out prey by gliding from perch to perch. Although it is the largest of the African owls, the Verreaux's eagle owl is not as powerful as the large African eagles. Nevertheless, they can catch diurnal prey up to the size of vervet monkeys, though nocturnal primates, such as bushbabies, are probably more common in their diet.[62] Owls come in large sizes, but they do not have the strength of eagles. Notwithstanding their great size, their almost-artistic predatory mechanisms, and their proclivity for primates, we calculate that the influence of owls on hominid evolution was slight if any.

That is not the case with eagles in our opinion. The crowned hawk-eagle is capable of killing 66-pound prey—this is as large as Lucy, an adult female *Australopithecus afarensis*.

If we were to make an educated guess based on the fossil and living primate evidence, we would unhesitatingly state that eagles with the power of the present-day crowned hawk-eagle were significant predators on young hominids and may even have played a role in evolutionary adaptations that served to protect infants. On this topic we'll defer to the expert and let Leslie Brown speak in his own words:

> I would now even reserve judgment on such thoroughly unlikely tales as that eagles take babies—not that it happens nowadays, but it may have happened once. I would not put it past an eagle to take and kill an infant left out in the open, perhaps uncovered and wriggling. . . . A baby is not as big as a bushbuck calf or a duiker, both of which can be killed by large eagles. And though I will not nowadays believe that a swaddled baby in a pram in Switzerland will be snatched up into the air by a non-existent Lammergeier [the magnificent bearded vulture], I will accept that at some dim and distant time in human memory some such thing may have happened as a factual basis for fable.[63]

The list of predators on living primates numbers over a hundred species right now and probably replicates the predation pressure on early hominids—running primates down over land, ambushing them, exploding out of the water while they drink, dive-bombing them from the air. But so far we have only told the predator's story. Our hominid ancestors survived quite well as a species because all predation attempts are not successful. Our ancestors weren't passive creatures who were just waiting to be eaten—they had a few tricks of their own to evade being consumed.

8

WE WEREN'T JUST WAITING
AROUND TO BE EATEN!

Just how easy was it for predators to serve up hominid *du jour?* The fossil history tells us little, if anything, about behavior and virtually nothing specific about defensive behavior against predators. We may find the fossilized remains of the *losers* in a predator–prey encounter, but we do not have enough fossils to draw any conclusions about the predation rate on hominids or their successful strategies to outwit predators. Obviously if we had been passive victims we would not have survived as a species. True, rabbits and other small mammals are examples of prey that are on the menu of every carnivore, snake, and raptor—and they still survive as species—but animals such as rabbits depend on strategies of quick escape and quick "littering" (short gestation periods combined with large numbers of young born simultaneously). Hominids, on the other hand, are not overly quick at escape: bipedal individuals simply cannot outrun swift four-legged predators, nor was fast and furious reproduction in the hominid plan.

We've put a lot of emphasis so far on the success predators had in making a meal of ancient hominids. But our ancestors weren't just standing around waiting to be eaten. Staying alive is the goal of all creatures, and those individuals who do things that facilitate staying alive are the

161

ones who pass on their genes to the next generation. We have only to look at our primate relatives to see strategies that have emerged to foil predation.

In his classic 1967 field experiment, Adriaan Kortlandt of the University of Amsterdam presented wild chimpanzees with a stuffed leopard. What did the chimpanzees do? They obviously were aware that the leopard was not in the act of hunting, since it was neither hidden nor moving. They may even have sensed that an immobile, staring leopard is certainly not normal, and they should take advantage of the situation. They vocalized to each other and communicated about this bizarre situation. Then one of them picked up a stick and rushed in to whack the leopard. Another one uprooted a small tree and used it as a weapon. One by one they all attacked the leopard with sticks and small trees, screaming and hooting to keep up their collective adrenaline rush.[1]

Such staged experiments have been validated repeatedly in field and laboratory conditions with many different primate species. Given a situation where the predator can be vanquished, many primates will attack preemptively.[2] For example, baboons have thrown stones at human observers in conjunction with other typical fear-and-escape behaviors. Captive capuchins, the wily little "organ-grinder" monkeys of South America, were found to be capable of throwing rocks with pretty good aim.

What about non-staged encounters with predators—the real thing? The ultimate act of defense, killing the predator, is atypical but not unknown. A wild white-faced capuchin actually clubbed a venomous snake to death, a daring event witnessed by field researcher Sue Boinski in Parque Nacional Manuel Antonio, Costa Rica. Baboons and chimpanzees have both been known to put up a struggle and win against carnivores. Chimpanzees in the Mahale Mountains of western Tanzania were seen on several different occasions harassing a female leopard, and they finally succeeding in killing her cub, although these attacks occurred during the day (researchers maintain that at night the tables would have been turned in favor of the leopard).

A single male baboon is a powerful adversary. With nearly 2-inch-long canines and a weight of up to 70 pounds, a male baboon with an attitude is formidable. Lukas Stoltz and G. S. Saayman, two zoologists working in the Transvaal section of South Africa, observed one dominant male baboon maim or kill three large dogs when they attacked his troop. When we

looked at scientific papers and compiled just the instances of aggressive retaliation by baboons against leopards, we found that out of eleven such
battles, the leopard was killed in four of them. This, of course, is a small
sample but it serves to show that when baboons feel it is in their capacity to
use aggression, they will not only thwart the predator but permanently
eliminate it nearly one-third of the time.

For primates undergoing severe predator pressure, a combination of
many anti-predator defenses may be necessary.[3] One example of a
species that employs a veritable multitude of anti-predation strategies is
the savanna-dwelling patas monkey. Sometimes called the military monkey because of the male's white moustache, colorful red coat, and
martial posture, patas monkeys are a ground-dwelling primate of the
African grasslands. They are renowned for:

1. Their speed during flight from predators: over 30 miles per hour

2. Their bipedal stance to scan the dry savanna for predators

3. A silent, furtive life in small, highly-dispersed groups

4. A conspicuous male who stays on the periphery of the group to dis-
   tract any potential predator's attention—sort of an altruistic decoy
   to draw predators away from the core of the social group, the females and young

5. The camouflage coloration of female and infant patas—they are
   practically invisible in the dry grasses

6. Altering the primate norm of nocturnal birthing by giving birth
   during the day.

On this last point patas give birth in the daytime because their small-
group composition and open-savanna habitat make them particularly
vulnerable at night. Nine species of carnivores are potential nocturnal
predators of patas: lions, leopards, two small African wild cats (caracals
and servals), golden jackals, blackbacked jackals, side striped jackals,
spotted hyenas, and striped hyenas. To counter this array of nocturnal

Because they live in the open grassland habitat with very few trees, patas monkeys employ a multitude of anti-predation strategies. (H. Kummer)

predators, patas have adapted by emphasizing unpredictable behavior, wide dispersal, and concealment in their sleeping patterns. Nocturnal births of baby patas might provide legions of hungry night-stalking predators with odorous cues to the location of female patas in the darkness and thus undermine the other defense strategies. So, daytime birth evolved as a defense strategy.[4]

While primates can be multi-faceted and even fierce in their own defense, we can't deny they also can be caught in a hopeless, hapless state of shock. In the late 1940s Colonel J. Stevenson-Hamilton, a warden at Kruger National Park in South Africa, recorded what he deemed a "massacre" of baboons by two lionesses. In his own words, "A pride of lions was taking its midday siesta close to a drinking-pool when a troop of baboons was heard approaching." Most of the lions just woke up and lay still, except for two females who placed themselves in a patch of vegetation close to the trail. The baboons were unaware of the big cats and walked into the "trap" set by the two lionesses. When the lions rushed out, the baboons were panic-stricken and ran straight toward the main part of the resting pride. "A complete massacre ensued. The baboons were apparently too terrified even to try to escape up any of the surrounding trees, and hid their faces in their hands while the lions simply struck them down right and left with blows of their paws."[5]

What can we glean about early hominids from the observations of living non-human primates? Here is a rundown on how primates were offsetting predation at the time the first hominids arrived on the scene: Generally body size had dramatically enlarged from the first small proto-primates, social grouping was the norm, alarm calls allowed communication between group members, primates had been spurred to greater cognitive development in order to outsmart predators, and attack as a last resort was a fallback position. These behaviors and changes were already in place as generic primate adaptations by the time hominids appeared.

All of these strategies—size, society, vocalizations, intelligence, threat behavior—have broad implications in their own right, but they all function as extremely competent defensive adaptations. Hominids came equipped with the hardwiring for these defenses and continued using and refining them.

If you are a smallish primate itching to get out of the trees and forge a new evolutionary path, what in the world do you do to defend yourself? We propose that two uniquely human traits—bipedalism and speech—

were also just *extensions* of inherent primate-ism. Stimulated by predation and helpful in coping with it, these human attributes of upright
walking and language evolved from the generic primate-defense system.
You could say that the early hominid "package" of body size, group living
with multiple males, communication, bipedality, complex threat behaviors, and cognitive skills were in a sense born of caution and honed by
predation. Some parts of the package were much more effective than
others; some were uniquely embraced by human ancestors and not by
other primates (walking upright); many package items were evolving
concurrently and none were mutually exclusive; and many were rede-
fined completely by humans (speech from alarm vocalizations). Let's
consider the effectiveness of the strategies included in the human anti-
predator package one at a time.

HEAVYWEIGHT CHAMPIONS

Wow! . . . all those predators waiting to eat early hominids. Considering
the fact that many of the smaller primates have more predators than do
large monkeys or apes, it was fortunate that our ancestors were too large
to be eaten by the mongooses, civets, genets, tayras, coatis, raccoons,
opossums, and little birds of prey that eat our smaller cousins.

Was increased size a primate adaptation to minimize predation? It appears that the first primates were arboreal and small and that increased
size was a later adaptation.[6] "Large body size may be seen as an evolutionary response to greater predation risk that has resulted in lower
predation rates," noted primate researcher Lynne Isbell of the University
of California–Davis.[7] And, indeed, the emergence of larger arboreal primates may have been, in part, an evolutionary response to predation in
the trees. Observations presented in this chapter are consistent with the
hypothesis that size increase was, at least in part, an evolutionary response to predation. However, it is unlikely that predation is the *sole*
explanation for primate species' size increases because size increase only
works up to a certain point to ward off predators.

Using body-weight data on primates and predators, we explored size
relationships and size increase as an anti-predation strategy. Our data set
consisted of almost 2,000 instances of recorded predation events (involving over 100 different species) gathered from questionnaires and the

scientific literature where both the weight of the predator and the weight of the primate prey were available.[8] Non-human primates range in size from 2 ounces to nearly 400 pounds; their predators range from 2.5 ounces to more than 500 pounds. In our research we asked the question: What correlations, if any, exist between the relative sizes of primates and the animals that prey on them? Our examination of the primate weights and predator weights suggested that most of the "gain" (escape from predators through growth) is in the 2-to-12-pound weight range of primates. Below this range, there must be advantages to small size that outweigh greater vulnerability to predation (perhaps better access to fruit and insects on tiny branches or small size simply makes it easier to hide?). Above this range, there is little gain in terms of safety from predators because predators are even larger, so it seems likely that size increase above 12 pounds was driven by different rewards.

But still, smaller primates are more susceptible to predation than larger ones. After all, the limits of many predators' abilities to kill and consume prey are based on size relationships. As a result, the number of predators on primate species should decrease as body weight increases.[9]

There are 81 species of raptors, owls, and other predatory birds known or suspected to prey on primates.[10] Many of the smaller birds weighing under 2 pounds (the toucans, small owls, kites, cuckoos, vangas, crows, small hawks, and falcons) prey on only the very smallest primates.[11] A clear consequence of most arboreal primate species' evolution of increased body size is that they are too large to be attractive prey to the very predators most active in their arboreal habitats—small predatory birds. Two dozen primate species weighing less than 5 pounds were preyed upon by 32 confirmed avian predators, while 2 dozen primate species weighing over 12 pounds had half that number of winged predators.

So, yes, size increase was an advantage initially in primate evolution. But, putting it bluntly, whether hominids weighed 35 pounds or 135 pounds, they were still prey to the *large* predators. Primates, including our ancestors, could outgrow most birds of prey (*except the crowned hawk-eagle types who can kill prey many times their own weight*), but that only eliminated a fraction of the potential attackers.

Unlike avian predators, most carnivores outweigh the majority of primate species, yet the weight of mammalian predators varies considerably by group. The weights of what we term "small carnivores"—mongooses, civets, genets, tayras, coatis—are lower than many primates. The single species in this category outweighing many primates is the fossa, the largest predator in Madagascar. Our research showed that many arboreal primates have outgrown the small, carnivorous mammals and are protected from them by increased size.

Few primate species are larger than wild cats, and even the largest primates—gorillas—are within the size range of a leopard attack. In fact we calculated that 94% of wild-cat species are larger than all but the top 10% of primates, plus cats are able to kill prey larger than themselves. Hominids have been in the past (and are right now) within a very suitable size range for a variety of cats, both extinct and living. The leopard is an illustration of this; a yummy 100-to-120-pound hominid is the perfect size for a leopard to attack, kill, and pull up onto a tree branch to eat.

Similarly, very few primates are protected from wild dog and hyena predation by size alone. The distribution of weights for dog species and hyenas is similar to cats: 85% of the dogs or hyenas are larger than all but the top 10% of primates, plus these fellows often hunt in packs.

The distribution of reptile weights is also similar to wild cats and dogs in the sense that reptilian predators include *extremely* large animals. All snakes are possible tree climbers; however, only the smaller snakes (those under 6 feet in length) are truly arboreal. Furthermore, most snakes, like most raptors, tend to hunt prey significantly smaller than themselves. There is a very good reason for this size limit: snakes are inhibited in their intake of large prey both because they must swallow their prey whole and because "satiated immobilization" may occur after ingestion of animals above a certain ratio to the snake's own weight. The snake can literally be so stuffed it cannot move. Most primate species are too large to be attractive prey to the smaller snake species that hunt arboreally, but large *terrestrial* snakes—for example, the reticulated and African pythons—are major predators of terrestrial primates.[12] Most primate species are also within the size range of monitor lizards, and *all* are within the size range for crocodiles.

Habitat is a critical consideration for any discussion concerning size of primates and their predators. There are differing theories concerning the effects and interplay of habitat and body size. One theory contends that terrestrial primates are more subject to predation than arboreal species because not only are terrestrial species at risk from raptors, snakes, arboreal carnivores, and large terrestrial carnivores in open territory, but they are also far from trees where they might run for safety.[13]

Arboreality, in and of itself, has been hypothesized to confer some protection from predation because all primates (with the exception of gorillas, the largest species, and modern humans) sleep in trees, cliffs, or off the ground in some manner.[14]

To summarize, examining the size relationships of primates and predators with arboreality in mind suggests that primates can avoid many arboreal predators—but few terrestrial predators—by being larger than they are. While the number of total predators will decrease, results of data analysis show that size increase may confer protection for primates only within some groups of predators. There is a clear tendency for primate species to be larger than most arboreal birds and small carnivores but smaller than most terrestrial predator species. The evolution of larger body size in arboreal primates may have conferred some protection from raptors and small carnivores, but seems to have had little effect on the levels of predation inflicted by cats, hyenas, dogs, or reptiles on primates living in the trees or on the ground.

Obviously, hominids did not outgrow any predators but raptors and small carnivores. Increased size does not seem to be the route we took to avoid predation. We got bigger over time—the famous australopithecine fossil, "Lucy," weighed only 60 pounds and may have stood only 3 and one-half feet tall, fully grown—but our subsequent size increase didn't do us much good predator-wise.

And before you can say, "Wait a minute! Lucy was a female!" we'll offer a little information about size differences between male and female apes and fossil hominids. Sexual dimorphism is a state of dissimilar size between the male and female of a species. Adult male animals are usually the larger, but there are many exceptions: hyenas, raptors, some of the civets and genets, and the large pythons are species in which females may be significantly larger. In primates, though, either the sexes are nearly the same size or the adult male is the larger. If the adult male primate (or hominid) is bigger than the female, does he play a special role as a defender? It's tough to give a definitive answer to that question. Alison Jolly, one of the most respected American primatologists, has proposed that there are two types of primates where defense is concerned: those in which the male seeks to lure the predator away while the females and young hide (an example is the patas monkey) and those in which the females and young draw in toward the males at the sign of danger (example, baboons).[15] It probably doesn't much matter that the male patas is larger than the female—his job is ultimately to get eaten instead of her. In the case of baboons, there is much dispute over whether adult males position themselves to protect the troop or whether they run helter-skelter away from predators, leaving the females to protect themselves and their infants. Great deeds of individual chivalry have been noted in male primates, but the jury is still out on whether sexual dimorphism is an anti-predator device or just an attractive contrivance to seduce females.

From fossil finds, we know that Lucy's male counterparts could have been much larger than she. To further complicate the issue, Lucy, as an individual, is at the low end of the unearthed specimens of *Australopithecus afarensis;* those at the high end were individuals 5 feet tall who could have weighed much more than 100 pounds. There is considerable variation both between the sexes and between individuals of the same sex in fossils of Lucy's kind.[16] Besides australopithecines, sexual dimorphism appears in gorillas, chimpanzees, and orangutans; it is not found, however, in bonobos, the pygmy chimps.

WHY HERMITS SEEM ODD

The society of others is a human universal—all cultures are formed from social groups. Society is natural; society is comforting. But why? The answer to this question may lie in the fact that group living equals safety in numbers. For a long time in our evolutionary history we undoubtedly would have died if not for group protection. More eyes, ears, and noses meant less risk of unseen, unheard, unsmelled predators sneaking up to eat you. (And, more teeth and hands could repel predators that did get close.)[17]

When we look at the number of individuals in a primate group and the corresponding predation rate, it suggests that predation may have played a key role in the evolution of basic primate attributes, such as group living.[18] Primates living in small groups—particularly the tiny New World tamarins and marmosets—tend to sustain relatively high degrees of predation,[19] as do small nocturnal prosimians, such as mouse lemurs. Much discussion has also centered around the related topics of group size and those unusual groupings called polyspecific associations. Polyspecific associations, you'll recall, are permanent or semi-permanent mixed-species combinations of primates. For example, there are mixed-species groupings of several tamarin species; combined squirrel monkey and capuchin troops; several different species of African forest monkeys called guenons often travel and feed together; and guenons associate in large groups with colobus and mangabeys.

There's also been research focused on predation as an explanation for the existence of more than one resident adult male in a primate group. With baboons, for instance, the presence of many protective adult males with their large body size and huge canine teeth might give a group the advantage over predators. However, in some instances conspicuous males are actually more likely to be selected by predators—sort of martyrs to the group. The advantages of many males per group have shown mixed results; one study found correlations between the number of males in a group and the level of predation, but another found no statistical connection.[20]

Only in the last few years has there been a study that enlightened the evolutionary impact a particular predator may have upon its primate prey. Klaus Zuberbühler of the University of St. Andrews in Scotland and David Jenny of Universität Bern, Switzerland, have worked for many years in the Tai Forest of Côte d'Ivoire in West Africa. The emphasis of their ongoing study is the relationship between leopard predation and primate evolution.[21] The upshot of Zuberbühler and Jenny's research is that none of the proposed evolutionary adaptations (not multi-male troops, not large groups, not increased body size) may be useful against *certain* predators. Their study has found that leopards actually *prefer* to kill large primates who live in larger groups sporting many adult males. This seems counterintuitive but, as are so many aspects of predation, the conventional wisdom may be dead wrong.

Protection of the more vulnerable immature individuals surely must be enhanced by a large social group. Hanuman langur adolescents have been found to avoid the periphery of sleeping trees and huddle close together. In baboon troops, the young sleep closest to the top of the tree, with the strongest adults close to the trunk to prevent leopards from climbing up. This is also the positioning that white-handed gibbons take in sleeping trees, with infants placed on thinner branches and higher sections of the tree. Black and white colobus monkeys were observed to cluster more tightly in their sleeping trees for mutual protection on nights with a full moon, when visibility gave predators a greater advantage.[22]

Does our esthetic pleasure when viewing grand, open landscapes have something to do with predator protection mechanisms? Open areas allowed early humans to see predators *before* it was too late to react. (C. Rudloff)

Scanning is one of the big benefits from group living since the more detectors, the higher the probability of detecting the predator before it detects its prey—more eyes mean more predators sighted. This reliance on scanning is consistent with the fact that primates depend more on visual cues than odors.

The ability to scan is also one of many deeply engraved aspects of human behavior. Why is it that some scenery, whether real life or in a painting, is universally pleasing and causes a feeling of tranquility? The eighteenth-century European masters caught this sublime sentiment in their artistic portrayal of gently rolling pastures, foothills, and scattered copses of trees. Cornell University's Nicholas Nicastro investigated the human preference for open vistas—landscapes that allow few obstacles to the eye—and concluded that open areas allowed us to see predators *before* they were on top of us and it was too late to hatch a plan.[23] Amazing, indeed, that our esthetic delight in grand expanses of nature was a function of pinpointing what wanted to eat us!

One of the most vulnerable periods in a primate's life is the time of dispersal from the group into which he or she was born. (Depending on the species, either the male, female, or both may leave their parental group—just like the variable patterns found throughout human cultures.) Being able to stay within the natal, or birth, group throughout adulthood is a great advantage to a primate since the individual is completely familiar with a home range and, therefore, doesn't need to learn about predators in a new territory.[24]

Even within the home range of a terrestrial primate group, when the troop moves to different feeding spots, the members may be at risk. The order in which baboons travel to maximize safety was identified as a defensive strategy in pioneering primate field studies back in the 1960s. Similar to our discussion of male defensive behavior based on their larger body size, initially the dominant males were thought to be protecting adult females and infants clustered in the center of the group, while subordinate males and juveniles were a first line of defense in the front and back. This "idealized" order was disputed by later research that found only a random order in troop progressions. But it may be that troop progressions are more creative than stylized. We suggest that a key to the code of where and when age or gender places a baboon in transit if predators are around may lie in female friendships with large males; these adult males will stay beside their female friends—and the females' infants—no matter how the group splits up. Although no particular placement of age or gender was noted, chimpanzees formed larger parties containing adult males as a defense strategy when traveling through open, non-forested habitat in Senegal under the eyes of potential predators.[25]

When placement and order fail, then the existence of large social groups confer another advantage: it causes confusion. A so-called saturation effect can occur during the flight of an entire primate group from a predator, in which the predator's senses are saturated and overwhelmed by so many choices. A flurry of animals running in every direction at once makes it difficult for a leopard to catch another baboon if it misses its first intended victim. The same goes for an "explosion" of vervets as the result of an attack by a leopard.[26]

As we see it, nocturnal birth—which is the norm for all diurnal primates except the patas monkey mentioned earlier—is connected to the existence of protection in social groups, too. The solitary, nocturnal prosimians (lorises, galagos, and lemurs) tend to give birth during the day in the safety of their sleeping shelters, but most female primates experience the birth process at night while their group is resting.[27] Night birthing allows a female time to be in labor, give birth, and provide initial care to an infant before she has to move with her group again. She is not left behind nor does she become vulnerable to predators, and she can then rejoin her fellows in their daily foraging trek the next morning. Most human babies are also born during the night. A sample of normal human births shows a clear nocturnal peak at 2:00–3:00 A.M. Labor, believe it or not, is statistically shorter for human births that take place at night than those during the day.[28] Likely this is another holdover from our distant past when it was necessary to give birth in the safety of the group.

A social group does not stop every predator (for example, leopards who prefer to kill primates from large groups), but being a member of a group has countless social and ecological advantages to the individual primate (and human). There is little doubt that the group's enhanced ability to deflect predation was paramount in our transition into social animals.

WE SAW . . . FOOD. WE CAME . . . DOWN FROM THE TREES. WE CONQUERED . . . GRAVITY

What are the boundary lines of being human? Well, for one thing, they keep shrinking. Not too many decades ago we were human because we were Man the Hunter. But many species of primates hunt, so that couldn't really work as a boundary between us and the rest of the animal kingdom. Then the definition shifted to Man the Toolmaker, but Jane Goodall observed chimpanzees making and using tools, so that boundary was erased. Then, it was Man the Food-Sharer, but bonobos and chimps share their food. How about Man the User of Language? Uh-oh, those pesky chimps, bonobos, and gorillas could be taught American Sign Language! Surely, Man the Possesser of Culture will work to describe us?

No, again: many primates may fulfill the tenets of possessing at least protoculture (learned behaviors passed on from generation to generation). Eventually, we have settled on Man the Bipedal Ape, and that finally seems to be a *real* boundary between ourselves and the rest of our primate cousins.

Let's tackle the big one then—the issue of standing, walking, and running upright. All paleontologists believe we were bipedal long before our brains got larger or our manual dexterity increased, because the hominid fossils show this. There are about six different "models" that have been proposed to account for bipedalism as a hominid adaptive strategy.[29] In no particular order these are the *carrying* model, the *vigilance* model, the *heat-dissipation* model, the *energy-efficiency* model, the *display* model, and the *foraging* model.

What are the pros and cons of each model? The carrying model asserts that freeing our front limbs from use in locomotion allowed our ancestors to carry children (better survival of offspring), carry food (transporting it back to a safer place for consumption), and carry weapons (protection from predators). One important obstacle to this explanation of bipedalism, however, is evident from the fossil record. The lower vertebrae features seen in modern humans that allow the carrying of heavy objects were not an early evolutionary trait.

The vigilance model? Yes, elevation of the head allows a better view. But many primates, and many other mammals such as squirrels, *stand* upright for scanning their environment—but they do not *move around* in an upright position.

Heat dissipation? Vertical orientation (that is, standing upright) allows less of the body to catch the direct rays of the sun and more of the body to catch cooling breezes. This model had more impact when it was thought that hominids initially were savanna animals. Current theory, however, holds that we evolved in open woodland and the edges of forests where the sun's rays and heat would not have been so much a factor. Furthermore, there are many quadrupedal mammals (including primates) living on the savanna, so why would just one species evolve bipedalism to counter the sun?

Energy efficiency? Bipedalism while walking requires less energy than quadrupedalism. Experts feel that the anatomical changes that made bipedal walking efficient, though, came after the establishment of our two-legged locomotion. Furthermore, bipedalism is an energy-*inefficient* method of running, and running away from predators was an important thing.

Displaying? For male chimpanzees, both dominance and sexual display are enhanced when they stand upright. Obviously, looking larger is advantageous when encountering possible mates, or competitors for those mates, or predators. It also allows an animal to wave its forelimbs around to attract attention or to threaten others.

Foraging? This model involves harvesting clumps of food on bushes or trees that were not as readily attainable unless upright posture and walking were employed. Our common ancestor with chimpanzees theoretically was competent both in the trees and on the ground without walking upright, but, if bipedal, benefits might accrue in the form of food on trees that were difficult or impossible to climb.

Each one of the models has some merit, but none of the theories seems to catch the significance of *changing* a method of locomotion from quadrupedalism to bipedalism. This is not a common occurrence although there are examples: Birds started flying and some became terrestrial again. Whales and seals were terrestrial quadrupeds and then became swimmers with vestigial hind limbs. But those changes were certainly not swift. Our bipedalism seems to have been a relatively quick alteration. Our common ancestor with the chimps was arboreal and then—presto-chango—hominids were bipedal. Since this seems an unlikely instantaneous mutation and none of the above theories is without holes, how about a brand-new interpretation of this standing-upright business?

A question that has plagued students of human evolution for some time is, "What factors or selective forces led to bipedalism?" Why did the earliest humans get up on their hind limbs in the first place, instead of remaining quadrupedal like other terrestrial primates? We think this is a moot question. There are a number of primate species that, because of their overall locomotor anatomy and behavior, are upright in their posture, both in the trees and on the ground.

In Madagascar, closely related indris and sifakas use their long hind limbs to propel themselves as they leap to and from vertical tree trunks. They are referred to as vertical clingers and leapers. When on the ground, because of their anatomical specializations (long legs, short arms, and an upright posture), these prosimians are unable to walk quadrupedally and they hop bipedally in an upright position. Spider monkeys and their relatives are highly adept at suspensory locomotion, with very long arms and relatively long legs and an upright posture. On large branches and on the ground, they hold their arms in the air (so they won't drag on the ground) and walk bipedally like trapeze artists in a high-wire act. The lesser apes, gibbons and siamangs, have perfected suspensory locomotion and propel themselves with a speedy hand-over-hand swinging locomotion (called brachiation) as they "fly" through the trees. On the ground, much like the spider monkeys, they lift their long arms and walk bipedally.

It is difficult to separate consequence from causation. We cannot conclude that any of the six suggested models outlined above *caused* hominids to be bipedal. We disclaim any one of the theories as causative. We claim instead that all the theories are results, undoubtedly very propitious results, for a primate who was already preadapted to being bipedal. We weren't any more preordained to be bipedal than chimps, gorillas, bonobos, or orangutans. All the great apes are *preadapted* and predisposed to bipedality. When our ancestors came down from the trees, bipedalism was possible because of body proportions and suspensory adaptations; that is, the longer arms and shorter legs that allow gibbons, orangutans, and chimpanzees to hang from trees and pluck fruit. The gorilla and chimpanzee are semi-erect knuckle walkers—in other words, their long arms, with weight placed on the knuckles, stabilize them as they walk. All apes have varying capacities for erect posture and are able to walk upright for short periods of time. Bonobos, especially, will stride upright with human-like posture when carrying food, carrying infants, and carrying on with dominance displays. In fact, all apes are adapted for upright posture because of their generally suspensory adaptations.

However, all of the great apes have evolved tremendously large and heavy upper torsos and it is "natural" for them to put much of their weight onto their very long and enormous arms when moving on the ground. We believe that the ancestors of modern apes and our earliest ancestors were adapted for suspensory locomotion but did not possess such large and long upper torsos. They did not have to rise from all fours when they moved on the ground. Rather, they were *preadapted* for bipedal locomotion—this was their natural posture due to their suspensory and upright-adapted anatomy.

The difference between other species and humans is that hominids were forced (challenged? enticed?) to the ground by a mosaic and changing environment that included climate change. We came down from the trees because our common ancestor with chimps was living on the edge of the forest and there was a whole wide world of ground-level plants to be eaten as the climate morphed from the tropical to dryer and colder. Those delicious things were available to quadrupeds, but there was less chance of being molested by predators if you incorporated scanning, looking larger, walking quickly and efficiently, carrying food back to a safe place, and carrying an infant by moving on *two* legs instead of four.

Did predation *cause* bipedalism? We can only theorize that it made life much *safer* to be bipedal. Bipedality made us successful defenders because it freed our hands. It was also a successful strategy because we could look bigger. It allowed us to be intimidating and chaotic by standing up, throwing things, and jumping up and down just as chimps do today. Other primates and many mammals (domestic cats, for instance) use piloerection or puffing up to make themselves look larger. We used bipedality. To quote Alison Jolly: "Two or three good reasons for evolving a trait is better than one."[30]

The question of why we are bipedal is made terribly complicated when it is really terribly simple. If the chimp branch of the family had taken the random serendipitous route that human ancestors took, they would be bipedal also, because the whole group of great apes has the capacity to adopt bipedality. *But,* bipedalism is only advantageous if you leave the trees and descend to the ground for the majority of your activities, and if you do it *before* you have evolved enormous torsos and arms.

If we are correct, rather than looking for the factor or factors that caused our ancestors to make those initial bipedal steps, we can simply accept that it was a combination of many factors that likely made bipedal locomotion advantageous in the particular habitat in which the first hominids lived. Such things as carrying food, tools, or weapons, sitting upright while eating, feeding on tall bushes, hunting, gaining better vision over the tall grass, or thermoregulatory needs did not cause other edge- or arid savanna-living primates to abandon their quadrupedal postures. Bipedal locomotion was a given; the successes or added advantages were simply a by-product. These advantages, plus the ability to exploit both arboreal and terrestrial habitats, added to the success of those versatile creatures, our ancient ancestors.

A reconstruction of two *Australopithecus afarensis*. The successes or added advantages of bipedal locomotion were simply a by-product of a preadaptation to upright posture. (Used by permission of American Museum of Natural History, AMNH Library 4936[2])

ON THE PATH TO EINSTEIN

Intellectual development, to the extent that our modern brain is quite large relative to our body, was a continuing process for the entirety of hominid evolution. Chimps have a cranial capacity of 400–500 cc; ours is about 1,300–1,400 cc. (But we can't puff out our chests too much because Neanderthals had even larger brains.) All of this brain acquisition may have occurred to outsmart predators. Primates are intelligent and resourceful animals and, as such, they have evolved both preemptive and reactive responses to predation. Recall again the leopards studied in the Tai Forest, the ones who preferred to hunt large primates living in large groups. The Swiss team's scientific findings about this situation possess a further tantalizing emphasis—they surmise that the principal effect of leopard predation has been on non-human primates' cognitive evolution.[31] Dealing with a large, strong predator may spur the brain to become larger and more complex since the only way to live is literally to *outsmart* the predator. We extrapolate that getting smarter was also the evolutionary adaptation that best forestalled death by leopard, or any other predators, for early hominids.

Behaviorist John Endler has divided all acts of predation into six sequential stages: encounter, detection, identification, approach, subjugation, and consumption.[32] The predators of primates—every predator for that matter—employ *all* of the six stages of predation. Prey have available numerous behaviors, strategies, and adaptations to avoid predation; these are specifically oriented to certain phases of the sequential predation stages, since not all anti-predation defenses are appropriate for all of the stages. Primates, as a group, respond by adopting a repertoire of anti-predator defense behaviors to interrupt the process at only *four* of the six stages of predatory activity: *encounter, detection, approach,* and *subjugation.* To cite a few initial examples, alarm vocalizations are a common primate anti-predator strategy to offset the *encounter* stage of predation; crypsis (freezing) is a typical anti-predator strategy observed in small primates to prevent *detection* by predators; male baboons employ aggressive threat behaviors to foil the *approach,* or attack, stage of predation. Chemical defense mechanisms, such as toxins, which might cause a predator to spit out its distasteful prey, have also evolved in a few prosimians and deter the *subjugation* stage of predation.[33] In our research we investigated the behavioral and morphological defenses used by primates to counter predators; in other words, we integrated primate defense strategies into the context of *responses* to sequential events initiated by their predators. When primate anti-predator strategies are placed within the context of a hunting preda- tor's behavior, certain patterns of defense can be seen. Primates, constantly spurred on to greater cognitive development, are especially adept in coun- tering predation through alarm vocalizations, group living, and constant visual scanning of the environment. As intelligent mammals, primates fo- cus on the prevention of predation at the earliest stage of predatory action. There's even an equation for why this is smart: The advantage lies with prey that interrupt the predation sequence at the earliest stage because: (a) the risk of a successful predation is reduced, causing (b) less current energy to be expended in defensive behavior, allowing (c) future fitness to be en- hanced through the channeling of saved energy into growth and reproduction, given the fact that (d) the relative frequency of the early stages of predation will be higher than later stages.[34]

Prey animals face the dilemma of being preyed on by more than one species or group of predators. Their difficulty lies in evolving defense strategies that are effective in all circumstances. Early predation stages are more general; therefore, more different types of predators can be coun- tered with a small repertoire of defensive strategies if prey respond in the earliest stages. The general primate anti-predator adaptations are cen- tered on the first stage of predator activity when the predator encounters the prey. Alarm vocalizations, constant scanning, social grouping, and polyspecific associations to enhance vigilance are all methods to achieve what Endler has termed "one-upmanship," or detection of the predator before the predator has detected the prey. Primates try to one-up the predator by seeing it before it sees them.[35]

Total avoidance of predators is the ultimate goal in the game of one- upmanship, since it completely interrupts the encounter stage. Many instances of total avoidance as a strategy have been recorded in the pri- mate literature. In India, rhesus macaques rapidly shifted a distance of 36 miles after hearing the roar of a tiger. In Ethiopia, hamadryas baboons silently moved away from the zone of predator activity in 33 of 34 ob- served dangerous situations.[35]

Okay, but if primates always successfully one-upped predators, they would never be eaten. What happens when a primate is having an off day, or when the predator just isn't one-upable? Then the next stage of the predation process ensues. The detection stage of predation involves a reduction in the distance between the predator and prey; the prey has now been located but is unaware or minimally alarmed by the predator. For wild cats, in particular, this is the critical stage in predation. Once prey has been located by the cat, if there is any reciprocal detection on the part of the intended prey, the cat will almost inevitably abandon the hunt.[36]

Mechanisms (such as scanning) used by prey at this stage are in the category of primary defenses because they go into force *before* a potential predator launches pursuit or attack. This is a key counteractive stage for prey since primary defenses reduce the possibility that prey will need to actively fight off the onslaught of the predator. Predatory mammals usually have a success rate of less than 50% once they have been spotted by potential prey, while snakes have zero chance of a successful kill if prey discover them at this stage.[37]

The approach, or attack, stage of predation actively maximizes the probability of predator–prey one-on-one contact. At this point, the predator tends to ignore discovery by the prey. Stealth is used, but there may be follow-through even if the prey becomes aware of the predator. The exact point of awareness by prey will influence whether the predator takes up a chase, continues it, or just gives up.[38]

If the chase continues and the prey is captured, few victims—including primates—can fight off predators at the subjugation stage. So, what does all this mean in real-life terms for a smallish bipedal primate? There is every reason to think that ancestral humans used much the same defenses (particularly one-upmanship at the early stages of predation) as other primate species in their continuing struggle to survive.

DAYTIME TALK SHOWS

Once upon a time, long, long ago—even before Oprah was on television—we started talking. Many anthropologists feel that speech originated from alarm vocalizations, and alarm vocalizations from one hominid to another were actions used for defense. Alarm vocalizations alert other members of the social group that a predator has been sighted. They also alert the predator that it has been noticed, which for many predators (such as wild cats and snakes) interrupts the predation process and sends it back to square one (that is, casting randomly around for prey still unaware of the predator's presence). Speech, which came much later in our evolution, not only allowed the same advantage of warning between hominids; it also permitted hominids to formulate plans in advance on how to avoid predation rather than just reacting to the predator.

Obviously, it is a great advantage to be aware of a predator before the predator is aware of you, since early detection of the predator usually means successful escape. But, one-upmanship in the form of alarm calling is a delicate balance of self-preservation versus altruism. Alarm calls are typically given after a predator has been sighted. While alarm calling enables prey to adjust to the presence of a predator (rather than being caught unawares and forced into panic flight), it also draws attention to the individual sounding the alarm. It is not unexpected that primate alarm vocalizations—often individually disadvantageous, but socially advantageous—might exceed other forms of anti-predation behaviors in highly social species, such as primates.

We sent questionnaires to field researchers containing an inquiry about anti-predation behaviors exhibited by primates. Alarm vocalizations were the most frequently observed defense strategy used by primates (31% of the instances recounted by the researchers). According to questionnaire respondents, alarm calls were used by all types of primates for which data were available and were used against *all* kinds of predators. In our survey, scanning was the second most frequently used defense strategy (16%) and was also used against all categories of predators. These two were followed in decreasing frequency by mobbing (group display and bluffing) (14%), fleeing to trees or cliffs (13%), charging or attacking the predator (8%), crypsis (freezing in place) (5%), defensive posturing (5%), pursuit by predators that triggered running on the ground (5%), fleeing through the canopy to a tree trunk (1%), breaking or dropping branches (1%), diving to the ground from the trees (0.2%), chestbeating (0.1%), strong body odor (0.1%), and disruption of ranging and sleeping behavior (0.1%).

Almost 40 years ago Tom Struhsaker of Duke University identified specific alarm calls for different types of predators given by vervet monkeys; these could be divided into distinct sounds associated with various aerial and terrestrial predators.[39] There were "leopard alarm barks" that translated into "get to a tree fast!" There were "eagle rraups" that meant "take cover!" And "snake chutters" that seemed to say "everyone come out to throw things at this snake!" Subsequent to Struhsaker's discovery of these very specific alarm calls, a long-term study of vervet monkey vo-calizations has been carried out in Kenya's Amboseli Reserve by Dorothy Cheney and Robert Seyfarth and their students from the University of Pennsylvania. An entire repertoire of learned (as in passed on from gener-ation to generation) predator-specific alarm signals have been identified. Vervets signal the presence of leopards, small carnivores, eagles, snakes, baboons, and unfamiliar humans with unique calls. The ability to vocal-ize these species-specific alarm calls is not limited to vervets either. Captive Japanese macaques also exhibit specificity in alarm calling, and free-ranging rhesus macaques let loose on an island near Panama re-sponded with alarm calls to the unusual appearance of a raptor, but never gave alarm calls to other large, non-predatory birds. Many of the New World monkeys also exhibit predator-specific alarm calls. Neither is this sophisticated defense mechanism limited to monkeys or apes, since species-specific alarm calls have also been recorded when ringtailed lemurs sight potential predators.[40]

Alarm vocalizations also may be given and interpreted *between* species. Ringtailed lemurs respond to predator alarm calls given by Verreaux's sifakas; vervets respond to the alarm signals of a bird, the superb starling; and captive Geoffroy's marmosets have recognized and distinguished recorded raptor calls versus other non-predatory bird calls.[41]

The prey flees and the predator follows was the phrase that we used to illustrate the principle of coevolution. In the constantly evolving adap-tations between predator and prey, some predators have learned to *counter* the counteractions with a capacity to localize alarm calls given by prey species. As a primate example, the alarm vocalizations emitted by Kloss's gibbons are wide-frequency, extremely loud, and repetitious, giv-ing rise to speculation that predators can home in on their sounds. This is a prime example of the conundrum of one-upmanship. The loud calls of the Kloss's gibbons have evolved to warn neighboring relatives (possi-bly adult offspring holding their own territories) of danger. Yet, the sirening and alarm trills loud enough to be heard outside of the immedi-ate family group also allow predators to find and target the individual calling gibbon.[42]

But how and why did alarm vocalizations turn into speech? Speech as we know it is a rather recent phenomenon. Speech is not just communi-cation about the here and now—the problem being faced at this moment. It is about the past and the future and concepts that are not tangible. It is also the process of combining meaningless subunits of sounds into infinite combinations that are meaningful.

The dictionary definition of referent is "the thing that a symbol (as a word or sign) stands for." One new theory from Nicholas Nicastro centers on referents as the key to the evolution of alarm vocalizations into speech.[43] Moving to a more open environment—the edge of the forest which now seems the most likely birthplace of the bipedal hominid,—gave us a lot to talk about. This is not a facetious statement. Logically, where can you see the most things? You can see more and farther in open areas, so alarm vocalizations did not need to be as immediately reactive for those in open environments as they did for forest dwellers. The chimp–human ancestor in the forest scanned the thick foliage constantly but spied predators pretty much one at a time and when the threat was close at hand. There was little time to mull over the distance or the options—just alarm call like crazy and get out of there! The bipedal hominid with a view had the luxury of debating whether this or that predator sighted 100 yards away was looking hungry or just out for a stroll. Nicastro has found evidence that when referents (things seen) rise beyond a threshold number, conceptual speech may be needed. If necessity is the mother of invention, Nicastro has theorized that speech would evolve if there were enough complex things that needed to be communicated.

Speech—complex ideas that could be shared—evolved over time, but true speech in the sense of the myriad sounds we as humans compose into language is relatively new. Surely Neanderthals, who buried their dead with rituals that suggest a budding religion 50,000 years ago, were capable of some form of speech. But Neanderthals could not make the sounds of modern humans; they may have had speech but they did not speak as we do.

Two anatomical circumstances determine the sounds that are possible from the modern human throat: (1) whether the base of the skull is flat or angled, and (2) the position of the larynx (the resonating chamber or voice box) that holds the vocal cords. The first refers to the way the base of the skull is configured: it can be in a straight line almost even with the upper jaw (as in chimpanzees), or the base can be deeply angled in relation to the upper jaw (as in modern humans). These angled versus straight profiles, in turn, determine the position of the larynx. The second circumstance—the position of the larynx—refers to whether it is located high or low in the throat. Chimpanzees have flatter skull bases than do humans; they also have larynges sitting much higher in their throats than modern humans do. A baby human also has a larynx placed high in the throat—it moves down as the child matures, which is why speech is not possible until a baby reaches 18 months or 2 years of age. Neanderthals had a skull-base angle intermediate between chimpanzees and modern humans; they may not have been able to make some of the vowel sounds that we can due to the higher position of their larynx. One of our most successful ancestors, *Homo erectus* (who inhabited the earth for more than a million years), had an angled skull base more like modern humans. Who knows what their capacity for linguistics might have been. Oddly enough, while the position of our larynx low in the throat is a definite plus for making a large range of sounds, it is also the reason we are prone to choke on food. With a higher larynx, you can talk (or cry in the case of babies) without the chance of having food slip into the respiratory chute instead of the esophagus.

Nevertheless, it is the ability to warn others, hail others, and keep together by exchanging sounds that protected hominids. Anatomically modern human speech may not be solely a result of predation, but there is little question that vocal communication is a result of predation and is used as a protective tool by all primates, including hominids.

MAKING A LAST STAND:
COUNTERATTACK AND CHUTZPAH

If all else fails, chutzpah is the primate last-ditch effort. Under certain circumstances early hominids could ably defend themselves and probably used unaltered rocks and sticks as weapons. When conditions were in favor of early humans, they were as likely to succeed as are modern baboons and chimpanzees in facing down a predator. Tim White, who has been discovering fossil hominids for 30 years, mused one day while he was examining the fossil Lucy and her relatives, "Although I'm bigger than a chimp, I'm not nearly as strong. I would not want to go one-on-one unarmed and in a locked room with one; he'd certainly kill me before I could kill him. Our hominids look to have been at least as strong as chimps."[44]

Active defense has a long evolutionary history. Some of the prosimians even do a bang-up job of defending themselves. One, the little African potto, makes violent thrusts at the predator with its bony shoulder blades called a scapular shield. Another African prosimian, the angwantibo, will lift its leg while tucked into a tight ball and thrust its head out to bite its attacker on the nose when in this defensive posture. Even tiny mouse lemurs have bitten people when cornered.

Active defenses aim to inflict serious injury on the predator. This last line of defense, termed "protective aggression," is intended to drive the predator completely away or sufficiently interrupt the predation attempt so the prey can escape.[45]

Mobbing is a common primate counterattack strategy. It can be described as several or all individuals of a group gathering around giving alarm cries, approaching, and even rushing or hitting a predator. Mobbing usually is chaotic and confrontational. Snake mobbing has been reported in groups of tamarins, langurs, and lemurs. In addition, the primate literature contains information about langurs mobbing a leopard and gibbons mobbing a tiger. (Talk about chutzpah!) As well, tiny marmosets mob small nocturnal wild cats, and capuchin monkeys mob the weasel-like tayra.[46] Mobbing was cited in our survey as employed by primates in 14% of the witnessed encounters with predators.

Approximately 8% of the observed primate anti-predator behaviors from our questionnaire respondents were classified as authentic charges or attacks. With their larger size and longer canines, adult male primates in particular will, under certain circumstances, charge and attack raptors, wild cats, wild and domestic dogs, and small carnivores. Mature silverback gorillas are a good example of the protective male. George Schaller reported that a silverback gorilla and a leopard were both found dead from mutually inflicted wounds.[47]

There are always extraordinary events that draw incredible acts of bravery from ordinarily cautious animals and people, and defending young is guaranteed to be at the top of the list for turning the meekest female into a tigress. Adult female primates will act aggressively toward predators, particularly in defense of an infant. George Schaller in his book, *The Serengeti Lion*, comments thus: "The size relation between predator and prey is a critical factor in determining whether an animal will defend its young. If prey outweighs a [carnivore] predator by a ratio of at least 3:1, then it may feel secure enough to attack, if only briefly."[48] Schaller was expressing his understanding of antelope, buffalo, and rhinoceros of the Serengeti. Did early hominids abide by this same ratio? If so, they were only comfortable defending their young against very small predators one-third their own size. Or, did an entire group of hominids (including the larger males) join together in protecting infants from predators?

Defense of the young in grazing animals is limited to the mother, a tableau sometimes reflected in the anti-predator strategies of the primate world. For example, most threat and attack behaviors by female baboons involve protection of an infant; a female indri (one of the largest of the lemur species) was observed successfully stopping an attack by a Madagascar harrier hawk on her infant. Sometimes females even take the lead in general defense of the group. A captive ruffed lemur matriarch regularly attacked carnivores that came into the lemur compound at Duke University Primate Center, and a female chimpanzee being rehabilitated into the wild in Mt. Assirik, Senegal, took the lead in charging a leopard that was flushed from cover.[49]

Even though the most frequently observed defense behavior for the great apes in our survey was alarm calling, wild cats evoked several charges and/or attacks, and mobbing by chimps and gorillas was evenly divided between cat and reptile predators. Gorillas used three entirely unique behaviors against predators—chestbeating, strong body odor, and disruption of sleeping and ranging behavior.[50] Chestbeating, accompanied by screams, is used as a warning threat by gorillas, but was only elicited by wild dogs and hyenas; strong body odor seems to be related to fear as much as bravado; and the disruption of ranging and sleeping behaviors by western lowland gorillas when predators were in the vicinity is an example of unpredictable or random movement to mess with the predator's mind and cause confusion.

If we assume that mobbing and charge-attacks were employed as active defense at about the same rate by early hominids as by living primate species, then a little less than one-fourth of the time, predators might have been challenged by our ancestors.

Then there is always the strategy of *blustering* your way through a disastrous situation. Defensive posture, or threat stances, were calculated in our survey to be used in approximately 5% of witnessed events. Standing bipedally gave our human ancestors a distinct advantage in this arena, since the purpose of the threat stance is to look as big and horrible as possible. Being bipedal also freed the arms to be used in chaotic, wild, and threatening gestures. We are reminded of the tales told by human survivors of lion and bear attacks—sometimes standing your ground, jumping up and down, waving your arms, and yelling is an effective method to shock a predator. "Hey, prey don't act like this!" they say to themselves. Of course, we have only heard the *survivors'* tales; maybe a certain portion of predators are shocked by outlandish behavior on the part of intended prey, but we never hear about the ones that blew it off and ate the jumping-waving-yelling prey anyway.

WEAPONS OF MASS DESTRUCTION

These, then, were the defenses used for most of our evolution: increase in size, socialization, vocalizations, bipedalism, increasing complexity of the brain, confusing and active defensive behaviors. Active defenses by primates may be in a general mammalian category; that is, employing teeth or nails and claws—like the angwantibo (a slow and steady prosimian) biting a predator on the nose—or they may be uniquely primate, such as using sticks or branches as weapons.

The truly singular retort at which primates excel is the use of weapons against predators. Breaking off or dropping branches was only observed in members of the New World capuchin monkey group by our survey respondents (and all aggressive retaliation of this kind was directed at wild cats and reptiles), but we know from reports and journal articles that unaltered weapons are used frequently by macaques and many other primate species.

At some point, hominids became weapon users. But the earliest weapons should not be thought of as any more than sticks and thorny branches. Anthropologists Lisa Rose and Fiona Marshall suggest that early hominids employed collective defense (just like non-human primates do), and "would have responded similarly to the risk of carnivore predation by intensifying cooperative behaviors, perhaps using branches or stones as simple defensive weapons."[51] There is no evidence that the early hominids made or used stone tools—no link between the oldest fossils and any tools has yet to be found. As stated earlier, stone tools did not appear for almost 5 million years into our evolution, and they were not weaponry at that point.

The sticks and branches or the occasional rock used as a weapon wasn't a danger to predators—it was simply the primate method of defending ourselves as best we could (although sticks and stones *can* break bones). We were not on the offensive, we were on the defensive. And, we must not confuse tools, or even weapons, with the ability to *avoid* predation. Hominids after 2.3 million years ago had stone tools, but that did not keep them from being preyed upon, as was so obvious with the *Homo erectus* remains of hyena meals found in the caves of China.

Considering all this evidence, why is it then that so many scientists, scholars, and members of the general public have a view of our ancestors as bloodthirsty brutes, not just defending themselves but aggressively entering into combat with every living creature? We feel this picture of early humans is based on three things we tackle in the next chapter: perverted Western views of modern humans, the Christian concept of original sin, and . . . just plain sloppy science.

9

GENTLE SAVAGE OR
BLOODTHIRSTY BRUTE?

Let's take stock of what we can say about early humans: They were tasty items for cats, dogs, bears, hyenas, raptors, and reptiles. They were bipedal. They communicated by vocalizations. They lived in groups. Their brains got larger over millions of years (although this was not a steady process—there were long periods of stasis through much of the early Pleistocene epoch). But how did they act? Would we recognize features of ourselves if we got to know them? What was your average smallish bipedal hominid really like?

Many anthropologists and biologists have theorized about the behavior of the earliest hominids and how this behavior might be related to the biological basis of modern human behavior. There seem to be only very extreme depictions of Mr. or Ms. Average Hominid. People take radical positions on this issue; there aren't many centrist opinions. On one side of this theoretical chasm, our human ancestors are painted as gentle versions of Jean-Jacques Rousseau's noble savage. On the other side, our ancestors are portrayed as blood-lusting demons. As we said, not much middle ground!

In an earlier chapter we explained that the killer-ape theory easily toppled the gentle vegetarian-ape theory in the midyears of the twentieth century. This is what one of the fathers of modern physical anthropology and American field primatology, University of California professor Sherwood Washburn, wrote about the dichotomy:

> The world view of the early human carnivore must have been very different from his vegetarian cousins. The desire for meat leads animals to know a wider range and to learn the habits of many animals. Human territorial habits and psychology are fundamentally different from those of apes and monkeys.[1]

In the inaugural decades of the twentieth century, it was thought the first humans must have had large brains and primitive, ape-like bodies. Easy acceptance in 1912 of the Piltdown Man, with its human skull and ape-like jaw, as the "missing link" between humans and apes was facilitated by a preconceived bias about our large brains.[2] Just such a preconception concerning the characteristics of early humans also fostered resistance to accepting *Australopithecus africanus*, uncovered in Africa in 1924 by Raymond Dart, as our earliest ancestor. However, in the early 1950s with the discovery that Piltdown Man was a fraud—and with many more australopithecine fossils recovered—scientists realized that our earliest ancestors were more like non-human primates than like modern humans. That realization, in turn, led to a number of attempts to reconstruct the behavior of our earliest hominid ancestors, often using primate models.

It seems that in each decade since the acceptance of australopithecines in our evolutionary past, a recurrent theme has emerged and reemerged, focusing on the importance of hunting and its relationship to an innate propensity for human violence. Many scenarios concerning the evolution of violence and its biological basis in modern humans have been constructed based upon Man the Hunter.

In the 1960s Sherwood Washburn was among the first to develop a hunting-man theme for human evolution and behavior. In the 1970s E. O. Wilson, one of the major founders of sociobiology, explained that much of current human behavior is an outcome of our hunting past. In the 1980s with the discovery of earlier hominid fossils in Ethiopia, anatomist Owen Lovejoy and Donald Johanson (the paleontologist who discovered Lucy) explained many of the features of hominid evolution with a modified version of male hunting and provisioning. A more recent version of this recurrent theme is authored by Harvard professor and primatologist Richard Wrangham and science writer Dale Peterson in their book *Demonic Males*. Describing his theory, Wrangham links human hunting to an inherent propensity for violence shared alike by humans and common chimpanzees. Craig Stanford has also emphasized comparable ideas in *The Hunting Ape*, as has Michael Ghiglieri in *The Dark Side of Man*.[3]

What are all these theories of hunting and innate violence? Coincidence? Valid scientific theory? Ethnocentrism? Our view is that the recurrent theme of Man the Hunter has more to do with the myths of Judeo-Christian culture than with objective science.

Let's go back again to Raymond Dart and how Man the Hunter became the paradigm for human origins in Western society. Dart's view of human evolution was infused with moral judgment. Dart believed that the earliest hominids, with their innovative new subsistence pattern (hunting), also created a new moral code devoid of altruism. The hunting hypothesis, as it is often referred to, was deconstructed by Matt Cartmill, a physical anthropologist who has studied the history of human hunting. He calls the hunting hypothesis a "bleak, pessimistic view of human beings and their ancestors as instinctively bloodthirsty and aggressive."[4]

Dart waxed poetic with his claims of australopithecine primal urges: "confirmed killers . . . carnivorous creatures that seized living quarries by violence, battered them to death, tore apart their broken bodies, [and] dismembered them limb from limb, greedily devouring livid writhing flesh." He had arrived at a point where he could explain "[t]he loathsome cruelty of mankind to man is explicable only in terms of man's carnivorous and cannibalistic origin."[5] Our ancestors were branded with the mark of Cain and were more allied with bloodthirsty carnivores than their primate relatives.

Dart's vision of early human morality, however, is not new in Western myth, religion, or philosophy. Cartmill in his 1993 book, *A View to a Death in the Morning: Hunting and Nature through History,* shows that it is reminiscent of the earlier Greek and Christian views of human morality.[6] Dart himself began his seminal Man the Hunter paper with a quote from a seventeenth-century Calvinist preacher: "Of all the beasts the

man-beast is the worst, / to others and himself the cruellest foe." In 1772
James Burnet reaffirmed the Man the Bloodthirsty Brute theme, arguing
that "when necessity forced man to hunt, the wild beast part of him became predominant, war succeeding hunting, and he became fiercer than
any other animal—when not subdued by laws and manners."[7] As
Cartmill states, the early Christian philosophers believed that free will
gave human beings the choice to be good or bad; therefore, humans can
be corrupted, a distinctively Christian philosophy that extrapolates to
nature itself having gone rotten. This view of the depravity of human nature is related to the idea of man's fall from grace and of the Christian
notion of original sin. As we shall see, these medieval myths still pervade
many modern, so-called scientific interpretations concerning the evolution of human behavior, human nature, and human morality.

Although more spectacular than the claims of contemporaneous scientists, Robert Ardrey, the writer who popularized Dart's theory, held
views of human nature that did not differ greatly from the scientists, nor
from the ancient Christian beliefs of a fall from grace and original sin. To
Ardrey, however, sin is good. It is a strength that "Cain's children" possess
by virtue of their enlarged brain and their carnivorous lifestyle: "Man is a
predator whose natural instinct is to kill with a weapon." Ardrey argues
that humans are not the product of special creation; they have naturally,
rightfully, and nobly inherited genes that carry the "scars of the ages."[8]
For Ardrey it is war and the instinct for territorial acquisition that led to
the great accomplishments of Western man.

THE HUNTING MYTH AND SOCIOBIOLOGY

Ardrey's statements might be considered the beginning of what has been
called evolutionary ethics,[9] a genre developed with the next major scientific statement on the importance of hunting in the formulation of
human nature. This theory was introduced in the mid-1970s by the famous Harvard biologist E. O. Wilson and other proponents of
sociobiology. Wilson describes a number of behavioral traits that he
claims are found in humans generally and are genetically based human
universals. These include: (1) territoriality, (2) aggressive dominance hierarchies, (3) male dominance over females, (4) permanent male–female

bonds, (5) matrilineality (female offspring stay with the troop they are born into while males leave to find a new social group when they reach sexual maturity), and (6) extended maternal care.[10]

The argument Wilson uses to support his idea that these traits are biologically fixed and genetically based characteristics is their relative constancy among our primate relatives—and their persistence throughout human evolution and in human societies. But, other than the last—extended maternal care—these behavioral characteristics are *neither* general primate traits *nor* human universals. Let's look at the first five, one by one.

Is Territoriality a Human Universal?

The concept of "territory" was first developed in studies on birds. The essence of the concept is that an animal or group of animals "defends" all or part of its range. Thus there are two major components: the space itself and the active defense of that space. However, many animals maintain exclusive areas simply by vocalizing, displaying, or in some way signaling to possible intruders, and very rarely, if ever, actually fight at borders.[11] The concept of territoriality is not in any way simple, and there are real difficulties in relating various spacing methods used by different species to one single, strict concept. In any case, for primate groups, spacing mechanisms are extremely variable. Groups of gibbons and the South American titi monkey could be considered territorial in that they actually have ritualized "battles" at borders of their almost-exclusive ranges. A number of other primates have specialized loud calls that presumably help them maintain exclusive areas (this includes orangutans, howler monkeys, African colobus monkeys, and Madagascar's largest lemur, the indri). However, most species of primates have overlapping group ranges and often share resources. This is especially true of many savanna forms such as baboons and chimpanzees. In ringtailed lemurs and gorillas several groups may have almost coincident home ranges. Thus, in primates territoriality in the strict sense of the word is very rare.[12]

In humans the concept of territory, as used to define the way birds defend an area, is not at all useful. Most hunters and gatherers do not have exclusive, defended ranges. Agricultural peoples have a multitude of ways of dealing with land use. Lumping these into a simple concept of territoriality is nonsensical. And, finally, modern warfare usually has little to do with directly defending borders. Think about it—how is a political decision to send troops to Somalia, Bosnia, or Iraq similar to a bird or a gibbon displaying at the border of its range?

Are Aggressive Dominance Hierarchies Human Universals?

Again, we are dealing with a very complex concept. Dominance hierarchies in animals are defined by a number of criteria, including priority of access to food, space, or mates, and by such delicate social situations as who grooms and who gets groomed, who is the leader of group progressions, or who will be the winner in aggressive encounters. These often are not positively correlated—that is, the animal who wins fights does not always lead the group.[13] In fact, defining the group hierarchy by any one of these criteria usually does not in any way help us to understand the complexities of primate group organization or structure.

Furthermore, there are many primate species in which dominance hierarchies are unclear, ambiguous, or absent altogether. For example, they have not been demonstrated in most prosimians, or in many New and Old World arboreal monkeys, or in terrestrial patas monkeys, or in gibbons. They do seem to be present in baboons, macaques, and chimpanzees. But even among the latter primate species, hierarchies are often unstable, and the genetic influence and consequences of hierarchies are unknown. For one example, in a baboon troop, rank changes may occur on an average of every 2 weeks among males; in many studies of baboons and macaques in which paternity is known, little correlation between rank and reproductive success has been found. Generally, the relationship between rank and reproductive success remains obscure.[14]

When we consider humans, the presence of dominance hierarchies based on aggression becomes even more problematic. In the science of ethology (the study of animal behavior), an aggressive dominance hierarchy is determined by winners and losers of head-to-head aggressive encounters and is normally defined within a closed social group. You might ask yourself the following questions: Is your status in society based on your fighting ability or aggressiveness? As you walk down the street or the halls of your school or workplace, do you "display" aggressively to the people who you pass so they cower from you? Or, in the same situation, are you forced to give way to them and allow them to pass? How many face-to-face fights have you had in your lifetime? What is your status (based on aggressive encounters) in your social group? And, by the way, what are the limits of your own closed social group? Are these questions meaningful in human societies? We think not.

Is Male Dominance over Females a Human Universal?

Male dominance over females is not by any means one of those traits that permeates the primate order. Barbara Smuts, a field researcher who studied the male–female relationships in baboons, has identified five major types of adult male–adult female dominance relationships in non-human primates.[15] In three of the five, males are not dominant to females. These include species in which sexual differentiation in body size is slight and in which females are clearly dominant to males (for example, many lemurs); species in which body-size differences are slight and the sexes are co-dominant (many bushbabies, lorises, lemurs, marmosets, tamarins and many other New World monkeys, and gibbons); and species in which males are larger than females but females sometimes dominate through female–female coalitions (squirrel monkeys, talapoins, vervets, many macaques, and possibly patas monkeys and some guenons). In fact the only species in which females rarely dominate males are those in which the males are much larger than females. These species include baboons and the great apes (*except* the bonobo—the pygmy chimp). Not so coincidentally these are also the only primate species that most sociobiologists know a great deal about. Of course, size difference (sexual dimorphism) in humans is slight, and female coalitions are quite common. If this *is* a human universal, we would need to believe that male dominance over females is ubiquitous; in other words, "women prove everywhere to be second-class citizens in the public-political domain."[16] (Tell this to Margaret Thatcher, Hillary Rodham Clinton, Oprah Winfrey, or the former and current prime ministers of Norway, Pakistan, Sri Lanka, India, Israel, and Indonesia.) Perhaps male dominance *is* a *near*-universal in Western and Islamic cultures, but many traditional societies have a more egalitarian distribution of power. For example, tropical hunters and gatherers, such as the !Kung San[17] of the Kalahari Desert and Mbuti pygmies of Central Africa, are known for a fairly equal distribution of domestic and public power between males and females.

Are Permanent Male–Female Bonds and the Nuclear Family Human Universals?

Permanent male–female bonds and nuclear families are extremely rare among non-human primates, most primates having promiscuous mating systems. Among humans, of 862 cultures listed in the cultural encyclopedia entitled *Ethnographic Atlas*, just 16% participate in monogamous marriages, while 83% are polygynous (one male having more than one wife). Pair-bonded monogamy, by the way, is *not* the current designation for the marriage systems of the United States and Canada. So-called serial monogamy (sequential marriages after sequential divorces) is the social science category for our current states of wedded bliss.

Is Matrilineality (or Matrilocality) a Human Universal?

For humans, matrilineality (tracing the line of family descent from mother to daughter) and matrilocality (married couples residing with the wife's family) are unusual. In most cultures the woman leaves her family and moves to the location or inside the household of the husband. We bent over backward in an attempt to find examples of this as a human universal by limiting our search to foraging peoples, since their pre-agricultural, pre-urban pattern is often more egalitarian than other modern cultures. Consulting the same atlas of cultures, we found that only 16 of the 179 hunting-and-gathering societies are matrilineal.

Thus, we must conclude that these supposed evolutionary and "genetically conservative universal" traits are neither conservative nor universal. Yet all of these traits were believed to be a product of our hunting past. Wilson figured that for more than a million years, man was a hunter and "our innate social responses have been fashioned largely through this lifestyle."[18]

The problem with the sociobiologists' approach to the old nature–nurture question is that they do not have any better criteria by which to formulate the key to human nature than did the earlier Social Darwinists of the Victorian era. Social Darwinism proclaimed that human morality should be based on the evolutionary process of the survival of the fittest.[19] Individuals, ethnic groups, races, or societies that were most fit would survive and those that were weak would be eliminated, and this was good! Competition—especially winning through competition—was the basis of human ethics and morality. Herbert Spencer, a contemporary of Darwin and the father of Social Darwinism, argued that we should cherish the evolutionary process that allowed the fittest to survive and the inadequate to be rigorously eliminated. Robert Ardrey's proclamations on the benefits of war are reminiscent of this approach.

Sociobiologists don't find fault with the fact that Social Darwinists linked evolution to ethics but simply that, when Social Darwinism was popular, the mechanisms of evolution were so poorly understood. Given sociobiological tenets, they claim we now can proceed to ethics from "known facts" rather than from mere theory. Here are two of these "known facts": The first is that the goal of each and every living organism is to pass on its own genes at the expense of all others. The second is that an organism should only cooperate with others if they carry some of his or her own genes (the process of kin selection), or if at some later date the "others" might support, aid, or help the organism (the theory of reciprocal altruism). However, since animals cannot make these calculations consciously, evolution has endowed our genes with a moral ethic to facilitate kin selection and altruistic reciprocation because, ultimately, this may help us perpetuate and multiply our own genes. In their own words Wilson and his collaborator, Michael Ruse, explain:

> It used to be thought, in the bad old days of Social Darwinism when evolution was poorly understood, that life is an uninterrupted struggle—"nature red in tooth and claw." But this is only one side of natural selection, the same process also leads to altruism and reciprocity. Morality is merely an adaptation put in place to further our reproductive ends. . . . Ethical codes work because they drive us to go against our selfish day-to-day impulses in favor of long-term *group survival*. . . . and thus, over our lifetimes, the multiplication of our genes many times. [emphasis ours][20]

Following this logic, evolutionary morality ultimately allows us to build group cohesion *in order* to successfully compete with strangers and thus pass on our genes. We should not look down upon our war-like, cruel nature but rather understand that it has led to success, in an evolutionary sense, when coupled with "making nice" with some—but not with other—individuals or groups of individuals. The "making nice" part is genetically driven and the real foundation of human morality.

Wilson's observations present the non-consoling thought that "some of the 'noblest' traits of mankind, including team play, altruism, patriotism, bravery on the field of battle, and so forth, are the genetic product of warfare." If a determinedly peaceful society was to try to steer members away from the "conflicts that once gave the destructive phenotypes their Darwinian edge," we might be throwing out the baby with the bathwater. In other words, looking at things through the genetic lens, we got the good traits *because* of our constant battles, conflicts, and blood-thirsty encounters.[21]

Let us pause to state clearly that we're not proposing a complete absence of a biological basis to human behavior. But, as Franz Boas—a sane voice in the decades of Social Darwinist theory—stated over 70 years ago, "unless the contrary can be proved, we must assume that all complex activities are socially determined, not hereditary."[22]

E. O. Wilson, himself, criticizes the Social Darwinists, accusing them of being misleading and basing wide, extrapolated explanations on a small sample of animal species. Yet sociobiology's favorite children—kin selection and reciprocal altruism—are always dressed up and adored as the only explanations for friendly social interactions. Again, in sociobiologist Michael Ruse's own words:

> Where kin selection fails, reciprocal altruism provides a back-up. But as one grows more distant in one's social relationship, one would expect the feeling to decline. . . . [I]t is silly to pretend that our dealings across countries are going to be intimate or driven by much beyond self-interest. . . . Jesus did not suggest that the Samaritan was in the general business of charity to strangers.[23]

This sounds very much like the claims of Dart and Ardrey, and the Social Darwinists before them. Furthermore, the scientific evidence for human universal traits or for sociobiological tenets is just as weak as was the evidence provided by Ardrey or Dart to support their theories of human morality. And how do these theories relate to the Western European Christian views of morality? Ruse admits that reciprocal altruism, especially, begins to sound like "warmed-over Christianity." He also attributes Christianity's raging conversion rate at the beginning of the first millennium as due to its neat fit into our genetically programmed behaviors.[24]

Hmmm . . . so Christianity was popular because it fit so nicely into universal biological instincts? Well, here's another way to look at it that we feel compelled to lay out: Are the professed Christian morals *generated* by the scientific evidence for biologically based morality, or do we think they are biological universals *because* they happen to fit our own Christian ethics? Ruse goes on to say he is not much of a relativist—he condemns as much as anyone else "rapes in Yugoslavia and the atrocities of Hitler."[25] But it seems to us that morality is often in the eye of the beholder. Western codes of ethics can be mightily flexible, as is obvious from the mainly Christian soldiers who carried out the rapes in Yugoslavia as well as the atrocities of Hitler.

CHIMPANZEE AND HUMAN MALES
AS DEMONIC KILLERS

One of the new claims to the importance of killing and the biological basis of morality is that of Richard Wrangham and Dale Peterson in their book, *Demonic Males: Apes and the Origins of Human Violence*. Their argument rests on the fact that 20–25 years ago we thought human aggression was unique because research on the great apes had revealed that those species were basically unaggressive, gentle creatures. Although early theorists proposed that hunting, killing, and extreme aggressive behavior were biological traits inherited from our earliest hunting, hominid ancestors, many anthropologists still believed that patterns of aggression were environmentally and culturally determined—learned behaviors. Our sins were thought by most to be acquired and not inherited characteristics. Our sins were no more original than all the other acquired and culturally transmitted traits manifested by the human species. Wrangham and Peterson argue that new evidence indicates the killer instincts are not unique to humans—we share this characteristic with our nearest relative, the common chimpanzee. In fact it is this inherited propensity for killing that allows hominids and chimps to be such good hunters.

Here's the demonic male theory in a nutshell: The split between humans and common chimpanzees happened at least 8 million years ago. Furthermore, humans may have split from the chimpanzee–bonobo (pygmy chimp) line after gorillas, with bonobos separating from chimps only 2.5 million years ago. Because a chimp-like being may be the common ancestor of all these forms, and because the earliest australopithecine was quite chimpanzee-like, Wrangham speculates that: "The most reasonable view for the moment is that chimpanzees are . . . an amazingly good model for the ancestor of hominids . . . [and if] we know what our ancestor looked like, naturally we get clues about how it behaved . . . that is, like modern-day chimpanzees."[26] Finally, if modern chimpanzees and modern humans share certain behavioral traits, these traits have "long evolutionary roots" and are likely to be fixed, biologically inherited components of our nature and not culturally determined.

Further to the demonic male theory, there are a number of cultural traits shared by early hominids and chimpanzees. However, it is not these cultural traits that are of the most interest; rather it is presumed shared patterns of aggression between chimps and humans. The authors of *Demonic Males* claim that only two animal species—chimpanzees and humans—live in patrilineal, male-bonded communities that exhibit intense territorial aggression, including lethal raids that seek vulnerable enemies to kill. Wrangham asks:

> Does this mean chimpanzees are naturally violent? Ten years ago it wasn't clear. . . . In this cultural species it may turn out that one of the least variable of all chimpanzee behaviors is the intense competition between males, the violent aggression they use against strangers, and their willingness to maim and kill those that frustrate their goals. . . . As the picture of chimpanzee society settles into focus, it now includes infanticide, rape, and regular battering of females by males.[27]

Since chimpanzees and humans share these violent urges, the demonic male paradigm emphasizes that chimpanzees and humans also share an inborn morality. Those long evolutionary roots of blood lust, those aggressive urges, those Dostoevskian demons, rise out of a 6-million-year-old curse we share with our closest kin! We are *apes of nature!*

Whoa! Let's calm down for a moment and look at a few details before we proceed any further with demon chimps and devil humans. Certainly humans hunt, and chimpanzees are also hunters who have specific predatory strategies in specific geographic populations—different cultural approaches, so to speak. But humans and chimpanzees are not the only primates that hunt for food. Some prosimians (certain lemurs, lorises, and tarsiers) are highly insectivorous, and many catch and eat small snakes, lizards, and amphibians. Neither are humans and chimpanzees the only primate hunters of mammals. The baboons of Africa and the capuchin monkeys of South America are hunters of small mammals. And chimpanzees and humans are not the only "higher" apes who hunt. Chimpanzees are the most carnivorous of our close relatives, but orangutans have been observed out on successful hunting forays, as have bonobos and gibbons.

Humans and chimpanzees are not even the only primates that hunt and eat other primates! Orangutans prey on lorises and gibbons; baboons eat bushbabies and vervet monkeys; blue monkeys prey on bushbabies; capuchin monkeys prey on titi monkeys and owl monkeys; red ruffed lemurs prey on infant ringtailed lemurs; and dwarf lemurs have been observed hunting and eating smaller mouse lemurs.[28]

But, only a few instances of primates preying on other primates are relatively well studied, and the emphasis has been on chimpanzee predation. At Gombe National Park in Tanzania, chimpanzee predation on red colobus is extensive, alleged to result in the death of a minimum of one-sixth to a maximum of one-third of the red colobus monkey population every year since the study began. (We won't even deal with the fact that if the higher end of this killing rate went on for long, there would, eventually, be no more red colobus monkeys.) There are other locations where chimpanzees also prey on red colobus monkeys (chimpanzees, for the record, have been seen preying on twenty different primate species), but not at the heavy rate observed in Gombe. Christophe Boesch, who with his wife Hedwige has researched chimpanzees in the West African nation of Côte d'Ivoire, believes that human presence had a much stronger impact on chimpanzee hunting of red colobus in Gombe than in the Tai Forest where Christophe and Hedwige's investigations take place. Nonetheless, the Boesches have identified red colobus as the most significant prey item for chimpanzees in the Tai Forest.[29]

So, there seems to be no doubt that many primate species will eat meat and hunt for meat—sometimes opportunistically, sometimes with purposeful intent. Where we differ from Wrangham and Peterson, Craig Stanford, and Michael Ghiglieri (and Raymond Dart, Sherwood

The bonobo, one of our closest relatives, has been used as an example of an ape that "lost" the desire to hunt and kill. (N. Rowe)

Washburn, and E. O. Wilson before them) is the theory that *killing and violence* are inherited from our ancient relatives. And we further disagree with their argument that killing and violence are traits shared by hominids and chimpanzees not as by-products of hunting, but rather the inverse: it is this violent nature and natural blood lust (say the sociobiologists) that makes both humans and chimpanzees such *good* hunters.

The bonobo (the "gentle" pygmy chimpanzee) helps them to this conclusion. Sociobiologists claim that bonobos have lost the desire to kill, as well as losing the desire to hunt; that they have suppressed both personal and predatory aggression; that even though bonobos evolved from a chimpanzee-like ancestor who was both a hunter of monkeys and a hunter of its own kind, during the evolution of bonobos the males *lost* the desire to kill each other and the desire to kill prey; and finally, that bonobos and chimps tell us murder and hunting are very similar.

Wrangham believes that blood lust ties killing and hunting tightly together, but in his scenario it is the desire to kill that drives the ability to hunt. Like other sociobiologists, he believes this lust to kill is based upon the *selfish gene.*

The selfish gene is an "elegant" sociobiological theory made popular by Richard Dawkins in his book of the same name.[30] (Scientists use the word *elegant* to describe theories that explain complex natural phenomena in a very polished and minimalistic style.) Dawkins' theory is so elegant that it has been accepted, incorporated, and has now reached the level of conventional wisdom in biology. Dawkins' selfish gene explains animal behavior in truly elegant style because it provides an umbrella explanation for *every* single thing that animals do—all behavior serves selfish ends. The selfish gene theory can be used to explain why humans that hated and killed their enemies were survivors. Natural selection would favor those that killed over those that might hesitate and be killed.

The selfish gene theory is also used to explain why bonobos don't kill their enemies. Is this level of generality elegant or hopelessly simplistic? To us it has about the same explanatory power as that of the eighteenth-century philosopher Jeremy Bentham's "moral philosophy," which claimed that human behavior is governed solely by pleasure and pain. Bentham believed that all behavior is dictated by seeking to enhance pleasure and to minimize the likelihood of pain. Both the selfish gene and Bentham's moral philosophy attempt to explain everything—and therefore explain almost nothing.

As with many of the sociobiological theories, we find problems with both the theory itself and with the evidence used to support it. The book *Demonic Males* states that humans and chimpanzees might share biologically fixed behaviors based on two assumptions: First, humans and chimps are more closely related to each other than chimps are to gorillas; secondly, chimps are a good model for our earliest ancestor and retain so-called conservative (*conservative* in the biological context basically means "relatively unchanged by recent evolution") traits shared by both.

The first of these statements is still a hotly debated topic because the chimps, gorillas, and humans are so close genetically that it is difficult to tell exact divergence times or patterns between the three.[31] The second statement is just not true. Chimpanzees have been evolving for as long as humans and gorillas, and there is no reason to believe that ancestral chimps were highly similar to present-day chimps. The fossil evidence is extremely sparse for the great apes. It is likely that many forms of apes have become extinct during millions of years—just as many forms of hominids have become extinct. Furthermore, even if chimpanzees *were* a good model for the ancestor to chimpanzees and humans and a "conservative" representative of this particular branch of the evolutionary bush, it would not follow that humans would necessarily share specific behavioral traits. As the authors of *Demonic Males* emphasize, chimps, gorillas, and bonobos are all very different from one another in their behavior and in their willingness to kill others of their species. It is exactly because of these differences, in fact, that the authors agree that conservative retention of traits alone cannot explain the drastic behavioral similarities and differences.

Let's examine the "proof" of Wrangham and Peterson's theory that, we must reiterate, doesn't rest on theoretical grounds but depends solely on the circumstantial evidence that violence and killing in chimpanzees and humans are behaviors that are similar in pattern, have ancient shared evolutionary roots, and are inherited. *Humans and chimpanzees kill members of neighboring groups of their own species*—we can't argue that this happens, particularly with humans. *This is a startling exception to the norm for animals*—actually, there are many exceptions, such as lions, wolves, spotted hyenas, and a number of other predators. *Fighting adults of almost all species normally stop at winning: They don't go on to kill*—the fact is that most species do not have the weapons to kill one another as adults. Aggressive, unfriendly behavior between adults of many species is common in various circumstances,[32] but certainly it would take two adult squirrels, rabbits, or aardvarks much more energy than it is worth to kill their opponent rather than to drive it away. They just don't have the tools. Chimpanzees and humans do, although the tools they use are radically different.

CHIMPANZEE AGGRESSION

Just how common is it for chimpanzees to kill other chimpanzees? This is where the real controversy may lie. During the first 14 years of study at Gombe National Park in Tanzania (1960–1974), chimpanzees were described as a peaceful, unaggressive species. In fact, during a year of concentrated study, Jane Goodall observed 284 agonistic (aggressive) encounters. Of these, 66% were due to competition for introduced (that is, human-provided) bananas, and only 34% could be classified as "attacks occurring in 'normal' aggressive contexts."[33] Furthermore, as Jane Goodall recorded:

> Only 10 percent of the 284 attacks were classified as "violent," and even attacks that appeared punishing to me often resulted in no discernable injury. . . . Other attacks consisted merely of brief pounding-hitting after which the aggressor often touched or embraced the other immediately.[34]

Chimpanzee aggression before 1974 was considered no different from patterns of aggression seen in many primate species. Goodall explained in her monograph, *The Chimpanzees of Gombe*, that she uses data mainly from after 1975 because the earlier years presented a behavioral contrast of the Gombe chimps as being "far more peaceable than humans."[35] Other early naturalists' descriptions of chimpanzee behavior were consistent with those of Goodall prior to 1975 and confirmed her first 14 years of observation. Even different communities were observed to come together with peaceful, ritualized displays of greeting.[36]

However, between 1974 and 1977, five adult males from one subgroup were attacked and disappeared from the area, presumably killed by other chimpanzees. Why after 14 years did the patterns of aggression change?

Recent claims of chimpanzee aggressiveness may be greatly exaggerated. Male chimpanzees bond closely with brothers and friends. (C. Sanz)

Was it because the stronger group saw the weakness of the other and
decided to improve its genetic fitness (the sociobiological explanation)?
Surely there were stronger and weaker animals and subgroups before this
particular time. We can look to Goodall's own observations for an answer. In 1965 Goodall began to provide "restrictive human-controlled
feeding." A few years later she realized that:

> [T]he constant feeding was having a marked effect on the behavior of the
> chimps. They were beginning to move about in large groups more often
> than they had ever done in the old days. They were sleeping near camp and
> arriving in noisy hordes early in the morning. Worst of all, the adult males
> were becoming increasingly aggressive. When we first offered the chimps
> bananas, the males seldom fought over the food; . . . [now] not only was
> there a great deal more fighting than ever before, but many of the chimps
> were hanging around camp for hours and hours every day.[37]

By this time the social behavior and ranging patterns of the animals were already disrupted, and the increasing aggression eventually created so many problems that observation was almost ended at Gombe.[38]

The possibility that human interference was a main cause of the unusual behavior of the Gombe chimps was the subject of a well-researched academic book by Margaret Power, entitled *The Egalitarians, Human and Chimpanzee: An Anthropological View of Social Organization*.[39] In *Demonic Males* Wrangham and Peterson essentially ignore this book, stating that yes, this might have been unnatural behavior if it weren't for new evidence of similar behavior occurring at Gombe since 1977 and "elsewhere in Africa." What is this evidence? We will summarize the four examples they provide:

Exhibit A: Between 1979 and 1982 the Gombe group extended its range to the south and conflict with a southern group (named "Kalande" by researchers) was suspected. One day in 1982 a so-called raiding party of males reached Goodall's camp and "some of these raids may have been lethal." However, Goodall described the *only reported* raid in *The Chimpanzees of Gombe: Patterns of Behavior* as follows: One female "was chased by a Kalande male and mildly attacked. Her four year old son . . . encountered a second male—but was only sniffed." Wrangham and Peterson imply that these encounters were similar to previous lethal attacks at Gombe, but in this single observed raid, no violence was witnessed. Along with their discussion of raids, they also report the death in 1981 of an adult male named Humphrey, whose body was discovered near the home range border. They fail to mention that Humphrey was approximately 35 years old, and wild chimpanzees rarely live past 33 years.[40]

Exhibit B: From 1970 to 1982 six adult males from one community disappeared at a Japanese study site in the Mahale Mountains of Tanzania, west of Gombe. The six disappeared one by one over this 12-year period. None of these animals was ever observed being attacked or killed, and one was sighted later roaming as a solitary male. Tom Nishida and his colleagues who study the chimps at Mahale puzzled over the gradual, successive disappearance of the adult males. They went on to speculate that at least some of these males may have been killed by chimpanzees from another group.[41] The only rationale for Nishida's research group to pinpoint other chimpanzees as the perpetrators was the well-known

Gombe intergroup conflict resulting in five male deaths between 1974 and 1977. (As mentioned earlier in this book, we now are aware that lions often pass through Mahale and regularly eat chimpanzees. A more logical explanation for missing chimps is that any unaccounted for males were eaten by lions.)

Exhibit C: In the Tai Forest in Côte d'Ivoire, West Africa, Wrangham and Peterson report that researchers Christophe and Hedwige Boesch believe that "violent aggression among the chimpanzees is as important as it is in Gombe."[42] Referring to the original paper by the Boesches, we found that the authors simply state that encounters by neighboring chimpanzee communities are more common in their site than in Gombe and that this may lead to larger, more cohesive, group structure and a "higher involvement of the males in social life"[43]—there is no mention of any violence or killing during these encounters.

Exhibit D: Finally, at a site that Richard Wrangham began studying in 1984, an adult male was found dead in 1991. This incident is dramatically reported in *Demonic Males:* "In the second week of August, Ruizoni was killed. No human saw the big fight. . . . the day before he went missing, our males had been travelling together near the border exchanging calls with the males of another community, evidently afraid to meet them. Four days after he was last seen, our team found his disintegrating body hunched at the bottom of a little slope."[44] There is no other mention of violence at this site during the 7 years before or the 6 years following this particular event.

This then is the total amount of evidence of male–male killing among chimpanzees after 37 years of research by an army of field primatologists. The data for infanticide and rape among chimpanzees are even less impressive. Data are so sparse for these behaviors among chimpanzees, in reality, that the authors of *Demonic Males* were forced to use examples from the other great apes—gorillas and orangutans. And, guess what? Just as for adult killing in chimpanzees, both the evidence and the interpretations of rape and infanticide in gorillas and orangutans are suspect and controversial.[45] Recently, the claim of chimp violence has been updated to ten verified and another ten suspected cases of killing among chimpanzees in four out of nine sites where chimps have been the subject of long-term research. This sums up to 10–20 cases in 170 years of combined observation by all of the researchers involved at all nine sites, or one killing every 8.5–17 years.[46]

Our digression into the alleged "demonism" of chimpanzees and early humans does not mean we argue that chimpanzees or humans are *not* violent under certain circumstances, as we all know, but simply that the claims of inherent demonism may be as greatly exaggerated as were earlier claims of noble savages and peaceable kingdoms. And furthermore, research seems to indicate that the neurophysiology of aggression between species (in other words, predation) is quite different from the spontaneous violence linked to *intra*specific aggression by humans (that is, murder). Even if hunting were a common subsistence technique among early hominids, this does not necessitate uncontrolled aggressiveness in human interactions.

GETTING OUT OF OUR GENES

So far, you could say we have been the devil's advocates, or adversaries, depending on your point of view. But, you might ask, what if the portrait of us and our chimp cousins in *Demonic Males* is correct and both chimps and humans are inherently sinners? Are we doomed to be violent forever because this pattern is genetically coded? Is original sin an inborn, fixed pattern that will ultimately destroy us, or can we go beyond our past?—get out of our genes, so to speak. According to Wrangham and Peterson, we can look to the *bonobos* as our potential saviors from demonic male genes.

Bonobos, although more closely related to the common chimpanzee than humans, have become a peace-loving, love-not-war-making alter ego of the chimpanzee–human paradigm of violence. How did this happen? In the demonic male scenario chimpanzee and human females select partners that are violent. "While men have evolved to be demonic males, it seems likely that women have evolved to prefer demonic males. . . .[A]s long as demonic males are the most successful reproducers, any female who mates with them is provided with sons who themselves will likely be good reproducers."[47] In the decidedly non-demonic world of bonobos, females form alliances, reduce male power, and have chosen to mate with less-aggressive males. So after all, it is not violence that has caused human and chimpanzee males to be their inborn, immoral selves. It is rather poor choices by human and chimpanzee females!

In any case, after millions of years of human evolution, can we rid ourselves of our inborn evils? Wrangham believes so, and it's pretty easy. We look at chimpanzees to see the worst aspects of our past, and we look at bonobos for the path of escape from it. In other words, humans can learn how to behave by watching bonobos. But—we can't resist asking— if humans can change our inherited behavior so simply, why haven't we been able to do so before the authors of the demonic male theory enlightened us? Surely, there are variations in the amount of violence in different human cultures and individuals. If we have the capacity to change by learning from example, then our behavior is determined by socialization practices and by our cultural histories, and not solely by our biological nature. This is true whether the examples come from benevolent bonobos or from pacifists and conscientious objectors during a war.

The theory of the demonic male, although it includes chimpanzees as our murdering cousins, is very similar to Man the Hunter theories proposed in the past. Further, it does not differ greatly from early Euro-Christian beliefs about human ethics and morality. We are forced to ask: Are these theories generated by good science, or are they just "good to think" *because* they reiterate our traditional cultural beliefs? Are the scientific facts being interpreted in such a way as to reinforce our traditional Euro-Christian myths of morality and ethics? Is the theory generated by the data, or are the data manipulated to fit preconceived notions of human morality and ethics? Since data supporting these theories are extremely weak—and yet the stories continue to repeat themselves—we are inclined to believe that Man the Hunter—the myth—may continue in Western European views on human nature long into the future.

Theories similar to Wrangham and Peterson's on the nature of human hunting and killing have been touted recently by chimpanzee researchers Craig Stanford and Michael Ghiglieri (although there seem to be some contradictions between the three views). Stanford believes that it is not hunting per se that is important for chimps or early humans but the sharing of meat. It is this meat-sharing that, to Stanford, has led to the development of the human brain (but not the chimpanzee brain), sophisticated tool use, our complex patterns of social interaction and structure, and the power of men to manipulate and control women. He portrays the roots of human behavior as manipulation and social cunning that arose from the use of meat by our ancestors. Stanford states:

"This is very different than saying that because of a meat-eating past, we have an innately aggressive nature. . . . Humans are not demons by nature. . . . in spite of the attention that we focus on human violence."[48] Thus, from Wrangham and Peterson's and from Stanford's chimpanzee-based scenarios, we are left with completely different conclusions. What is missing from these "just-so" stories of human evolution based on chimpanzee analogies is a careful analysis of the actual fossil evidence of our earliest human relatives. We have to agree with an earlier statement of Stanford (with co-author John Allen) that current models of hominid evolution are "either implicitly chimpanzee-referent models or restatements, updated and improved, of the 'man-the-hunter' hypotheses of the 1950s and '60s."[49]

Michael Ghiglieri believes that human violence—rape, murder, war, genocide, and even robbery—are all just extensions of the sexual strategies and the desire to pass on genes not only in chimpanzees and humans, but in all sexually reproducing organisms. He equates the life history traits of strangler figs that suck nutrients from trees with that of hard-core human felons. Both are involved in the universal sexual strategy of robbery. He states: "Robbery is not unique to people. . . . Ants do it, birds do it, even strangler figs do it. To call these robberies 'sociopathic' misses the point that nature *equipped* these creatures with a tremendously useful strategy of seizing resources by force." [original emphasis][50] To Ghiglieri most robberies occur in the context of who gets the "resources vital to attracting sexual partners to mate with them."[51] Need we state that we disagree?

Referring to "rape" in dragonflies, "robbery" in ants and strangler figs, or "murder" in chimpanzees may sound like science, but as stated by Jonathan Marks in his book, *What It Means To Be 98% Chimpanzee*, "It's a science of metaphorical, and not biological, connections."[52]

THE OTHER 50%

Demonic *males! Man* the Hunter! What about the other 50% of the species? Female hominids: were they killer apes, too?

Obtaining meat may have been significant in later human evolutionary history, but there is considerable debate concerning the importance of hunting versus scavenging or scavenging versus gathering, during even these later stages of human evolution. Many feminist anthropologists emphasize a Woman the Gatherer scenario of human evolution over the Man the Hunter scenario.[53] Empirical investigations continue.

Adrienne Zihlman is a physical anthropologist at the University of California at Santa Cruz. Besides being internationally known for her research on bonobos, her studies on fossil humans and her writings on the role of women in evolution bring a refreshing perspective to what has been a tediously male-oriented bias. Zihlman also is in the unique position of having been a student of Sherwood Washburn—father of American field primatology and staunch advocate of Man the Hunter philosophy. She has rigorously applied the Washburn legacy of modern scientific approach and methodology in the field of human paleontology, but she has come up with some very alternative views to her mentor's concept of Man the Hunter. Zihlman has been a pioneer in helping us understand the role of women in human evolution—a new holistic and exciting interpretation of the early human fossil record.

Studying the behavior, anatomy, and ecology of the bonobos—and of modern-day foraging cultures—Zihlman has constructed what we believe is the most tenable characterization of the way earliest hominids might have exploited savanna or woodland edge environments. She has done this by comparing the way humans use their hands, arms, backs, legs, and so on with the various behavioral patterns found among closely related apes, specifically, and other non-human primates.

In an article entitled "Women in Evolution," Zihlman and co-author Nancy Tanner examined the way in which tools are used by modern foragers and by chimpanzees. Rather than being utilized in hunting, most tools used by chimps are for gathering such things as termites and ants (long twigs and digging sticks), or cracking nuts (rocks or sticks), or soaking up water from puddles (wads of leaves)—and female chimpanzees use tools more than males. Most food is obtained by gathering plant foods; hunting is almost always a transitional and chance phenomenon and makes up a very small proportion of the chimpanzee diet.[54]

At around 2.3 million years ago in the fossil record the first stone tools appear, but that is a relatively recent event since our hominid ancestors probably first appeared at least 7 million years ago (and, since chimps use tools made of many materials, it is highly probable that our common human–ape ancestor used them long before 7 million years). What were they using? And *who* was using them?

Among modern human hunter–gatherer cultures, most tools, again, are used not for hunting large prey but rather for gathering plants, eggs, honey, small insects, and small burrowing animals. Women's tools include digging sticks, poles for knocking down fruit or nuts, and rocks for cracking nuts or tough fruit rinds. Containers can be tools also: baskets and slings are used for carrying babies and gathering roots, nuts, berries, and grains. And, again, most of these tools *are made and used by women*, not men. We have known for 4 decades that some 60%–90% of the food used and collected by most modern human foragers in the tropics is provided by women. Although the Man the Hunter hypothesis may still be conventional wisdom, it does not fit the evidence of chimpanzees or modern hunter–gatherers.

To our way of thinking, Zihlman has come up with the most reasonable theories on the social organization of early hominids. Simply put, the Man the Hunter paradigm assumes that men go out and hunt and bring home the bacon to women and children. In order to do this and not be cheated into feeding another man's children, pair bonds developed early in human evolution. However, this doesn't fit what we know from other primates or from modern foragers. By doing a broad comparative analysis, Zihlman envisions a flexible early hominid society in which women carried the young, conducted most of the socialization of the young, were repositories of group knowledge, had cognitive maps of the home range and its resources, were the center of society and the core of group stability, and spread innovations, techniques, and knowledge through the group and onto the next generation. Finally, she poses the theory that female choice of sexual partners existed, not sex through male coercion or aggression. (Ditch the cliché of the hairy cave man holding a club in one hand and dragging his literally stunned mate by her hair.) Successful mating behavior involved being appealing to females, which translates into females choosing less, rather than more, aggressive males with whom to mate.

Adrienne Zihlman was among the first to address the male-biased theory in human evolution and has provided a feasible alternative theory—one that best fits *all* the evidence. But her theory of Woman the Gatherer is still ignored, misunderstood, and underappreciated by many contemporary paleontologists. Sex-biased theories of killer apes and killer humans still pervade the popular literature. She stated in a recent article, with the whimsical title, "The Paleolithic Glass Ceiling": "The role of women in evolution has undergone a number of permutations, but paradoxically, in spite of challenges to the contrary, the outcomes have resulted in little change. . . . [A]nthropologists reach a wide audience through textbooks, television specials, and museum exhibits [but] women in evolution are rendered either invisible nonparticipants or as the handmaidens to men in prehistory."[55]

Passive handmaidens or compliant harem girls sum up the extent of the first descriptions of female non-human primates studied in the wild, also. Sherwood Washburn and Irven DeVore undertook the first modern field studies of primates, specifically baboons, in the early 1960s. They took one look at the larger size of the males with their impressive shoulder mantles and huge canines and became fixated on male behavior. The rather innocuous-looking females were dismissed completely while males were bestowed with the regal power to hold the baboon troop together by sheer force. This almost-complete misperception is why Washburn and DeVore so totally misunderstood baboon sociality.

Ironically, another of Washburn's female graduate students, Shirley Strum, went to the field and looked past the imposing appearance of male baboons that had so captivated her mentor.[56] Strum was baffled at first by why her own observations were so at odds with previous research on baboons. After years of field study and rigorous analysis, she could not dismiss the fact that the guys before her had gotten it all wrong. The females were the core of baboon society: they stayed with their mothers, sisters, aunts, and grandmothers from birth to old age. Each lineage of baboon females, the matriline consisting of several generations of females, could be placed in a dominance hierarchy. The males left as adolescents and entered new troops as often as every 5 years. This had been known before Strum's field study; what she discovered was that dominant, aggressive behavior got the males *nowhere* with females. The successful males—that is, the ones who got to mate with females—*finessed* themselves into female society through friendship and amicable behavior. The unsuccessful males were the ones who threw their considerable weight around and scared both females and their young offspring. Here's the way Strum described those findings in her book, *Almost Human*:

As I recapitulated my years of male baboon studies, I grew more and more sure that social strategies, not aggression, were the ingredients of male success. One type of social strategy was useful in competition, as between males for sexually receptive females; the other was useful in defense, as when a male used an infant or female as a buffer. Social strategies had to be engineered and learned, and that was why the long-term males [who had emigrated into the troop several years earlier] were the most successful. Newcomers had few options because they lacked both social ties and experience. Their aggression—one of the few options they *did* have—made them feared, and thus dominant, but neither dominance nor aggression gave them access to much of what they wanted. Short-term residents [those males who had been in the troop less than a year] were on the way up; they had made friends and gathered social information, but it was the long-term residents who showed how much time and experience was needed in this male world. They were the lowest-ranking, least aggressive and most successful. They had wisdom, friendships and an understanding of the subtle tactics necessary.[57]

Just like Adrienne Zihlman's portrait of early hominid lifestyle, in baboons it is female choice of sexual partners and not male coercion or aggression that is important in successful mating behavior. Females choose less, rather than more, aggressive males with whom to mate, and as field research has shown, female choice is the most common mating pattern among species in the primate order.[58]

Were our ancestors gentle savages or bloodthirsty brutes? They were social animals; they were primates; they were complex beings in their own right who were not necessarily headed in a foreordained direction. They were trying to adapt to their environment and reproduce successfully. Most primate societies and individuals exhibit cooperation as a social tool, not aggression. Success is not synonymous with brutality; it comes through finesse and friendship.[59]

We think early hominids were prey items for a great number of large, fierce, hungry creatures. Man the Hunted needed to make friends (not enemies) and supporters (not slaves), and needed to work together with females (not dominate them). In the final chapter to this book, we will give you our picture of how our long-dead ancestors might have lived.

MAN THE HUNTED 10

Throughout this book we have posed a question: Were our early ancestors *hunters* or the *hunted*? How do we finally and definitively answer such a question? There have been copious attempts to reconstruct the behavior and ecology of our earliest ancestors, but the most common theory, and the one that is widely accepted today, is the Man the Hunter hypothesis.

Cultural anthropologist Laura Klein expresses the current situation adeptly: "While anthropologists argue in scientific meetings and journals, the general public receives its information from more popular sources. . . . In many of these forums, the lesson of Man the Hunter has become gospel."[1] Klein has chosen the right word to use—*gospel*.

There's something about the pessimistic image of killer apes, naked apes, war-like apes, cannibalistic apes that seems a comfortable, albeit ugly, judgment on humanity. Maybe the infusion of Puritanical philosophy in the early history of the United States makes the general public's propensity to view our ancestors as innate killers a foregone conclusion. Certainly the Puritan fear and hatred of the wilderness that was North America in the seventeenth and eighteenth centuries translated into a profound belief that wild places, wild predators, and "wild Indians" characterized a so-called natural state. The human potential for reversion to

219

this nefarious condition needed constant prevention through the strictest of theological dicta.[2]

Nevertheless, as we have seen, the evidence to support a Man the Hunter hypothesis has been, and continues to be, very weak. Raymond Dart based his "killer-ape" hunting theory on the holes and dents in some fossil australopithecine skulls that he conjectured were the murderous actions of fellow hominids. But we now know these holes and dents were undoubtedly caused by the fangs of predators and the processes of fossilization. Sherwood Washburn's theory of Man the Hunter was based mainly on the first behavioral field research on baboons, a species with extreme contrast in size between males and females in which the males are highly visible with their impressive canines and aggressive actions toward one another. Nineteenth-century concepts of "cultural survivals" (those behaviors that no longer perform an indispensable function but still continue as residual activities) were employed to prop up the Man the Hunter archetype. Washburn espoused cultural survivals as the reason modern man hunted for sport, contending that the fundamental nature of hunting as a life or death activity no longer existed, but it had permeated so many aspects of human behavior that the pleasure and inclination to hunt were still a part of human nature.

As we pointed out earlier in this book, dancing is also a pleasurable activity found in all human cultures. We could start from the same premise as Washburn, of course; that humans were innately dancers and evolution had been spurred by dancing not hunting. We could postulate that the origin of many modern human behaviors emanated from an ancestral obsession with *dancing* just as Washburn postulated that they emanated from a focus on hunting. Is our Man the Dancer theory then a legitimate reconstruction of the past? Well, we don't really think so, but it is no more hypothetical than Man the Hunter. The reality is that we have no more evidence to prove Man the Hunter is true as an explanation for human origins than we do to prove Man the Dancer is true.

Robert Ardrey's hunting hypothesis was based more on a pessimistic view of modern humans and Christian paradigms of "original sin" than on fossil evidence. The current view of Man the Hunter, provided mainly by a few chimpanzee researchers, is based on hypothesized analogies between one group of chimpanzees (existing under conditions that are artificial where foraging is concerned) and early humans. This currently fashionable view is based on many assumptions, both about chimpanzee behavior (see the discussion in Chapter 9) and about human fossils that we believe are unsubstantiated.[3]

Now, back to how to answer the question of *hunters* or *hunted?* What kinds of evidence should be used in attempts to reconstruct the behavior of our earliest ancestors? We consider the most important and legitimate body of evidence to consist of the fossil remains themselves. Let's be fair: In a court of law a criminal prosecutor would hardly get away with minimizing or totally ignoring *tangible* evidence in favor of maximizing tenuous analogies or psycho-religious hypotheses. Should we not give the same benefit of tangible evidence to our ancestors who have been accused, in some cases, of being not one degree better than sociopathic killers? (And, needless to say, if we evolved from sociopaths, why do we forge any complaints about historical or modern examples, such as Caligula, Ivan the Terrible, Hitler, or Pol Pot? By this rationale aren't they just doing what comes naturally?)

True evidence includes careful examination and understanding of the actual skeletal remains of the creatures. However, it also includes other fossil evidence (such as tools or footprints) left by our earliest relatives, as well as fossil materials that give us clues about the environment in which they lived (other animals, plants, or water sources). These fossils provide the most important data for an accurate reconstruction. Interestingly, Man the Hunter theories fall short (if they are used at all) in the critical examination of the fossil evidence. Even Craig Stanford, a primatologist who is one of the strongest proponents that hunting done by chimps sheds light on our human origins, noted this lack of fossil evidence in such evolutionary theories: "models of hominid evolution are, appearances notwithstanding, virtually fossil-free."[4]

Besides fossils, any other types of secondary evidence used in reconstructions are less reliable but, nonetheless, offer insights. We would rank these in the following order as far as applicability to reconstructing early hominid lifestyles:

1. The behavior of non-human primates living under similar ecological conditions (wet forest, savanna, or edge environments, as the case may be) to those of our earliest ancestors. It's best to keep timing in mind with this approach. Forests change and so do climates . . . and

so do species, as well. Hominids likely began as edge species but moved out onto the savanna about 2 million years ago.

2. The behavior of our genetically closest primate relatives, such as chimpanzees, bonobos, and gorillas. But, handle with caution! Lumping all the great apes together as one analogue when they are so diverse is dangerous; many species may look essentially the same skeletally but are behaviorally quite different.

3. Characteristics shared by certain (or all) modern humans that might also be similar to our earliest ancestors. Watch out for a common trap, though: so-called primitive peoples who are living today are just as advanced and evolved within their own culture and environment as any cell phone–using city dweller.

Our least confident recommendation is:

4. The behavior of other animal species that might be living under similar conditions or share some aspects of the lifestyle of early humans, such as carnivore species or prey species. With this one it's best to remember that a dog is still a carnivore, even if it eats some grass. If early hominids had a few vertebrates in their diet, their occasional meat-eating did not make them carnivores.

In using any of these types of secondary evidence, if we are not extremely careful (because in many cases similar looking behaviors are *not* the same), we can end up comparing apples with oranges, lions with hominids, or even strangler figs with purse snatchers! (Yes, the analogy of invasive rain-forest fig trees to robbers *has* been made.) Obviously, words with loaded meaning for humans—war, rape, and genocide, to name a few—must be used with extreme caution when referring to the activities of non-human species. In this regard it doesn't hurt to repeat what Jonathan Marks of Yale University warned against: "a science of metaphorical, not of biological, connections."[5]

We cannot, therefore, necessarily impute correlation between human ancestors and data based on extant carnivores, modern human foragers, or great apes. For example, even the *concept* of hunting in chimps and humans is quite different.[6] Present-day human hunters purposely search for animal prey, but chimpanzees do not. As described by Craig Stanford, "Instead, they forage for plant foods and eat prey animals opportunistically in the course of looking for fruits and leaves."[7] Furthermore, reconstructions must always be compatible with the actual fossil data—the fossils are *real* but the models we construct are *hypothetical* and must constantly be tested and reconfirmed. Lastly, when attempting to construct models of our early ancestors' behavior, it is necessary to be precise about timing. If we say our earliest human ancestors (those who lived nearly 7 million years ago) behaved in a certain way, we cannot use fossil evidence from 2 million years ago, nor can we confuse those creatures from 2 million years ago with those who existed 500,000 years ago. A case in point about timing: Could hunting have occurred without stone tools? The first evidence of stone tools comes from around 2.3 million years ago.[8] The earliest human fossils, however, date from almost 7 million years ago, some 4 million years before the first recognizable tools.

In seeking to understand why Man the Hunter was so captivating and easily adopted as *the* paradigm for hominid evolution, it's helpful to remember that the first hominid fossils to be found in the nineteenth century were European specimens well under 100,000 years in age, and most of the artifacts found with them were finely crafted spear points or tools used for slaughtering animals. The Paleolithic cave paintings in Europe also depicted a metaphysical connection between humans and hunting. Actually, anthropology was introduced first to the very *latest* twigs on the messy bush of human evolution, and those latest forms were hunters.

Fossil evidence speaks louder than any number of reconstructions based on pure speculation. When we look at the fossil evidence, hunting appears to have come quite late to our human family. Interpretations of hominid behavior, therefore, should be conservative and cautious in the vein of this advice from a popular college-level physical anthropology text:

> [T]he mere presence of animal bones at archaeological sites does not prove that hominids were killing animals or even necessarily exploiting meat. Indeed, as was the case in the earlier South African sites, the hominid remains themselves may have been the meal refuse of large carnivores.[9]

Then when *was* there a transition to hunting as a dominant way of life? It definitely didn't start until after the appearance of our own genus, *Homo*, and did not even begin with the earliest members of our genus. *Homo erectus* has been given credit in the past for existing as a large animal hunter, and dates as far back as 1.75 million years ago have been hypothesized for such a lifestyle. But if you take a conservative approach to this subject—looking only at facts and fossils and not imaginative speculations—the first indications of hunting are amazingly recent. The first unequivocal evidence of *large scale, systematic* hunting, according to the *Cambridge Encyclopedia of Human Evolution*, is available from paleoarchaeological sites possibly only 60,000–80,000 years old.[10] Hominid fossils dated at nearly 7 million years old predate the first factual evidence of systematic human hunting by more than 6.9 million years.

No hard archaeological evidence; in other words, no *fossil* evidence of tools for hunting exist that is earlier in time than a finely shaped wooden spear over 6 feet long excavated at Schöningen, Germany, dated at approximately 400,000 years of age. The efficacy of this spear (and others like it), however, has been called into question. John Shea, an archaeologist at Stony Brook University, is an expert on the evolution of projectile weapons. "Picture yourself with an oversized toothpick trying to subdue an enraged wild bull," he says. "These weapons may have been used for hunting—it's hard to think of other uses for something like the Schöningen javelins—but they weren't very effective." The suggestion that the javelins were used as thrusting spears and, therefore, were not thrown at all, has been proffered by Steven Churchill of Duke University. Investigation seems to lean in the direction that large-scale, systematic hunting was not carried out with these wooden points.[11]

Just as this spear alone does not indicate the presence of large-scale, systematic hunting, neither do the famous Torralba and Ambrona sites in Spain, dated at 500,000 years ago, contain huge numbers of large-mammal bones. They were thought to represent unquestionable evidence of mega-fauna, such as the straight-tusked woodland elephant, killed by Pleistocene hunters. Now these two sites are being reconsidered in light of better archaeological analysis. Elephant bones at these sites could just as likely represent natural deaths or carnivore kills as they could remains of human hunting.[12]

It is the consensus of archaeologists that an emphasis on hunting probably did not start earlier than 400,000 years ago. No hominids were

A finely shaped, 400,000-year-old wooden spear from a fossil site in Germany may represent the earliest evidence of human hunting; however, its efficacy as a weapon has been questioned. (C. Rudloff, redrawn from Tattersall and Schwartz 2000)

large-scale hunters before they had the use of fire (because of their dentition and alimentary tract; points we will elucidate below), although
possibly insects, small vertebrates, lizards, and birds were eaten when encountered opportunistically. *Homo erectus* probably depended mainly on
vegetation rather than meat and modern hunting ability (in the manner
of contemporary foragers) did not occur until 60,000–80,000 years ago.

In the same undergraduate textbook quoted previously we find the
following admonishment: "The assumption of consistent hunting has
been challenged, especially by archaeologists who argue that the evidence
does not prove the hunting hypothesis. . . . [I]t is crucial to remember
(although not as exciting) that probably the majority of calories [came]
from gathering plant foods."[13]

SINK YOUR TEETH INTO THIS!

Whether *Homo erectus* or any other hominid before 400,000 years ago
hunted *or* scavenged may be just another moot question. Hunting would
only be an activity undertaken if you could *eat* what you killed—and to
eat meat you need to be able to masticate meat.

We will now trek down another path paved with fossils that dispute
Man the Hunter as anyone but a Johnny-come-lately. One reliable
method to reconstruct eating patterns of early hominids is to investigate
their fossil teeth. Teeth fossilize well and are represented more than any
other feature in the hominid record. Obviously, Man the Hunter models
of human evolution assume that a significant portion of our earliest ancestors' diets must have come from killing and eating meat from
relatively large mammals.

That isn't what the experts claim. Highly respected paleoanthropologist C. Owen Lovejoy, in an article called "The Origin of Man,"
characterized the possible common ancestor of chimps and humans as an
omnivorous generalist occupying a patchy environment. Lovejoy proposed
that the use of a variety of food sources can be viewed as a behavioral element serving to increase survivorship and birthrate.[14] This generalist
dietary strategy was a behavioral adaptation that might have facilitated
the development of a new ecological niche by the hominid line.

First, it appears highly unlikely that a quick switch to a narrow diet—
with an emphasis on meat-eating—would have arisen. Secondly, by

comparing the characteristics of the dental and jaw morphology of various living primates with those of fossils, we can make inferences about the diets of early hominids. Biological anthropologists Mark Teaford and Peter Ungar carried out just such a comparison in an attempt to reconstruct the early hominid diet.[15] They used such features as tooth size, tooth shape, enamel structure, dental microwear, and jaw biomechanics and found that the earliest humans had a unique combination of dental characteristics and a diet different from modern apes *or* modern humans.

Australopithecus afarensis (whom we introduced under the less formidable name, "Lucy") is characterized by jawbones that are thick, with relatively small incisors and canines in relation to her molars—molars that, by comparison with other primates, are huge, flat, and blunt and that lack the long, shearing crests necessary to mince flesh. Lucy also had larger front molars than back molars. Her dental enamel was thick and microwear on her fossil teeth is a mosaic of gorilla-like fine-wear striations (indicating leaf-eating) and baboon-like pits and microflakes (indicating fruits, seeds, and tubers in her diet). These are definitive pieces of evidence coming from fossil dentition and they all point away from meat-eating.

When scientists compare mammalian omnivores, they find that the larger they are, the more they include plant protein in their diet in lieu of animal protein. When they feed on insects it is usually on social ones that come in large "packages." (This is because it takes a high amount of energy to capture individual insects or other animal prey.) In studies of mid- to large-sized primates, such as macaques, baboons, chimpanzees, and modern human gatherers, in which the amount of time spent obtaining animal protein has been quantified, the total is very low, usually making up less than 5% of time spent feeding.[16]

Given these facts, we can hypothesize that early humans were able to exploit a wide range of dietary resources, including hard, brittle foods (fruits, nuts, seeds, and pods), and soft, weak foods (ripe fruits, young leaves and herbs, flowers and buds). They were also able to eat abrasive objects, including gritty plant parts, such as grass seeds, roots, rhizomes, and underground tubers. As stated by Teaford and Ungar, "this ability to eat both hard and soft foods, plus abrasive and nonabrasive foods, would have left early hominids particularly well suited for life in a variety of habitats, ranging from gallery forest to open savanna."[17] Dental morphology indicates that the earliest hominids would have had great *difficulty* breaking down tough pliant plant foods, such as fibrous seed coats and the veins and stems of mature leaves. Interestingly, Teaford and Ungar stress that another tough pliant food that our early ancestors would have had difficulty processing was *meat!* These authors state: "The early hominids were not dentally preadapted to eat meat—they simply did not have the sharp, reciprocally concave shearing blades necessary to retain and cut such foods."

Another piece of the puzzle adds mightily to the picture of the early human diet. Both modern chimpanzees and humans have an alimentary track that is neither specialized for eating leaves nor animal protein, but instead is more generalized, similar to the majority of primates who are omnivorous and eat a mixture of food types.[18]

Modern humans, especially in Western cultures, think of themselves as meat-eaters. For Americans and a whole spectrum of other cultures, meat defines that ephemeral status of wealth and ease for which we strive. Meat is harder to come by than plant foods. Meat is what poor people cannot afford. Meat is what "cavemen," (read "real men") bring home. Because they, themselves, were rooted in these cultural stereotypes, anthropologists egregiously misnamed the modern forager cultures as *hunters* and gatherers and initially emphasized only the contributions of male hunters. Perhaps male anthropologists saw only the male role in provisioning because it involved weaponry. Or maybe the meat-as-a-metaphor idea was so ingrained that hunting seemed to produce the only *important* food. Or maybe they, the anthropologists, simply ignored the female contributions because women were usually ignored. Nevertheless, more than two-thirds of modern-day tropical foragers' food comes from plant foods gathered by women who, in the process, also opportunistically captured small mammals and reptiles. The meat portion brought in through dedicated hunting by men, constituting less than one-third of the diet, simply serves to supplement foraged nutritional intake. Yet, meat can have significance far beyond its mathematical contribution.

Richard Lee, chronicler of the !Kung[19] Bushmen culture in the Kalahari Desert of Botswana, researched the diets of modern-day foragers. Lee captured the mystique of meat-eating in his "Eating Christmas in the Kalahari" narrative when he quotes his Bushman friend saying, "we love meat. And even more than that, we love fat. When we hunt we are always searching for the fat ones, the ones dripping with layers of white fat: fat that turns into a clear, thick oil in the cooking pot, fat that slides down your gullet, fills your stomach and gives you a roaring diarrhea."[20]

Some researchers reject any nutritional basis to the human appetite for meat and argue that people simply like the taste. But, as has been pointed out by biologists, protein has no taste.[21] Ahh, but *fat* does! Think about the emphasis and desirability placed (until recent health concerns) on fat-streaked, "marbled" beefsteak. Fatty fishes, such as tuna and salmon, are also more alluring and meat-like than other fish. The question has been posed: Is a taste for fat an evolutionary adaptation in humans? Does it just *satisfy* (that is, "fill your stomach," as Richard Lee's Bushman informant said) more than other types of food?

After literally millions of years of human evolution in the category of food acquisition through foraging, with meat as a scarce supplement, the advent of agriculture only 10,000–15,000 years ago might have made meat a bit more accessible—at least for the higher strata in sedentary societies. *Modern* dietary concerns in industrial societies revolve around the amounts of both fat and red meat that are consumed by the average person. By the latter portion of the twentieth century there was a full-blown red alert from the medical community warning that meat should be ingested in limited quantities. "Diseases of affluence" caused by high-protein, high-fat diets include raised cholesterol levels, high blood pressure, heart disease, stroke, breast cancer, colon cancer, and diabetes—all correlated to a diet exorbitantly rich in red meat. With colon cancer, in particular, startling data are available: Daily red-meat eaters are 2 and one-half times more likely to develop this cancer as are people adhering to a mostly vegetarian diet.[22] Colin Campbell of Cornell University, who was involved in a landmark study of Chinese rural villagers (eating a traditional diet low in meat) and their urban compatriots (eating more meat), told the *New York Times*: "We're basically a vegetarian species and should be eating a wide variety of plant foods and minimizing our intake of animal foods."[23] Campbell's Chinese study even found that individuals following a low-fat, low-meat diet suffered less from anemia and osteoporosis (conditions commonly associated with food *low* in animal protein) than did individuals higher on the meat-consuming ladder.

Some modern, relatively recent inhabitants of northern latitudes—the Inuit of North America and Greenland—live in a climate where being a vegetarian isn't an option. The mostly meat content of the Inuit diet (which signifies a copious iron intake) may explain the elevated incidence of enlarged and cirrhotic livers found in many Inuit of early middleage. Another explanation for enlarged and malfunctioning livers in some Inuit groups may be related to monumental vitamin A amounts found in the traditional meat diet.[25]

Tens of thousands of years ago, the Neanderthal meat diet might have played a part in their demise. "Neanderthals were excellent hunters," Dr. Paul Pettitt of the University of Oxford, England, told reporters recently as he explained the newest information from his research site in Croatia. Fossil remains at that site indicate that hunting was, in fact, pretty much all Neanderthals did to acquire food in the extreme cold of the last glacial period. Pettit speculates whether their emphasis on meat, to the exclusion of most plant food, was one cause of their extinction. His new research questions what the results might have been of a diet composed of 90% meat. The more well-rounded and vegetative diets of anatomically modern humans may have allowed us to survive while certain groups of Neanderthals, in Europe vanished.[26] (There is always a danger of generalizing about the Neanderthals, though. They occupied a vast range of environments and habitats. Earlier studies in the Middle East found remains of berries, nuts, and other plants at Neanderthal sites.)

Lastly, let us mention the obvious—no hominids hunted on a large scale before the advent of controlled fire.[27] Again, we just do not have the dentition or the digestive tract of a carnivore; our anatomy and physiology did not particularly suit us for digesting meat until the mastery of cooking solved the problem. Our intestinal tract is short and pre-digestion by fire had to precede any major meat-eating (although that does not obviate the fact that we still require certain nutrients not obtainable from a meat diet).[28] Evidence for mastery and use of fire in one of the Zhoukoudian cave sites in China was based on evidence of burnt bones and stones, thick ash beds, and thin lenses of ash, charcoal, and charred bones that are representative of fossil hearths, but the conclusion that Zhoukoudian *Homo erectus* actually inhabited the cave or had hearths is very controversial and has been challenged repeatedly. Be that as it may, while the Chinese cave "hearth" is dated at around 400,000 years before the present, late-breaking news published in the April 2004 issue of *Science* reports on a fossil hearth unearthed in Israel that can be dated back to 790,000 years ago.[29]

No matter the point in time when human ancestors controlled fire, it might be wise to remind ourselves that mastery of fire does not equate with mastery over predation. Whether fire was mastered and meat could have been cooked at 790,000 years ago or 400,000 years ago, it doesn't change the fact that the hominids around the Zhoukoudian cave sites in China were the main course of many hyena meals.

PAINTING THE FAMILY PORTRAIT

By far the best known of early australopithecine species is *Australopithecus afarensis,* with many fossil remains dating from between 3.6 and 2.9 million years ago and possibly as far back as 5 million or more years ago. Collections from Hadar, Ethiopia, alone have yielded 250 specimens, representing at least 35 individuals, and there are a number of other East African digs that contain remains of this species. Specimens include the famous Lucy (dated at 3.2 million years old), which is the most complete adult skeleton from this time period and fossil footprints from Laetoli, Tanzania, ash deposits (dated at 3.6 million years). Furthermore, most hypotheses concerning human evolution position *A. afarensis* as a pivotal species from which all other later hominids, including *Homo,* evolved.[30] Given the above facts, we see *A. afarensis* as a good species to examine when attempting to reconstruct the appearance and behavior of one of our early human ancestors.

Terrestrial bipedalism is a hallmark of the whole fossil hominid family. This mode of locomotion can be inferred from fossil specimens nearly 7 million years old. It appears long before the vast growth of open grasslands in Africa and before the expansion of human brain size and recognizable stone tool-making. Besides the fossilized bones, direct evidence of early bipedalism comes from the footprints at Laetoli where two hominids were walking together in soft ash almost 4 million years ago—prints that are remarkably like modern human footprints. However, looking at the skeletal evidence, especially from Lucy, the locomotion of these early hominids was not exactly identical to ours. In fact, *A. afarensis* seems to have been a primate equally at home in the trees or on the ground.

This is indicated by a number of factors. First, the limb proportions are different from modern humans. The arms are similar in proportion to modern humans, but the legs are relatively much shorter—more ape-like—and this implies the use of suspensory locomotion in the trees (hanging by the front limbs to eat fruit or to move from branch to branch). Other aspects of the upper limbs also retain a number of features indicating an ability to move easily in the trees. The wrist and hand bones are quite chimpanzee-like; the finger bones are slender and curved as in apes, giving *A. afarensis* grasping capabilities compatible with suspensory behaviors; the toe bones are relatively longer and more curved than in *Homo sapiens;* and the joints of the hands and feet and the overall proportions of the foot bones all reinforce evidence for climbing adaptations and arboreal activity. Nevertheless, the relative thumb length of these hominids is closer to that of modern humans than it is to chimpanzees.

The pelvis and lower limbs of Lucy and her kind are a mixture of human-like and ape-like features. These features and the shorter leg length indicate that *A. afarensis* may have used less energy while walking, whereas transition speeds from walking to running may have been lower with slower running speeds than in modern, longer-legged humans. Overall, as the human paleontologist Noel Rak summarizes: "Although clearly bipedal and highly terrestrial, Lucy evidently achieved this mode of locomotion through a solution of her own."[31]

Because of this mixture of anatomical features, anthropologists have often assumed that these early humans were in a stage of transition, intermediate in their locomotor abilities between arboreal apes and modern, fully terrestrial humans. The theory has been that in this evolving stage (on their way to modernity), early human bipedal, terrestrial locomotor abilities were not exactly like ours and were, thus, in some ways inefficient. However, we must remember, *A. afarensis* existed from 5 million years ago until around 2 and one-half million years ago, a period of over 2 and one-half million years. Modern humans have only been around for less than 200,000 years, so maybe we shouldn't be so quick to judge the efficiency of our ancestors. They must have been doing something right.

We must assume that *A. afarensis* was a total package and was quite good at what he or she did. A propensity to question the efficiency of primate locomotion is not new to anthropology. It was also once thought that the diminutive New World monkeys—the marmosets and tamarins—were restricted in their ability to move on small branches because they have claws instead of the standard primate nails on their hands and feet. However, it has subsequently been proven that claws do not restrict a small monkey's locomotion on thin branches; indeed their claws also enable them to utilize large trunks, much like squirrels do. Claws allow them to be more versatile and they can use a wider range of arboreal habitats than most other New World monkeys. It appears that the combination of skeletal characteristics found in *A. afarensis* enabled this species to be versatile in a similar way. They were able to use the ground and the trees equally and successfully for a very long time. We believe these early humans were well adapted to their environment and not one bit inhibited by switching back and forth from bipedalism on the ground to some kind of suspensory locomotion in the trees.

As mentioned earlier, debating the questions of the ages—"what factors or selective forces led to bipedalism?" and "why did the earliest humans walk upright instead of being satisfied with the typical primate quadrupedal locomotion?"—is just hashing over moot points. Rather than seeking the factor or factors that *caused* early human ancestors to take the two-legged, upright journey down the path of life, let's shave off all the bombastic conjectures with Occam's razor and look at the simplest and most logical explanation for bipedality. As explained in Chapter 8, it was a preadaptation that already existed, and it was efficient in a new habitat; the successes or added advantages were simply a by-product.

Besides bipedalism and limb use, we also have a pretty good idea of what our earliest ancestors were like as far as general size, height, weight, and brain capacity.

From various *A. afarensis* specimens and by examining the almost-complete skeleton of Lucy, it seems there was a considerable size difference between males and females. Although the canines were quite small and not at all dagger-like, they were larger and longer in the males than in the females. The range of body size for *A. afarensis* individuals is estimated to be 60–100 pounds. The height of the adults ranged from 2 feet 11 inches to 4 feet 11 inches. Lucy stood around 3 and one-half feet tall and weighed around 60 pounds (she was definitely on the small side). If these weights are accurate, we can extrapolate that female *A. afarensis* were the size of male baboons and males were the size of female chimpanzees.

A reconstruction of how Lucy might have looked. (C. Rudloff, redrawn from Johanson and Shreeve 1989)

The cranial capacity of these hominids was around 400–500 cubic centimeters—about the size of a modern chimpanzee but twice as large as Miocene epoch fossil apes 20 million years earlier. On average, australopithecines and modern chimpanzees have brains that are two to three times larger than similar-sized mammals, whereas in modern humans, brain size is six to seven times larger.

Looking at brain size relative to body size (referred to by anthropologists as the "encephalization quotient" or EQ), the brain of *A. afarensis* was slightly larger in relation to its body than that of modern chimpanzees (EQ = 2.4 for *A. afarensis* versus 2.0 for chimps). Thus, our ancestors were mid- to relatively large-sized primates with brains that were slightly larger than any non-human primate, though only a fraction bigger than modern chimpanzees. The EQ rose as our ancestors evolved through millions of years, but with the appearance of our own genus, *Homo*, there is also a change in the *rate* of change. Noel Boaz, Director of the International Institute for Human Evolutionary Research, has noted, "*Homo* clearly has a larger brain than earlier hominids, and its size continues to change at a rapid rate. . . . We know of no other anatomical character in any part of the body that is changing so rapidly in human evolution."[32] Boaz's figures for brain-size change are pretty phenomenal: 20 cc of brain tissue (approximately 156 million neurons) were being added every 100,000 years.

There are many speculations about how Lucy really looked. If we saw her walking down the street, would we recognize her as a human or think she was an ape? Or is she in between—a kind of hairy, but petite, missing link? Donald Johanson, the discoverer of Lucy, added some details to the portrait of a living Lucy. He pictured her and her kin as small but extremely powerful—their bones were robust for their size, and they were probably heavily muscled. Their arms were longer in proportion to their legs and trunk than modern humans. Their hands were like ours but their fingers were curled more when in a relaxed position. Heads were more ape-like than human-like with thrusting jaws and no chin.[33]

HABITAT FOR HUMANITY

We've painted a portrait of the actor (or actress, if we are talking about Lucy). Now let's paint the scenery around our star. Although many theories on the evolution of our earliest ancestors stress the importance of arid, savanna environments, these do not seem to be the primary habitats of early humans, according to the fossil record, until after 2 million years ago. The African climate was becoming more arid as time passed between 12 and 5 million years ago, and equatorial forests were undoubtedly shrinking. However, the process that led to this climatic phenomenon also greatly enlarged areas of *transitional* zones between forest and adjacent savanna. Closed woodland forests were still widespread in East Africa 3.5 million years ago, whereas the proportion of dry shrub and grassland habitats begins to increase around 1.8 million years ago.[34]

It is in these transitional zones that the behavioral and anatomical changes were initiated in early hominid evolution. The flora and fauna remains that are found in association with fossil hominids of this time period indicate they lived in a mixed, mosaic environment—mosaic in the sense that it was ecologically diverse and subject to seasonal and yearly changes in vegetation. These environments were wetter than those in which later fossil humans are found, and most fossil sites of this early time period contained some type of water source, such as rivers and lakes. For example, at Hadar in Ethiopia, the mammalian fauna remains suggest that a lake existed, surrounded by marshy environments fed by rivers flowing off the Ethiopian escarpment. A mosaic of habitats existed there that included closed and open woodland, bushland, and grassland. Thus, the earliest hominids appear to be associated with variegated fringe environments or edges between forest and grassland. These habitats usually contain animal and plant species of both the forest and the grassland, as well as species unique to the borders between the two. The species adapted to these transitional habitats are often referred to as *edge* species. They also sometimes are called weed species because of their ability to spread quickly and colonize new and unstable habitats. During these earliest times, it appears that hominids began to take advantage of the growing fringe environments, lessening competition with their sibling ape species that were better adapted to exploit the dense forest, and thus partitioning the niche occupied by the parent species of both apes and hominids into two narrower and less-overlapping adaptive zones.[35]

Our early ancestors were able to exploit a great variety of food resources but were mainly fruit-eaters, probably supplementing this diet with some young leaves and other plant parts, social insects like termites, and a small amount of opportunistically captured small vertebrate prey—lizards or small snakes and mammals. They did well as they inhabited their fringe environments with a mosaic of habitat types, including relatively closed forest and open grassland, and also the intermediate habitats between these extremes.

Several other species of primates are intrinsically adapted to edge habitats and are, therefore, also able to take advantage of changing environments. African vervet monkeys and some Asian macaques and langurs are non-human primate examples. These, not coincidentally, are the most common and numerous of all living primates other than humans. Vervets are the most frequently seen monkeys in Africa—each little woodland oasis may have a vervet troop. The macaque genus, on the other hand, has the widest geographical distribution of any non-human primate in Asia. Many macaque species in Asia are endangered, but the ones that have healthy populations are the edge-adapted ones. Long-tailed macaques are often crop raiders near human settlements, while rhesus macaques are found at temples and near villages in India. And the most terrestrial of the leaf-eating monkeys—the Hanuman langur, the sacred monkey of India—is also an edge species that prospers in contact with humans.[36]

We are committed to the belief that certain ecological niches breed certain behavioral repertoires. Many argue that the closer the DNA comparison, the more similar the behaviors between two related species. If you believe this, then chimps and bonobos, who are genetically closest to humans, are obviously the best prototype for early human ancestors. However, if you believe, as we do, that you need to *live a certain way* because of *where* you live, then chimps and bonobos must be thrown out as prototypes, and edge species (even though they may not be as fascinating as the chimps) are definitely the best model for early humans.

We humans never were tropical-forest beings as are our chimp and bonobo cousins. We were opportunists living on the edge of the forests where our bipedalism was an asset. Back in the 1960s this was accepted as axiomatic. It was only after chimpanzees became so well known, so newsworthy, so "sexy" that they grabbed the public's imagination, that scientists forgot the importance of ecology in the equation.

Here is what Robin Fox, a theorist on human origins, declared nearly 40 years ago:

> But the problem of taking the great apes as models lies in the fact of their forest ecologies. Most modern students of primate evolution agree that we should pay close attention to ecology in order to understand the selection pressures at work on the evolving primate lines. This has been shown to be crucial in understanding . . . evolution.[37]

A common but not at all naïve question, "what makes us *humans* and not chimpanzees, bonobos, or gorillas?" is extremely hard to answer. Even if one were to learn everything about the hominid–ape common ancestor, many of the most crucial questions about distinctively hominid evolution would remain unanswered.[38] Why don't we think chimpanzees are the best model species for early human evolution? Even though there is a fairly impressive record of human fossils during these early time periods, no fossil chimpanzees are found at these early sites. In fact, there is a curious absence of fossil apes from about 7 million years ago to 2 million years ago. It seems likely, therefore, that chimpanzee ancestors did not inhabit these fringe environments and were likely restricted to wetter, more closed, forest ecosystems—areas where fossils are less likely to be preserved. Chimpanzees probably moved into more open, mosaic habitats relatively recently, after humans had moved into more arid environments. Furthermore, modern chimpanzees do not live in habitats in which modern humans lived in the past or are found today. The current geographic range of chimpanzees (we refer here to the species' historical range across Central Africa, not the tiny percentage of undisturbed land left in the twenty-first century after decades of human exploitation) is quite restricted, much more restricted than even that of early humans before leaving Africa.

In our opinion the best primate models to use as a basis for extrapolation about behavioral characteristics of our earliest ancestors are modern primate species living in similar edge habitats. There are a number of such species. Ringtailed lemurs in Madagascar, vervet monkeys and baboons in Africa, rhesus and long-tailed macaques in Asia are all edge species that spend a good proportion of time both in the trees and on the ground. They are all omnivores and are very versatile in their locomotion, though all are quadrupeds.

The two macaques are extremely good colonizers of edge habitats. The macaque genus spread throughout Asia before humans reached that continent. By the time *Homo erectus* arrived in Asia 1.8 million years ago, hominids were no longer edge species (our more recent human ancestors were exploiting open habitats) so hominids did not displace the macaques. True "weed" species, the macaques are excellent models for reconstructing how our early ancestors may have lived.

Macaques Я Us?

Why macaques? Two reasons: the ecological similarities and the social similarities. One of the best models we can think of is the long-tailed macaque
of Asia, *Macaca fascicularis* (also known as the crab-eating macaque in
honor of one of its favorite meals). Long-tailed macaques are a smallish
omnivorous edge species. The most widespread of any Southeast Asia
monkeys, they occur from Burma through Malaysia and Thailand to
Vietnam, while offshore populations are found on Java, Borneo, and numerous smaller islands as far east as the Philippines and Timor.
Throughout this area, broadleaf evergreen and other forest types are inter-
spersed with secondary and disturbed habitats, and it is in the latter that
long-tailed macaques preferentially occur. Virtually all of the studies of this
species make note that they are most commonly found in secondary-forest
habitats, preferably near water. Researchers emphasize that these monkeys
are extremely adaptable and able to flourish in highly disturbed land. The
success of the long-tailed macaque throughout its extensive Asian distribution is widely credited to its being an "adaptable opportunist."[39] One of
the authors (RWS) studied these primates on the island of Mauritius in the
southwest Indian Ocean, about 500 miles to the east of Madagascar.
Although the original transport of long-tailed macaques from Asia to
Mauritius is totally undocumented, it is likely they were on board the ships
when the Portuguese "discovered" the island, and the monkeys were inadvertently or purposely introduced to the primate-deficient ecosystem.
Cited from the first studies as an assertive colonizer of new habitat,[40] the
small number of original immigrants have increased to 40,000 animals—
successfully living up to their reputation as noteworthy squatters.

These are lithe, slender, slight, graceful monkeys. At an average
weight of 9 pounds for females and 13 pounds for males, they are the
featherweights of the macaque clan. White muttonchop whiskers (quite
Victorian) are found on both males and females. Aptly named, their tails
are *really* long, reaching all the way to the ground in a graceful arc. As
with all species in the macaque genus, they have a crest of hair on the
crown of their heads that is darker than the rest of their brownish-gray
fur. Long-tailed macaques are known for their high-volume calls, roars,
screeches, and shrieks, plus subtle facial gestures conveying information

The ecology and social organization of the long-tailed macaque might offer excellent models of how our early ancestors lived. (R. W. Sussman)

about environmental phenomena such as dangerous predators and food sources.[41] The long-tailed macaque society is organized around multi-generational families of related females. Each family, or matriline, has its own place in the social hierarchy of the troop, from the most dominant, high-ranking female and her daughters and granddaughters, down to the most subordinate. Females inherit the rank of their mothers so the troop organization remains relatively stable throughout time. These females are highly, constantly social and extremely interested in each other. Imagine, if you will, a small town peopled by women living with their mothers and daughters and young sons. They own their homes and the land around the little town. Each and every one of the households is intimately aware of the slightest emotion and mood of their own families and their neighbors. That's what female macaque society is like.

What is going on with adult males while the female macaques are so immersed in their social lives? There are always one or two dominant males visible within the group, as well as some lower-ranking adult males, plus the adolescent and subadult sons of the females. However, at sexual maturity sons will leave the troop they were born into and seek an entirely new group of females who hold a different home range (nature's built-in incest taboo). Female offspring, of course, will stay with their mothers, grandmothers, aunts, and sisters their whole lives, mating with unrelated males who join their troop.

In all primate species, males, females, or both sexes migrate between groups, thus maintaining genetic diversity within the population. Which sex migrates has a great deal to do with other aspects of the social organization. For example, if males migrate, females usually interact with their mothers and sisters, and matrilines ascend in importance. Males in this kind of society will continue to migrate between groups throughout their lifetime. This situation portends a constant need for males to develop new social networks; often the formation of "friendships" with females in a new group is the only sure entry.[42] Species in which females migrate and males remain in their natal groups display dissimilar social organization; males form close ties with one another and female matrilines do not develop. (Nonetheless, in recent studies of primates in which females do migrate—hamadryas baboons, bonobos, and chimpanzees—females have been found to develop long-term relationships with *unrelated* females. This likely occurs because adult females do not continue to migrate after giving birth to their first infant.)

In most primates adapted to edge environments it is the males who migrate. However, in the closest living relatives of humans, the gorillas, chimpanzees, and bonobos, and in the majority of current human societies, females normally change groups when they mature. This is a good example of a trait that just goes with the territory of being in a particular taxonomic group and having distant common ancestors. Because of this fact, it seems likely the case with our earliest ancestors that females, not males, migrated between groups.

The ability of edge species to exploit a wide variety of environments is accompanied, not unexpectedly, by a substantial flexibility of behavior. Long-tailed macaques appear to be primarily arboreal where suitable vegetation exists, but they come to the ground along riverbanks, seashores, and in open areas—and in some portions of their geographic range, such as Mauritius, they are highly terrestrial. They are eclectic omnivores with a distinct penchant for fruit. But the variety of habitat they exploit is reflected in the variety of their food choices—besides fruit, they gladly gobble up leaves, grasses, seeds, flowers, buds, shoots, insects, tree gum, sap, and bark.

Human-disturbed habitat is prime real estate for long-tailed macaques. Living close to human settlements is never avoided; rather, unfortunately, they tend to live in proximity to humans throughout their range, which results in crop raiding in fields of sugarcane, rice, cassava, and taro.

They live in large multi-male, multi-female groups of up to 80 individuals, although in some areas groups are much smaller than this. They show distinct flexibility in group structure; the large basic social unit tends to split up into smaller subgroups for daytime foraging activities. Subgroups sometimes are made up totally of males, but most often consist of adult males accompanying females and their young offspring. The number and size of subgroups tends to vary with the season and resource availability. The entire troop reforms each evening and returns to the same sleeping site each night, usually on the edge of a water source. Because of their unique behavior of returning to a home base each night, long-tailed macaques are referred to as a "refuging" species.

Put It All Together and What Do You Have?

Now we proceed to the task of combining the fossil evidence with the living primate model. Looking at the fossil evidence, we can say that human ancestors, living between 7 and 2.5 million years ago, were intermediate-sized primates, not smaller than male baboons or larger than female chimpanzees. Given their relative brain size, they were quite clever, at least as clever as the great apes of today. They had diverse locomotor abilities, using both terrestrial and arboreal habitats. They used suspensory postures and traveled in the trees but were bipedal when on the ground. We believe that their bipedalism was a preadaptation—walking on two feet freed the arms and hands and proved to be advantageous in a number of ways—and certainly was not a detriment.

Given their relatively small size and their petite canines, there is no reason to think that our early ancestors were any *less* vulnerable to predation than are modern monkeys in edge habitats—species that have yearly predation rates generally comparable to gazelles, antelopes, or deer living in similar environments.[43] Indeed, edge species are *highly* vulnerable to predation and because of this usually live in relatively large social groups with many adult males and adult females. Adult males often serve as sentinels and provide protection against predators.

We believe that, like long-tailed macaques, our human ancestors lived in multi-male, multi-female groups of variable size that were able to split up depending on the availability of food and re-form each evening at home-base refuges. However, certain facts, such as the exact size of the groups and subgroups, whether males or females migrated from the group when they reached sexual maturity, the internal structure of the group (whether matrilineal or formed along male kinship lines), would be impossible to determine accurately. These things can't be found in the fossil record and are quite variable even in closely related living primates.

Always of interest to anthropologists are the roles of males and females. It's remarkably sexist the way Man the Hunter vignettes adhere to male hunters as the leaders, the innovators, the toolmakers, and the tool users. Since these aspects of gender specificity may never be revealed in the fossil record, we assert that it's justifiable to construct theories based on our primate relatives. When Japanese macaques were first studied in the wild, it was the young females who started innovative behaviors, such as new ways of processing food. Anthropologist Adrienne Zihlman has commented that chimpanzee tools are made mainly by females and used mainly in gathering activities (such as nut-cracking and extracting termites from mounds). And, it is also the female chimps who teach the next generation how to use these tools. Furthermore, for most primates, females are the repositories of group knowledge concerning home ranges and scarce resources. Group knowledge and traditions are passed on from mother to offspring, and stability of the group, both in the present and over time, often is accomplished through female associations.

Do males sound almost dispensable? Well, in some ways . . . yes. A primate group with only one male and ten females can have the same reproductive output as a group with ten males and ten females. The male role in primate groups is to act as first line of defense; if he gets eaten doing his job—well, there are others to take his place. If a sexually mature female gets eaten, then she and all her potential offspring (and living dependent infants) are lost. Very logical to emphasize the female, when you consider it's the species that must survive and not the individual.

In sum the best archetype of early humans may be a multi-male, multi-female group-living, mid-sized, omnivorous, quite vulnerable creature who lived in an edge habitat near a large water source. They may well have been a refuging species returning to the same well-protected home base or sleeping site each night. This creature was adept at using both the trees and the ground, and when it did come to the ground, it had upright posture and was bipedal. It depended mainly on fruit, including some soft fruits and some that were quite brittle or hard, but also ate herbs, grasses, and seeds, and gritty foods such as roots, rhizomes, and tubers. A very small proportion of its diet was made up of animal protein; mainly social insects (ants and termites) and, occasionally, small vertebrates captured opportunistically. These early humans did not regularly hunt meat and could neither process it dentally nor in their digestive tracts.

Like all other primates, and especially ground-living and edge species, these early humans were very vulnerable to predators. The South African cave with its australopithecine skull perforated by leopard fangs demonstrate this. The Taung child with the evidence of eagle talons shows this. The *Homo erectus* remains of hyena meals at the Zhoukoudian site in China reveal this. The Dmanisi skulls found in the Republic of Georgia provide further evidence. Based on the predation rates of other primate species, who knows how many other fossil caches may represent the indigestible refuse of a ferocious animal's taste for hominid flesh?

Man the Hunted

Given that the earliest hominid ancestors were medium-sized primates who did not have any inherent weapons to fight off the many predators that lived at that time—and given that they lived in edge environments that incorporate open areas and wooded forests near rivers—then, like other primates, they were vulnerable to predation. Because of this we hypothesize that rates of predation were just as high in our early ancestors as they are in modern species of primates. Granted these facts, we feel that our origins are those of a *hunted* species and much modern human behavior reflects this.

Protection from predation is one of the most important aspects of group-living, and we believe this was true of our earliest ancestors. Long-tailed macaque groups are organized in a way that allows efficient exploitation of a highly variable and changing environment and also protects its members from predators. If the human species started out as Man the Hunted, what were the strategies for protecting ourselves from predators when we were such generally assailable animals?

Strategy #1: Live in relatively large groups of 25–75 individuals. Safety in numbers; one of the main reasons all diurnal primates live in groups is predator protection. More eyes and ears alert to the presence of predators is the first line of defense.

Strategy #2: Have very versatile locomotion. Use the trees *and* the ground. The advantage of agility in the use of diverse habitats is safety both in trees and dense underbrush. Add the advantage of upright posture that allows scanning, carrying, and the appearance of increased body size.

Strategy #3: Demonstrate flexible social organization. Gather scarce resources in small groups but reunite as a larger group when predation requires strength in numbers. Small groups can quickly disperse and hide in dense vegetation; large groups can mob and intimidate predators.

Strategy #4: Definitely have more than one male in the social group. This provides more males both when traveling through open areas and when the group settles in at evening or midday, when social interactions also take place. Even when large groups break into subgroups, always keep females and young in the company of one or more large males.

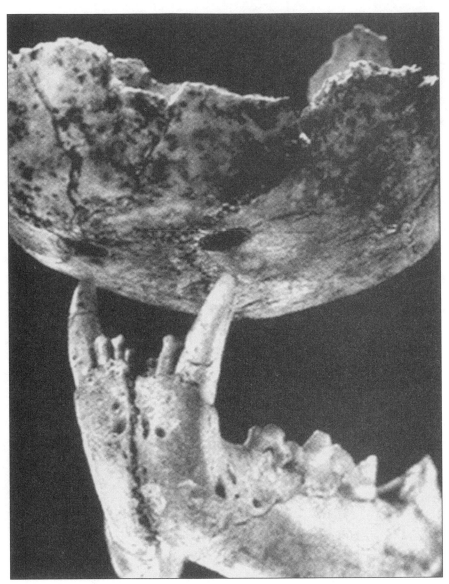

Evidence indicates that early hominids were prey species to many predators. Here paleo-detectives show how the canine teeth of a fossil leopard fit perfectly into paired holes in an australopithecine skull found in the same deposit. (Noel T. Boaz)

Strategy #5: Use males as sentinels. Sexually dimorphic males are larger than females. Upright posture adds to the appearance of large size and also allows for better vigilance; also waving arms, brandishing sticks, and throwing stones are good ideas. Males should mob or attack predators since they are the more expendable sex.

Strategy #6: Carefully select sleeping sites: As a refuging species, keep the whole group together at night and in a very safe area; at daytime resting sites, stay in very dense vegetation; move to and from sleeping sites through open areas, keep in large groups. Males stay on high alert.

Strategy #7: Be smart and employ one-upmanship: Intelligence endows the ability to monitor the environment, communicate with other group members, stay one step ahead of the predator, and implement anti-predator defenses in the first stages of predation.

Those were the survival rules and surely our earliest ancestors must have followed them. We can state that with total authority—if they hadn't exhibited the behavior of a hunted species, we wouldn't be here debating our origins.

Many circumstances have been proposed as a catalyst for the evolution of humankind: competition for resources, intellectual capacity, male–male conflicts, and hunting. We suggest that predation pressure was one of the major catalysts.

What have we always contended with? What do we fear? What still evokes the most gut-level panic and revulsion? The answer to all three questions is the hunger of predators for human prey. Ecologically and psychologically we were, until very recently, prey meat—meals for large, frightening animals. It was a fact of life for our ancestors, and it is a fact of life for many humans today. It is only within our artificially sanitized Western world that humans can think of themselves as the macho, meat-eating, kill-'em-dead Top Predator. And Western culture is less than a few moments of the 7-million-year span peculiar to the human species. If we can make the break with embedded stereotypes and view early humans more as potential prey than as hunters, we might break through and actually gain a better understanding of our ancestors and ourselves.

The Oldest Story

It is the dawn of time—human time, that is. A group of hominids sees the light begin to fill the sky. The daily routine of life begins again. Hunger is the first thought for all members of the group. Descending from sleeping trees—their refuging site overlooking a river—they set off to gather food from trees, bushes, and off the ground. Night is over; the wild cats should be resting in the heat of the day. If one is careful and cautious, the day can be a pleasant time of filling empty stomachs and socializing. One of the first activities of the day is a bout of grooming among the adults; each one grooms another while infants and young play in proximity to watchful and tolerant grown-ups.

As they set off to forage, some of the group will keep wary eyes on the sky above; males will rise to their tallest stature and scan the open woodland for predators. But, the actions are more routine than fearful. The large group breaks up into smaller groups to look for a variety of resources in the mosaic habitat. Some of the young males take off on their own, but no females or young leave the company of at least one or two adult males. When a large saber-toothed cat is seen from a distance as the hominids gather around a tree laden with fruit, there is little anxiety aroused. The span of grassy plain between them and the predator seems far too great to become seriously concerned.

Vigilance will be upgraded when the small group leaves the fruiting trees to find water. All are aware of the dangers at water holes when thirst forces them to stop foraging and drink. Healthy caution keeps the adults alert. When one of them sees the barely visible blink of hooded crocodile eyes waiting patiently in the water for a meal, they all back up and move to a different location along the edge of the pond.

Infants are held close whenever the group moves even a short distance; none are left on the ground for more than a moment, since small jackal-like predators might be hanging around waiting for the chance to snatch them. The babies are held with one arm and balanced on the hip of the females. It is a comfortable way for the infants to reach for their mother's breast whenever they are hungry. As they drink at the water hole, one of the males spies a jackal. He gives a warning call and a number of adult males pick up sticks and wave their arms, jumping up and down repeatedly. The wild dog is frightened away by the size and evident ferocity of the male primates.

After their thirst is quenched, they move away from the water hole and settle for a while to rest. The small group stays close together exchanging constant vocalizations that communicate what they see in the distance. A child gives a sudden alarm call as the shadow of a large bird falls upon him. The adults quickly assure themselves that the shadow is not that of an eagle but just a harmless stork. The sun is warm and high in the sky. Comforting body contact is acknowledged with sounds of pleasure—when one is surrounded by other group members, the feelings are those of total safety and relaxation. Being alone is not an experience any of the juvenile individuals have, in fact, ever known. Some adults have experienced it—at sexual maturity young adults may migrate either alone or with a partner—and this is the most dangerous time of their lives. Many perish from predators or, because they do not know the resources in a new area, perish before being admitted into a new social group.

After a time, the small group begins their foraging again. The oldest female knows the area well. She takes the lead and they reach a grove of trees that contains sweet fruit. They eat standing and each one without the burden of an infant gathers some of the fruit to transport back to the sleeping refuge. The old female keeps an eye on a herd of gazelles grazing at a short distance. She often is the one who measures the group's safety by her keen observations of other prey animals. Because of her caution and care, she has been successful in raising young. Several adults in the group are her offspring and look to her for guidance. She is the one who immediately picks up on a change in the gazelle behavior. Suddenly the peaceful grazing has stopped and the gazelles are shifting and turning, as if they were a stream of water running through the cracks and crevices of dry soil after a hard rain. She remembers seeing this weaving pattern before, and quickly marshals the group to find the reason for the gazelles' disturbance.

The males of the group are taller and stronger so they ease forward just a bit; everyone else is poised for flight toward the more wooded vegetation a short distance away. Then out of nowhere the hyenas, busy testing the gazelle herd for signs of a weak individual, see the hominid group and realize that easier prey may be available. There are several dozen of the huge hyenas and they are hungry—hungry enough to be hunting in the heat of the day. The phalanx of hyenas turns toward the hominid group. At first the hominid males stand their ground and try to deflate the hyenas' determined approach with their size and the noise and chaotic jumping that had worked so well earlier with the jackal. But these predators are not to be deterred. High-pitched screams erupt from the youngsters' mouths. Alarm calls fill the air. A few of the adult males run in opposite directions, which confuses the hyenas. The old female, her offspring, and most of the group start to run toward trees. She leads them to the nearest trees, and they all quickly climb to the highest branches; she knows that this kind of predator cannot follow up the tree. A few of the hominid group are slower and their panic is palpable. One of the young ones is dropped; its mother hesitates and she and the youngster are the first victims. One of the males trying to draw off the hyenas from the hominid group is soon overtaken and ripped apart by huge jaws. Two other adolescent males also are pulled down in a maelstrom of ripping teeth. The rest of the group has been given precious seconds needed to reach the trees. They make it to the grove while the hyenas are feasting upon their fellows. Within 30 minutes the carcasses are completely consumed; little is left for the jackals or vultures from these relatively small prey.

By late afternoon the old female feels safe enough to descend from the tree. The others trust her judgment and descend also. Vocalizing softly, all move together toward the safety of their sleeping refuge and meet other members of the large group as they get closer to the site overlooking the river.

Most days are not disrupted in such a grim way and the group may not have had a direct encounter with a predator for many, many months. Long periods go by without a lethal attack, but the danger is always present—and possible—and just one infrequent encounter evinces a devastating effect on the group.

As they did in the morning, the adults socialize. This time is spent reaffirming their bonds and easing the tension and loss of those who died. The young, who soon forget the terror of the afternoon, begin to play. Slowly, normalcy returns and the group settles in for the night.

ACKNOWLEDGMENTS

We would like to acknowledge family, friends, and academic associates for their help and support while researching and writing this book. Karl Yambert of Westview Press has been a wonderful editor as he guided the trajectory of the subject matter during gestation; Ellen Garrison, editor at Perseus Books, has nurtured the book through its actual birth. Christina Rudloff's drawings are valuable assets that bring predators of the past to life.

Fond thanks to Rachel Fredrick and Alex Hart; both were inspirational from the viewpoint of their personal interest in the subject of predation. Pam Ashmore, Dennis Bohnenkamp, Barb Rain, Ian Tattersall, and Mary Willis have been excellent sounding boards for diverse topics running the gamut from adjectives to brain functions to zoology. Glenn Conroy, Charles Hildeboldt, Jonathan Losos, Jane Phillips-Conroy, Tom Pilgram, and Tab Rasmussen were instrumental in the formation of our theories concerning predation on primates. Al Bruns, as always, was ready to step in when needed and put energy and time into getting a job done well.

Donna Hart thanks Bob Sussman, and Bob likewise thanks Donna for our harmonious working relationship academically and our personal friendship through many years of mutual enthusiasm regarding primates, predation, and human evolution.

To all the magnificent extant predatory animals mentioned in this book, we acknowledge worry over their continued existence and a dedication to protecting them legally and philosophically . . . because they are what makes this world exciting, beautiful, and real.

Notes

Preface

1. Quammen 2003.

Chapter 1

1. Deurbrouck and Miller 2001, *Christian Science Monitor,* 5/9/01, p. 9.
2. Capstick 1993, publisher's comments.
3. Lévi-Strauss 1966.
4. Capstick 1993, publisher's comments.
5. McDougal 1991.
6. Seidensticker 1985.
7. McDougal 1991.
8. Jackson 1991.
9. Brain 1981, 1970.
10. Berger and Clarke 1995.
11. Gore 2002.
12. Shipman 2000.
13. Cavallo 1991.
14. See Turnbull-Kemp 1963, Altmann and Altmann 1970, Saayman 1971, Goodall 1986, and Stoltz and Saayman 1970 for descriptions of baboon defense against leopards.
15. Busse 1980.
16. Brain 1981, 1970.
17. Brain 1981; Binford 1985; Cartmill 1993.

CHAPTER 2

1. Wilford 2001, *The New York Times*, 3/22/01, p. A1.
2. Darwin 1874.
3. Wood 2002.
4. Tattersall 1999, p. 45.
5. Gore 2002.
6. Ardrey 1976, p. 8.
7. See Boesch 1994 for a discussion of the differences in hunting strategies between the chimpanzees at Gombe Stream Reserve, Tanzania, and the Tai Forest, Côte d'Ivoire.
8. Sussman 2000.
9. Dart and Craig 1959, p. 195.
10. Ardrey 1961.
11. Brain 1981.
12. Brain 1970, 1978; Cavallo 1991.
13. Brain 1981.
14. Coryndon 1964; Simons 1966.
15. Washburn and Lancaster 1968, p. 303. A decade prior to this quote, Washburn (1957) had published a paper entitled "Australopithecines: The Hunters or the Hunted," in which he wrote: "The conclusion of this examination of the kills in the Wankie Game Reserve is that the high frequency of jaws, skulls, and upper cervical vertebrae in the australopithecine deposits is not necessarily evidence for hunting, herd hunting, or human activities, but may be due to selective eating by carnivores" (p. 613).
16. All quotes from Washburn and Avis 1958, pp. 433–434.
17. Washburn and Lancaster 1968, p. 303.
18. Tylor 1871.
19. Washburn and Lancaster 1968.
20. Ardrey 1961, p. 171, for quote about Hitler, p. 325 for quote about gorillas.
21. Ardrey 1976.
22. Oliwenstein 2000, reprinted in *Physical Anthropology*, 01/02, p. 216.

CHAPTER 3

1. Burns 1996, *The New York Times*, 9/1/96, p. 1.
2. Kruuk 2002.
3. Kala 1998, *Asiaweek*, 4/24/98.
4. Baumgartel 1976.
5. Fay et al. 1995.

6. Schaller 1963.

7. Baumgartel 1976.

8. Rijksen 1978; Rijksen-Graatsma 1975.

9. Jurmain et al. 2003.

10. McGrew 1976.

11. Tutin et al. 1983.

12. Tsukahara 1993.

13. Boesch 1991, p. 228.

14. Sunquist and Sunquist 1989.

15. Population ecology theory from Bryden 1976, Kruuk 1986, Vezina 1985.

16. Schaller 1972.

17. Endler 1991.

18. Principles of predation from Bertram 1978, 1979, Janzen 1980, Bakker 1983, Roughgarden 1983, Vermeij 1982.

19. Evolutionary effects from birds of prey from Gautier-Hion et al. 1983, Terborgh 1983, Peres 1990.

20. Zuberbuhler and Jenny 2002.

21. Terborgh 1983; Sussman and Kinzey 1984; Goldizen 1987; Caine 1993.

22. Le Gros Clark 1959.

23. Conroy 1990; Bloch and Boyer 2002.

24. Eisenberg et al. 1972, Bourliere 1979, Dittus 1979, Wrangham 1979, 1980, Cheney and Wrangham 1987, and Raemakers and Chivers 1980 represent the view that the effect of predation is minimal. Tilson 1977, Harvey et al. 1978, Busse 1980, Tutin et al. 1983, Sussman and Kinzey 1984, Anderson 1986a, Caine 1993, Terborgh 1983, Moore 1984, van Schaik 1983, Terborgh and Janson 1986, and Dunbar 1988 represent the view that predation is a powerful force in shaping primate evolution.

25. Hall 1966, Cheney and Wrangham 1987, Altman 1974, Hausfater and Hrdy 1984, Chapman 1986, Stanford 1989, Srivastava 1991, Peetz et al. 1992, Hrdy et al. 1995, Nunes et al. 1998, and countless other publications have mentioned that predation is rarely observed.

26. Wrangham 1980.

27. Cowlishaw 1994 for vulnerability of baboons; Isbell 1994 for ecological patterns; Boinski and Chapman 1995 for status of research; Hill and Dunbar 1998 for rate versus risk; Treves 1999 for arboreal primates; Busse 1980 and Isbell 1994 for changes in field methodology.

28. Anderson 1986a; Cheney and Wrangham 1987; Isbell 1994; Boinski and Chapman 1995; Busse 1980.

29.   Busse 1980.

30.   Primate territories: Aldrich-Blake 1970 for forest guenons; Sussman 1974 for redfronted lemurs; Wolfheim 1983 for chacma baboons.

31.   Predator territories: Seidensticker 1991 for leopards in general; Bothma and LeRiche 1984 for Kalahari leopards; Rabinowitz 1991 for tigers; Schaller and Vasconcelos 1978 for jaguars; Fuller and Kat 1990 for African hunting dogs; Kruuk 1975 for spotted hyenas; Collar 1989 for harpy eagles; Kennedy 1977 for Philippine eagles; Brown and Amadon 1989 for crowned hawk-eagles; Wright et al. 1997 for fossa.

32.   Hart 2000; meta-analysis of predation on non-human primates based on questionnaires, published research, and eyewitness accounts.

33.   D. Jenny 1996, personal communication.

34.   Hart 2000; see Appendix I for a complete listing of predatory species and sources.

35.   Hart 2000.

36.   Terborgh 1983.

37.   Terborgh 1983, p. 197.

38.   Dunbar 1988.

39.   Young 1994; Hill and Dunbar 1998.

40.   Terborgh 1983.

41.   Dunbar 1988.

42.   Anderson 1986a, p. 24.

43.   Terborgh 1983.

44.   Goodman et al. 1993.

45.   Hill and Dunbar 1998.

46.   Martin 1972.

47.   Stanford et al. 1994.

48.   Bernstein 1996, p. 153.

49.   Hill and Dunbar 1998.

50.   Vermeij 1982 discussed what underlies selection for defense behaviors; Cowlishaw 1997 conducted research on risk versus rate in baboons.

51.   Ehrenreich 1997, pp. 46–47.

CHAPTER 4

1.   Chicago Field Museum of Natural History 2001.

2.   Patterson 1925, p. 90.

3.   Elliot 2003, *National Geographic,* 8/03, for quote from Kerbis Peterhans.

4.   McDougal 1991 for Ankole man-eater; Schaller 1972, p. 220, for Manyara man-eater quotes; McDougal 1991 for Tundara man-eater; Chicago Field Museum of Natural History 2001 for Mfuwe man-eater; Saberwal et al. 1994 for Gir Forest man-eaters.

5. Corbett 1954; McDougal 1991.

6. McDougal 1991; Jackson 1991.

7. Seidensticker et al. 1975.

8. McDougal 1991, p. 204.

9. McDougal 1991, p. 206, for quote by John Taylor; Brain 1981 for Golis Range man-eater, Zambezi River man-eater, and baby-snatching man-eater; McDougal 1991 for Himalayas man-eater; Uprety 1998, *The Week* news magazine, 8/2/98, for Uttar Pradesh man-eater.

10. Fay et al. 1995; Turnbull-Kemp 1967 for sex distribution of man-eaters.

11. National Public Radio 2004; CNN.com, 2004.

12. Kruuk 2002.

13. Anonymous 1991, *St. Louis Post-Dispatch,* 2/24/91, p. 13D.

14. Kruuk 2002, pp. 52–53.

15. Alexander 1992.

16. Kruuk 2002; Turner 1997.

17. Gebo and Simons 1984.

18. Schaller 1972.

19. Zapfe 1981.

20. Fossil-cat descriptions from Ewer 1954, Maglio 1975, Leakey 1976, Brain 1981, Carroll 1988, Heald and Shaw 1991, Macdonald 1992, Turner 1997, and Packer and Clottes 2000; Kruuk 2002, p.110, for quote about *Smilodon.*

21. DeWaal and Lanting 1997, p. 3.

22. Petter 1973.

23. Leakey 1976; Howell and Petter 1976.

24. Brain 1970, 1978.

25. Cavallo 1991 for "tree" explanation; Brain 1981 for "cave" explanation.

26. Coryndon 1964; Simons 1966.

27. Tsukahara 1993 for lions; Boesch 1991, Tutin and Benirschke 1991, and Fay et al. 1995 for leopards; Rijksen 1978 for tigers.

28. Gabunia et al. 2000; Vekua et al. 2002.

29. Gore 2002; Wong 2003, p. 82.

30. See Shipman 1983; Marean 1989.

31. Marean 1989.

32. Kitchener 1991 for physical appearance of cats; Guggisberg 1975 for sensory information; Kruuk 1986, Kitchener 1991, and Hoogerwerf 1970 for size; Kruuk and Turner 1967 for lion social grouping.

33. Hunting techniques of cats from Kruuk 1972, 1986, Sunquist and Sunquist 1989, Ewer 1973, Rautenbach and Nel 1978, Marean 1989.

34.   Johnson 2003.

35.   Johnson 2003, p. 39.

36.   Srivastava et al. 1996.

37.   Emmons 1987.

38.   Leopard hunting techniques from Rosevear 1974, Turnbull-Kemp 1967, Kingdon 1974, 1989.

39.   See Bertram 1982 and Mills and Biggs 1993 for information about leopard prey base in general; in Africa leopards are known to prey on bonobos (Badrian and Malenky 1984), common chimpanzees (Boesch 1991, 1992), western lowland gorillas (Fay et al. 1995), many species of rain-forest guenons (Hart et al. 1996), vervets (Isbell 1990), geladas (Iwamoto et al. 1995), baboons (Stolz 1977), and drills (Rosevear 1974); in Asia leopards prey on langurs (Srivastava et al. 1996), golden snub-nosed monkeys (Schaller et al. 1985, 1987), many species of macaques (Seidensticker and Suyono 1980), and gibbons (Hoogerwerf 1970).

40.   See Hoppe-Dominik 1984 for Côte d'Ivoire; Schaller 1967 and Srivastava et al. 1996 for India; Isbell 1990 for Kenya; Seidensticker and Suyono 1980 for Indonesia.

41.   Information on clouded leopards from Rabinowitz 1988, Seidensticker 1985, Rijksen and Rijksen-Graatsma 1975, Rijksen 1978, Boonratana 1994.

42.   Information on cheetah from Lumpkin 1993, Sunquist and Sunquist 1989, Eaton 1974, Hamilton 1981.

43.   Information on tigers from Whitfield 1978, McDougal 1977, Sunquist and Sunquist 1988, Thapar 1986, Rijksen 1978, Seidensticker and Suyono 1980, Schaller 1967.

44.   Information on lions from Kruuk 1986, Schaller 1972, Packer et al. 1990, Kruuk and Turner 1967, Makacha and Schaller 1969, Pienaar 1969.

45.   T. Williamson 1997, personal communication.

46.   Macdonald 1984; Domico 1988.

47.   Macdonald 1984; Domico 1988.

48.   Macdonald 1984; Domico 1988.

49.   Herrero 2002.

50.   Evolutionary history of bears from Martin 1989, Domico 1988.

51.   Herrero 2002, p. 96.

52.   Herrero 2002, p. 96.

53.   Herrero 2002, p. 96.

54.   Herrero 2002, p. 97.

55.   Information on Asian bears from Domico 1988, Prater 1971, Nowak 1991, Herrero 2002.

CHAPTER 5

1. Mech 1970.
2. Kruuk 2002; Clarke's analysis of eighteenth-century France wolf attacks can be found in Grzimek 1975.
3. Kruuk 2002, p. 70.
4. Kruuk 2002, p. 70.
5. Kruuk 2002.
6. Burns 1996, *The New York Times,* 9/1/96, p. 1.
7. Defenders of Wildlife 2001.
8. Kruuk 2002, p. 69.
9. Gore 2002.
10. Information on hyenas from Kruuk 1970, Grzimek 1975, Cooper 1990, Macdonald 1992.
11. Brain 1981; Kruuk 2002.
12. Kruuk 2002.
13. Brain 1981; Werdelin and Solounias 1991; *Euryboas* is a synonym for *Chasmaporthetes*; both names refer to a cheetah-like hyena species found in South African hominid sites.
14. Discussion of *Pachycrocuta* in Africa from Werdelin and Lewis 2000 and Marean 1989; discussion of Zhoukoudian cave remains from Boaz et al. 2000, Boaz and Ciochon 2001, Boaz et al. [manuscript].
15. Romer 1955; Macdonald 1992; Voorhies 2002.
16. Turner 1997.
17. Discussion of African fossil canids from Maglio 1975, Leakey 1976, Marean 1989, Werdelin and Lewis 2000.
18. Bertram 1979; Caro and Fitzgibbon 1992.
19. Estes 1967 for morphology of canids and hyenas; Schaller and Lowther 1969 for speeds.
20. Information on African hunting dogs from Estes and Goddard 1967, Kingdon 1974, Fuller and Kat 1990.
21. Information on dholes from Hoogerwerf 1970, Johnsingh 1980, 1983, Macdonald 1984, Rice 1986, Seidensticker and Suyono 1989, Paulraj 1995, Srivastava et al. 1996.
22. Phythian-Adams 1939, p. 653.
23. Information on jackals from Estes 1967, Struhsaker and Gartlan 1970, Nagel 1973; for Kummer observation, Lamprecht 1978, Newton 1985, Stanford 1989, McKenzie 1991.

24.   Information on three species of hyenas from Pienaar 1969, Kruuk 1975, Skinner
       1976, Bearder 1977, Owens and Owens 1978, Mills 1978, 1989, Brain 1981,
       Cooper 1990, Kerbis Peterhans 1990, Werdelin and Solounias 1991; Stelzner and
       Strier 1981 for description of baboon kill; Starin 1991 for description of red colobus
       kill.

25.   Information on domestic dogs from Oppenheimer 1977, Barnett and Rudd 1983,
       Anderson 1986b.

26.   Kruuk 2002.

CHAPTER 6

1.   White 2000.

2.   Murphy and Henderson 1997.

3.   Rose 1962, pp. 326–327.

4.   See van Schaik and Mitrasetia 1990, Vitale et al. 1991, and Nunes et al. 1998 for
       research that confirms snake-avoidance behavior by primates; see Dittus 1977 for
       curious-approach behaviors.

5.   Evidence that fear of snakes is instinctive behavior based upon studies of Bolwig
       1959, Masataka 1993, and Ziegler and Heymann 1996; evidence that supports the
       theory that fear and avoidance of snakes are learned behaviors is based upon studies
       of Osada 1991, Joslin et al. 1964, Bertrand 1969, Mineka et al. 1980, Cook and
       Mineka 1990, and Bayart and Anhouard 1992.

6.   Jones and Jones 1928; Maurer 1965.

7.   Pope 1980, p. 77.

8.   Weights and lengths from Pope 1980 and Shine et al. 1998.

9.   Pope 1980, p. 12.

10.   Branch 1984.

11.   Murphy and Henderson 1997.

12.   Cloudsley-Thompson 1994.

13.   Mattison 1995 for information about the sit-and-wait ambush; Uhde and Sommer
       2002 for information about active search; Montgomery and Rand 1978 for burrow
       behavior; Greene 1997 for striking behavior; Murphy and Henderson 1997 for diet
       diversity; Grzimek 1975 for arboreality.

14.   Weights and lengths from Pope 1980 and Shine et al. 1998.

15.   Hoogerwerf 1970.

16.   *Man-Eating Snakes I* and *Man-Eating Snakes II.*

17.   Branch and Haacke 1980, p. 306.

18.   Branch 1984.

19. J. McNamara 1995, personal communication.
20. Murphy and Henderson, 1997.
21. Carroll 1988.
22. Romer 1955.
23. Hart 2000; based on the level of recorded predations as a function of the percentage of primates in a predator's diet, there were eleven primate specialists and two out of these eleven were the African and the reticulated pythons.
24. White 2000.
25. Isemonger 1962, p. 12.
26. Starin 1991; Starin and Burghardt 1992.
27. Wiens and Zitzmann 1999.
28. Rakotondravony et al. 1998.
29. Shine et al. 1998.
30. Murphy and Henderson 1997.
31. Pope 1980, p. 77.
32. Weights and lengths from Pope 1980 and Shine et al. 1998.
33. Heymann 1987 for anaconda; Chapman 1986 for boa constrictor; Boinski 1988 for clubbing behavior.
34. Greene 1997.
35. I. Malik 1999, personal communication.
36. Astill 1999, *The Jakarta Post,* 11/9/99.
37. Pfeffer 1989; Auffenberg 1981; Minton and Minton 1973.
38. Pfeffer 1989; Auffenbert 1981; Minton and Minton 1973.
39. Pfeffer 1989; Auffenbert 1981; Minton and Minton 1973.
40. Bennett 2003.
41. Discovery Channel 1996.
42. Blair and Blair 1991.
43. Bennet 2003.
44. Carroll 1988.
45. Pfeffer 1989; Auffenberg 1981; Minton and Minton 1973.
46. Carroll 1988.
47. Anonymous 1983.
48. Brasch 1993, *St. Louis Post-Dispatch,* 3/24/93, p. 3A.
49. Pooley et al. 1989; Alderton 1991.
50. Alderton 1991, p. 22.
51. Pooley et al. 1989, p. 172.
52. Pooley et al. 1989; Alderton 1996.

53.   Cott 1961.

54.   Pope 1980, p. 77.

55.   Pooley et al. 1989, p. 172.

56.   Cloudsley-Thompson 1994.

57.   Ross 1989; Pooley and Gans 1976.

58.   C. Olejniczak 1999, personal communication.

59.   See Starin 1991 for red colobus predation; see Cott 1961 for baboon and macaque predation; see Pooley et al. 1989 for information on false gharials; see Galdikas and Yeager 1984, Galdikas 1985, and Yeager 1991 for primates preyed on by false gharials.

60.   Hoogerwerf 1970.

61.   Pooley et al. 1989; Alderton 1991.

62.   See Mukherjee and Gupta 1965 for rhesus macaques preyed on by sharks; see Lineaweaver and Backus 1970, Ellis 1996, and Stafford-Deitsch 1987 for information on wolf and requiem sharks.

63.   Ellis 1996.

CHAPTER 7

1.   Steyn 1983, p. 111.

2.   Stjernstedt 1975.

3.   Dittus 1975; Struhsaker 1975; Charles-Dominique 1977; Rettig 1978; Terborgh 1983; Wright 1985.

4.   Steyn 1983 for vervet incident; Clifton 1977 for colobus incident.

5.   Brown and Amadon 1989.

6.   Whitfield 1978.

7.   Meshach 2004.

8.   Brown 1971.

9.   Everett 1977.

10.   Brown 1971, p. 268.

11.   Kemp 1990.

12.   See n. 5.

13.   Tarboton 1989.

14.   Jouventin 1975.

15.   Brown and Amadon 1989.

16.   Brown et al. 1982.

17.   Leland and Struhsaker 1993.

18.   Chapin 1925; Brown 1953.

19. Brown 1977.

20. Brown and Amadon 1989.

21. Fowler and Cope 1964; Voous 1969; Brown 1977; Rettig l977, 1978, 1995; Izor l985; Brown and Amadon 1989; Voous 1969; Brown 1977.

22. Brown 1977.

23. Hanif 1970, p. 24.

24. Kennedy 1981.

25. Gonzales 1968; Alvarez 1970; Kennedy 1977, 1985; H. Miranda 1999, personal communication.

26. Chapin 1932; Maclean 1993.

27. Skorupa l989; Struhsaker and Leakey l990; Leland and Struhsaker 1993; Sanders et al. 2003, Msuya 1993.

28. Tarboton 1989.

29. Brown and Amadon 1989.

30. Clark 1970, p. 77.

31. Daneel 1979 for team hunting; Maclatchey 1937 for whistling.

32. Brown 1966.

33. Gautier-Hion et al. 1983; Terborgh 1990.

34. Peres 1990; Voous 1969; Terborgh 1983; Eason 1989; Sherman 1991.

35. Goodman 1994.

36. Leland and Struhsaker. 1993.

37. Brown et al. 1977.

38. Tattersall 1982; Simons et al. 1995; Simons 1997.

39. Clark 1970, p. 77.

40. Sauther 1989; Macedonia 1990.

41. Burton 2001.

42. Goodman 1994.

43. Kemp 1990.

44. Olson 1985; Carroll 1988.

45. Kemp 1990, p. 22.

46. Kemp 1990.

47. Carroll 1988; Mourer-Chauvire 1981.

48. Berger and Clarke 1995.

49. Sanders et al. 2003.

50. Cambridge Educational Films 1999.

51. Sanders et al. 2003; Berger and Clarke 1995; Cooke et al. 2004.

52. Berger and Clarke 1995.

53.   Sanders et al. 2003.

54.   Coimbro-Filho 1978.

55.   Thiollay 1985.

56.   Boinski 1987.

57.   Mitchell et al. 1991; Terborgh 1983; Goldizen 1987; Peres 1991.

58.   Brown and Amadon 1989.

59.   Vernon 1965 and Gargett 1971, 1990 for black eagles in South Africa; Zinner and
      Peláez 1999 for black eagles in Eritrea.

60.   Goodman et al. 1993.

61.   Rasoloarison et al. 1995.

62.   Newman 1970; Pitman and Adamson 1978; Gillard 1979; Steyn 1983; Andrews
      1990.

63.   Brown 1971, pp. 270–271.

CHAPTER 8

1.   Kortlandt 1967.

2.   Hamilton et al. 1975 for baboons; Westergaard and Suomi 1994 for captive
      capuchins; Boinski 1988 for wild capuchins; Hiraiwa-Hasegawa et al. 1986 and
      Byrne and Byrne 1988 for chimpanzees; Stoltz and Saayman 1970 for baboons
      attack on dogs; Turnbull-Kemp 1967, Altmann and Altmann 1970, Saayman
      1971, and Goodall 1986 for specifics on leopard mortality from baboons.

3.   Sussman 2003.

4.   Kummer 1971; Hall 1965; Chism and Rowell 1988; Chism et al. 1983.

5.   Stevenson-Hamilton 1947, p. 262.

6.   Conroy 1990.

7.   Isbell 1994, p. 68.

8.   Hart 2000.

9.   Struhsaker 1967; Terborgh 1983; Vezina 1985.

10.   Hart 2000.

11.   Terborgh 1983; Boinski 1987; Mitchell et al. 1991; Goodman et al. 1993; and Hart
      2000, Appendix 1.

12.   Grzimek 1975 and Pfeffer 1989 for snake size; Shine 1991 and Mehrtens 1987 for
      snake behavior.

13.   Crook and Gartlan 1966; Dunbar 1988.

14.   Busse 1977; Isbell 1994.

15.   Jolly 1985.

16.   Johanson and Edey 1981.

17.   Jolly 1985.

18.   Alexander 1974; Terborgh 1983; Stacey 1986; Terborgh and Janson 1986.

19.   Terborgh 1983; Sussman and Kinzey 1984; Goldizen 1987; Caine 1993.

20.   For example, Crook 1970, Leutenegger and Kelly 1977 observed advantages for the group when males were present, but Stacey 1986, Boesch and Boesch 1989, Struhsaker and Leakey 1990 found that males seemed to be selected by predators. Anderson 1986a found correlation between number of males in a group and predation, but Cheney and Wrangham 1987 found none.

21.   Zuberbühler and Jenny 2002.

22.   Sommer et al. 1998 for langurs; Verschuren 1958 for baboons; Uhde and Sommer 1998 for gibbons; von Hippel 1998 for colobus monkeys.

23.   Nicastro 2001, p. 153.

24.   Philopatry (staying in the natal group) is such an advantage it may be selected for as an anti-predation adaptation; see Isbell et al. 1990, 1993; Isbell 1994.

25.   DeVore and Washburn 1963 for idealized order of baboon progressions; Altmann 1979 for random order of baboon progressions; Tutin et al. 1983 for chimpanzees in Senegal.

26.   Altmann and Altmann 1970 for baboons; Struhsaker 1967 for vervets.

27.   Jolly 1972.

28.   Jolly 1985.

29.   Park 2002; the discussion on models of bipedalism is found on pp. 237–239.

30.   Jolly 1985, p. 77.

31.   Zuberbühler and Jenny 2002.

32.   Endler l99l.

33.   Cheney and Wrangham 1987 for encounter stage; Charles-Dominique 1974, 1977, Terborgh 1983, and Caine 1987 for detection stage; Altmann and Altmann 1970, and Stoltz and Saayman 1970 for approach stage; Alterman 1995 for subjugation stage.

34.   Endler 1991.

35.   Lindburg 1977 for rhesus macaques; Sigg 1980 for hamadryas baboons.

36.   Schaller 1972; Bertram 1978.

37.   Kruuk 1986 for key stage; Vermeij 1982 for mammals; Owen 1980 for snakes.

38.   Elliot et al. 1977 for stealth; Curio 1976 for awareness.

39.   Struhsaker 1967.

40.   Work on vervets done by Seyfarth and Cheney 1980, 1986, Seyfarth et al. 1980, Cheney and Seyfarth 1981; work on Japanese macaques done by Fedigan 1974; work on captive rhesus macaques done by Chapais and Schulman 1980; callitrichids done

by Pola and Snowdon 1975, Moody and Menzel 1976, Vencl 1977, Neyman 1977; work on cebids done by Norris 1990, Fedigan et al. 1996; work on lemurs done by Sussman 1977, Sauther 1989, Macedonia 1990, Pereira and Macedonia 1991.

41. Oda and Masataka 1996 for ringtailed lemurs; Hauser 1988 for vervets; Searcy and Caine 1998 for captive Geoffroy's marmosets.

42. Harvey and Greenwood 1978 for theory; Tenaza and Tilson 1977 for gibbon example.

43. Nicastro 2001.

44. Johanson and Edey 1981, p. 274.

45. Archer 1988.

46. Bartecki and Heymann 1987 for tamarins mobbing snakes; Srivastava 1991 for langurs mobbing snakes; Colquhoun 1993 for lemurs mobbing snakes; Ross 1993 for langurs mobbing leopards; Uhde and Sommer 1998 for gibbons mobbing tigers; Passamani 1995 for marmosets mobbing Neotropical wild cats; Phillips 1995 for capuchins mobbing tayra.

47. Gonzales 1968, Boggess 1976, Eason 1989, Gautier-Hion and Tutin 1988, and Struhsaker and Leakey 1990 for attacks on raptors; DeVore and Washburn 1963, Hamburg 1971, and Baenninger et al. 1977 for attacks on wild cats; DeVore and Washburn 1963 for attacks on dogs; Klein 1974 for attacks on small carnivores; Schaller 1963 for silverback gorilla–leopard conflict.

48. Schaller 1972, p. 388.

49. Hamburg 1971 for baboons; J. Powzyk 1999, personal communication for indri; Macedonia 1993 for female lemur; Gandini and Baldwin 1978 for female chimpanzee.

50. Zahl 1960 and Schaller 1963 for chestbeating; C. Olejniczak 1999, personal communication for strong body odor and disruption of behavior patterns.

51. Rose and Marshall 1996, p. 314.

CHAPTER 9

1. From a 1956 statement by Sherwood Washburn at Princeton University, quoted in Ardrey 1976, pp. 10–11.

2. Sussman 2000.

3. *Demonic Males* by Wrangham and Peterson 1996, *The Hunting Ape* by Stanford 1999, *The Dark Side of Man* by Ghiglieri 1999.

4. Cartmill 1997, p. 511.

5. Both quotes from Dart 1953, p. 209.

6. Cartmill 1993.

7. James Burnet quoted in Bock 1980, p. 202.

8. Ardrey 1961, quotes from pp. 316 and 326, respectively.

9. Ruse 1994.

10. Wilson 1975.

11. Waser and Wiley 1980.

12. See Fedigan 1992 and Sussman 2003a, b, for a discussion of home ranges in primate species.

13. Bernstein 1981.

14. Walters and Seyfarth 1987 for a discussion of the ambiguity of dominance hierarchies; Hausfater 1975 for a discussion of baboon hierarchies; Bercovitch 1991 for a discussion of the relationship between rank and reproductive success.

15. Smuts 1987.

16. Brown 1991, p. 91.

17. The ! before words in the Ju/'hoansi (or !Kung) language denotes a clicking sound.

18. Wilson 1976.

19. Ruse and Wilson 1985.

20. Ruse and Wilson 1985, pp. 50–52.

21. Wilson 1975, quotes from pp. 573 and 575, respectively.

22. Boas quoted in Degler 1991, p. 148.

23. Ruse 1994, p. 102.

24. Ruse 1994.

25. Ruse 1994, p. 106.

26. Wrangham 1995, p. 5.

27. Wrangham 1995, p. 7.

28. See Hart 2000, Appendix 2, for a listing of primates that prey on primates.

29. Uehara et al. 1992, Stanford et al. 1994, Stanford 1995, and Stanford and Wrangham 1998 give descriptions of chimpanzee predation; Stanford et al. 1994 specifically details the extent of chimpanzee predation on red colobus monkeys at Gombe; Boesch 1994 discusses human presence as a variable on hunting by chimpanzees; Boesch and Boesch 1989 includes a discussion of chimpanzee hunting of red colobus monkeys in the Tai Forest.

30. Dawkins 1976.

31. Marks et al. 1988; Marks 1991a; A. Templeton 1997; personal communication.

32. See Small 1997.

33. Goodall 1968, p. 278.

34. Goodall 1968, p. 277.

35. Goodall 1968, p. 3.

36.   Goodall 1965; Reynolds and Reynolds 1965; Sugiyama 1972; Ghiglieri 1984.

37.   Goodall 1971, p. 143.

38.   Wrangham 1974.

39.   Power 1991.

40.   Goodall 1986.

41.   Nishida et al. 1985.

42.   Wrangham and Peterson 1996, p. 20.

43.   Boesch and Boesch 1989.

44.   Wrangham and Peterson 1996, p. 20.

45.   See Bartlett et al. 1993; Galdikas 1995.

46.   Sussman 2004.

47.   Wrangham and Peterson 1996, p. 239.

48.   Stanford 1999, p. 217.

49.   Stanford and Allen 1991, p. 58.

50.   Ghiglieri 1999, p. 47.

51.   Ghiglieri 1999, p. 48.

52.   Marks 2002, p. 104.

53.   Dahlberg 1981.

54.   Zihlman and Tanner 1976.

55.   Zihlman 1997, p. 91.

56.   Strum 2001.

57.   Strum 2001, p. 126.

58.   Quiatt and Reynolds 1995; Swedell 2005.

59.   Sussman and Chapman 2004.

CHAPTER 10

1.   Klein 2004, p. 10.

2.   Worster 1994.

3.   Sussman 1999.

4.   Allen and Stanford, unpublished manuscript.

5.   Marks 2002, p. 104.

6.   Tattersall 1998.

7.   Stanford 1999, p. 48.

8.   Conroy [in press]; Feibel et al. 1989.

9.   Jurmain et al. 2003, p. 306.

10.   Binford 1992; Klein 1999. Richard Potts, fellow of the Smithsonian Institution and leader of large-scale excavations at Olorgesailie in southern Kenya, was quoted in a

3/9/97, article in *The Sunday Times Magazine* (London): "The hunting scenario is now totally out of the window. There is clear evidence from studying the archaeological remains from early sites—that is, starting from around 2.5 million and especially around 2 million years ago—where we have nice bone preservation. And we see evidence that early humans were exploiting certain animals, but there is no indication that they were hunting them. There is clear evidence that they were getting the bones and cutting meat off them, and there is clear evidence that they were smashing the bones for bone marrow. But that's about as far as we can go. The first clear evidence we see of hominids as aggressive hunters is not until very late in the archaeological record: *within the last 100,000 years.*"

11. Tattersall and Schwartz 2000; Klein 2002, p. 160.
12. Klein 1999.
13. Jurmain et al. 2003, p. 305.
14. Lovejoy 1981.
15. Teaford and Ungar 2000.
16. Dittus 1974; Suzuki 1969; Lee 1969; Tanaka 1976; Sanz 2003; Sussman 1999.
17. Teaford and Ungar 2000, pp. 13,508–13,509.
18. Teaford and Ungar 2000, pp. 13,508–13,509.
19. Harding 1981; Chivers and Hladik 1984; Martin 1990; Milton 1999; Sussman 1999.
20. The ! before words in the Ju/'hoansi (or !Kung) language denotes a clicking sound.
21. Lee 1969, as reproduced *in Anthropology,* 03/04, p. 32.
22. Harrison et al. 1989.
23. Willett et al. 1999.
24. Junshi et al. 1990.
25. Lee 1969.
26. Carrington 2000.
27. Klein 1989.
28. Harrison et al. 1990.
29. Balter 2004; Goren-Inbar et al. 2004.
30. Conroy [in press].
31. Rak 1991.
32. Boaz 1997, pp. 140–141.
33. Johanson and Edey 1981.
34. Conroy [in press].
35. Conroy [in press].
36. Jolly 1985.

37. Fox 1967, p. 419.

38. Tooby and De Vore 1987.

39. MacKinnon and MacKinnon 1978.

40. Sussman and Tattersall 1981, 1986.

41. Burton and Eaton 1995.

42. Strum 2001.

43. Hart 2000.

BIBLIOGRAPHY

Alderton, D. 1991. *Crocodiles and Alligators of the World*. Facts on File, New York.

Aldrich-Blake, F. 1970. The ecology and behaviour of the blue monkey, *Cercopithecus mitis stuhlmanni*. Ph.D. dissertation, University of Bristol, Bristol, U.K.

Alexander, J. 1992. Alas, poor *Notharctus*. *Natural History* 9:54–59.

Allen, J. and C. Stanford. [no date] Evaluating models and theories of hominid evolution. [Unpublished manuscript, Stanford personal communication.]

Alterman, L. 1995. Toxins and toothcombs: Potential allospecific chemical defenses in *Nycticebus* and *Perodicticus*. In: *Creatures of the Dark: The Nocturnal Prosimians*, L. Alterman, G. Doyle and M. Kay Izard (eds.). Plenum Press, New York. pp. 413–424.

Altmann, S. 1974. Baboons, space, time, and energy. *American Zoology* 14:221–248.

_____. 1979. Baboon progressions: Order or chaos? a study of one-dimensional group geometry. *Animal Behaviour* 27:46–80.

Altmann, S. and J. Altmann. 1970. *Baboon Ecology*. University of Chicago Press, Chicago.

Alvarez, J., Jr. 1970. A report on the 1969 status of the monkey-eating eagle of the Philippines. IUCN (International Union for the Conservation of Nature and Natural Resources) Publication N. S. 18:68–73.

Anderson, C. 1986a. Predation and primate evolution. *Primates* 27(1):15–39.

Anderson, J. 1986b. Encounters between domestic dogs and free-ranging non-human primates. *Applied Animal Behaviour Science* 15(1):71–86.

Andrews, P. 1990. *Owls, Caves and Fossils: Predation, Preservation, and Accumulation of Small Mammal Bones in Caves, with an Analysis of the Pleistocene Cave Faunas from Westbury-Sub-Mendip, Somerset, United Kingdom*. The University of Chicago Press, Chicago.

Anon. 1983. A record size water monitor lizard in Sabah, East Malaysia. *Hamadryad* 8(3): cover.

_____. 1991. Mountain lions pose threat to residents of rugged west. *St. Louis Post-Dispatch* 2/24/91. p. 13D.

Archer, J. 1988. *The Behavioural Biology of Aggression*. Cambridge University Press, Cambridge, U.K.

Ardrey, R. 1961. *African Genesis: A Personal Investigation into Animal Origins and Nature of Man*. Atheneum, New York.

_____. 1976. *The Hunting Hypothesis*. Atheneum, New York.

Astill, J. 1999. Komodo dragon lures tourists, conservation. *The Jakarta Post* 11/9/99. p. 1.

Auffenberg, W. 1981. Behavioral ecology of the komodo monitor. Ph.D. dissertation, University of Florida, Gainesville, Florida.

Badrian, N. and R. Malenky. 1984. Feeding ecology of *Pan paniscus* in the Lomako forest, Zaire. In: *The Pygmy Chimpanzee: Evolutionary Biology and Behavior*, R. Sussman (ed.). Plenum Press, New York. pp. 275–99.

Baenninger, R., R. Estes, and S. Baldwin. 1977. Anti-predator behavior of baboons and impalas toward a cheetah. *East African Wildlife Journal* 15(4):327–330.

Bakker, R. 1983. The deer flees, the wolf pursues: incongruencies in predator-prey coevolution. In: *Coevolution*, D. Futuyma and M. Slatkin (eds.). Sinauer Associates, Inc., Sunderland. pp. 350–382.

Balter, M. 2004. Earliest signs of human-controlled fire uncovered in Israel. *Science* 304:663–665.

Barnett, R. and R. Rudd. 1983. Feral dogs of the Galapagos Islands: impact and control. *International Journal for the Study of Animal Problems* 4:44–58.

Bartecki, U. and E. Heymann. 1987. Field observation of snake-mobbing in a group of saddle-back tamarins (*Saguinus fuscicollis nigrifrons*). *Folia Primatologica* 48:199–202.

Bartlett, T., R. Sussman, and J. Cheverud. 1993. Infant killing in primates: a review of observed cases with specific references to the sexual selection hypothesis. *American Anthropologist* 95:958–990.

Baumgartel, W. 1976. *Up Among the Mountain Gorillas*. Hawthorn Books, New York.

Bayart, F. and M. Anthousard. 1992. Responses to a live snake by *Lemur macaco macaco* and *Lemur fulvus mayottensis* in captivity. *Folia Primatologica* 58(1):41–46.

Bearder, S. 1977. Feeding habits of spotted hyena in a woodland habitat. *East African Wildlife Journal* 15:263–280.

Bennett, D. 2003. Little book of monitor lizards. http://www.mampam.com.

Bercovitch, F. 1991. Social stratification, social strategies, and reproductive success in primates. *Ethology and Sociobiology* 12:315–333.

Berger, L. and R. Clarke. 1995. Eagle involvement in accumulation of the Taung child fauna. *Journal of Human Evolution* 29:275–299.

Bernstein, I. 1981. Dominance: the baby and the bathwater. *Behavior and Brain Sciences* 4:419–457.

_____. 1997. One man's view. *American Journal of Primatology* 41:151–154.

Bertram, B. 1978. Living in groups: Predators and prey. In: *Behavioural Ecology: An Evolutionary Approach*, First Edition, J. Krebs and N. Davies (eds.). Blackwell Scientific Publications, Oxford and London, U.K. pp. 64–96.

_____. 1979. Serengeti predators and their social systems. In: *Serengeti: Dynamics of an Ecosystem*, A. Sinclair and M. Norton-Griffiths (eds.). University of Chicago Press, Chicago. pp. 221–248.

_____. 1982. Leopard ecology as studied by radio-tracking. *The Symposium of the Zoological Society of London* 49:341–352.

Bertrand, M. 1969. *The Behavioral Repertoire of the Stumptail Macaque*. S. Karger, Basel, Switzerland.

Binford, L. 1985. Human ancestors: changing views of their behavior. *Journal of Anthropological Archaeology* 4:292–327.

_____. 1992. Subsistence—a key to the past. In: *Cambridge Encyclopedia of Human Evolution*, S. Johnes, R. Martin, and D. Pilbeam (eds.). Cambridge University Press, Cambridge, U.K.

Blair, L. and L. Blair. 1991. *Ring of Fire*. Bantam Press, London.

Bloch, J. and D. Boyer. 2002. Grasping primate origins. *Science* 298:1606–1610.

Boaz, N. 1997. *Eco Homo*. Basic Books, New York.

Boaz, N. and R. Ciochon. 2001. The scavenging of "Peking Man." *Natural History* 110(2):46–51.

Boaz, N., R. Ciochon, Q. Xu, and J. Liu. 2000. Large mammalian carnivores as a taphonomic factor in the bone accumulation at Zhoukoudian. *Acta Anthropologica Sinica* (Suppl.) 19:224–234.

_____. 2003. Taphonomy of Zhoukoudian *Homo erectus*: locality 1 as a hyaenid den. [unpublished manuscript]

Bock, K. 1980. *Human Nature and History: A Response to Sociobiology*. Columbia University Press, New York.

Boesch, C. 1991. The effects of leopard predation on grouping patterns in forest chimpanzees. *Behaviour* 117(3–4):220–242.

_____. 1992. Predation by leopards on chimpanzees and its impact on social grouping. *Bulletin of the Chicago Academy of Science* 15(1):5.

_____. 1994. Hunting strategies of Gombe and Tai chimpanzees. In: *Chimpanzee Cultures*, R. Wrangham, W. McGrew, F. de Waal, and P. Heltne (eds.). Harvard University Press, Cambridge, Massachusetts. pp. 77–92.

Boesch, C. and H. Boesch. 1989. Hunting behavior of wild chimpanzees in the Tai National Park, Ivory Coast. *American Journal of Physical Anthropology* 78(4):547–574.

Boggess, J. 1976. The social behavior of the Himalayan langur (*Presbytis entellus*) in eastern Nepal. Ph.D. dissertation, University of California, Berkeley, California.

Boinski, S. 1987. Birth synchrony in squirrel monkeys: a strategy to reduce neonatal predation. *Behavioural Ecology and Sociobiology* 21(6):393–400.

_____. 1988. Use of club by a wild white-faced capuchin to attack a venomous snake. *American Journal of Primatology* 14(2):177–179.

Boinski, S. and C. Chapman. 1995. Predation on primates: where are we and what's next? *Evolutionary Anthropology* 4(1):1–3.

Bolwig, N. 1959. A study of the behaviour of the chacma baboon, *Papio ursinus. Behaviour* 14:136–163.

Boonratana, R. 1994. The ecology and behaviour of the proboscis monkey (*Nasalis larvatus*) in the Lower Kinabatangan, Saba. Ph.D. dissertation, Mahidol University, Thailand.

Bothma, J. du and E. Le Riche. 1984. Aspects of the ecology and behaviour of the leopard in the Kalahari Desert. *Koedoe*, Suppl. pp. 259–279.

Bourliere, F. 1979. Significant parameters of environmental quality for nonhuman primates. In: *Primate Ecology and Human Origins*, I. Bernstein and E. Smith (eds.). Garland, New York. pp. 23–46.

Brain, C. 1970. New finds at the Swartkrans Australopithecine site. *Nature (London)* 225:1112–1119.

_____. 1978. Interpreting the bone accumulation from the Sterkfontein Valley caves. *Annals of the Natal Museum* 23:465–468.

_____. 1981. *The Hunters or the Hunted?* University of Chicago Press, Chicago.

Branch, W. 1984. Pythons and people: predators and prey. *African Wildlife* 38(6):236–241.

Branch, W. and W. Haacke. 1980. A fatal attack on a young boy by an African rock python, *Python sebae. Journal of Herpetology* 14(3):305–307.

Brasch, P. 1993. Woman loses arm to African crocodile. *St. Louis Post-Dispatch* 3/24/93. p. 3A.

Brown, D. 1991. *Human Universals*. Temple University Press, Philadelphia.

Brown, L. 1953. On the biology of the large birds of prey of Embu District, Kenya Colony. *Ibis* 95:74–114.

_____. 1966. Observations on some Kenya eagles. *Ibis* 108:531–572.

_____. 1971. *African Birds of Prey*. Houghton Mifflin Company, Boston.

_____. 1977. *Eagles of the World*. Universe Books, New York.

Brown, L. and D. Amadon. 1989. *Eagles, Hawks and Falcons of the World*. Wellfleet, Secaucus, New Jersey.

Brown, L., E. Urban, and K. Newman (eds.). 1982. *Birds of Africa Vol. I: Ostriches to Birds of Prey*. Academic Press, New York.

Bryden, B. 1976. The biology of the African lion (*Panthera leo*, Linn 1758) in the Kruger National Park. Master's thesis, University of Pretoria, South Africa.

Burns, J. 1996. India fighting plague of man-eating wolves. *The New York Times* 9/1/96. p. 1.

Burton, F. and M. Eaton. 1995. *The Multimedia Guide to the Non-Human Primates.* Prentice Hall Canada, Scarborough, Ontario.

Burton, R. (Translator). 2001. *The Arabian Nights: Tales from a Thousand and One Nights.* The Modern Library, New York.

Busse, C. 1977. Chimpanzee predation as a possible factor in the evolution of red colobus monkey social organization. *Evolution* 31:907–911.

_____. 1980. Leopard and lion predation upon chacma baboons living in the Moremi Wildlife Reserve. *Botswana Notes Records* 26:132–160.

Byrne, R. and J. Byrne. 1988. Leopard killers of Mahale. *Natural History* 97(3):22–26.

CNN.com. 2004. Mountain lion spotted stalking deputies.http://www.cnn.com/2004/US/West/01/09/mountain.lion/index.html.

Caine, N. 1987. Vigilance, vocalization, and cryptic behaviour at retirement in captive groups of red-bellied tamarins (*Saguinus labiatus*). *American Journal of Primatology* 12:241–250.

_____. 1993. Flexibility and co-operation as unifying themes in *Saguinus* social organization and behaviour: the role of predation pressures. In: *Marmosets and Tamarins: Systematics, Behaviour, and, Ecology*, A. Rylands (ed.) Oxford University Press, Oxford. pp. 200–219.

Cambridge Educational Films. 1999. *The Story of Hominid Evolution: Origins of Homo sapiens East African Roots.* Films for the Humanities and Sciences, Princeton, New Jersey.

Capstick, P. 1993. *Maneaters.* Safari Press, Huntington Beach, California.

Caro, T. and C. Fitzgibbon. 1992. Large carnivores and their prey: the quick and the dead. In: *Natural Enemies: The Population Biology of Predators, Parasites and Diseases*, M. Crawley (ed.). Blackwell Scientific Publications, Oxford. pp. 117–142.

Carrington, D. 2000. Taste for flesh troubled Neanderthals. *BBC NewsOnline* 6/12/00.

Carroll, R. 1988. *Vertebrate Paleontology and Evolution.* W. H. Freeman, New York.

Cartmill, M. 1993. *A View to a Death in the Morning: Hunting and Nature through History.* Harvard University Press, Cambridge, Massachusetts.

_____. 1997. Hunting hypothesis of human origins. In: *History of Physical Anthropology: An Encyclopedia*, F. Spencer (ed.). Garland, New York. pp. 508–512.

Cavallo, J. 1991. Leopards and human evolution. In: *Great Cats: Majestic Creatures of the Wild*, J. Seidensticker and S. Lumpkin (eds.). Rodale Press, Emmaus, Pennsylvania. p. 208.

Chapais, B. and S. Schulman. 1980. Alarm responses to raptors by rhesus monkeys at Cayo Santiago. *Journal of Mammalogy* 61(4):739–741.

Chapin, J. 1925. The crowned eagle, ogre of Africa's monkeys. *Natural History* 25:459–469.

_____. 1932. The birds of the Belgian Congo, I. *Bulletin of the American Museum of Natural History* 65(1):534–655.

Chapman, C. 1986. Boa constrictor predation and group response in white-faced cebus monkeys. *Biotropica* 18(2):171–172.

Charles-Dominique, P. 1974. Ecology and feeding behavior of five sympatric lorisids in Gabon. In: *Prosimian Biology*, R. Martin, G. Doyle, and A. Walker (eds.). Duckworth, London. pp. 135–150.

_____. 1977. *Ecology and Behaviour of Nocturnal Primates: Prosimians of Equatorial West Africa*. Duckworth, London.

Cheney, D. and R. Seyfarth. 1981. Selective forces affecting the predator alarm calls of vervet monkeys. *Behaviour* 76:25–61.

Cheney, D. and R. Wrangham. 1987. Predation. In: *Primate Societies*, B. Smuts, D. Cheney, R. Seyfarth, R. Wrangham, and T. Struhsaker (eds.). The University of Chicago Press, Chicago. pp. 227–239.

Chicago Field Museum of Natural History. 2001. Man-eaters at the Field Museum. http://www.fmnh.org/exhibits/exhibit_sites/tsavo/mfuwe.html.

Chism, J., D. Olson, and T. Rowell. 1983. Diurnal births and perinatal behavior among wild patas monkeys. *International Journal of Primatology* 4:167–184.

Chism, J. and T. Rowell. 1988. The natural history of patas monkeys. In: *A Primate Radiation: Evolutionary Biology of the African Guenons*, A. Gautier-Hion, F. Bourliere, J. Gautier, and J. Kingdon (eds.). Cambridge University Press, Cambridge, U.K. pp. 412–437.

Chivers, D. and C. Hladik. 1984. Diet and gut morphology in primates. In: *Food Acquisition and Processing in Primates*, D. Chivers, B. Wood, and A. Bilsborough (eds.). Plenum Press, New York. pp. 213–230.

Clark, J. 1970. Observations on the crowned eagle, *Polemaetus coronatus*. *The Lammergeyer* 12:74–77.

Clifton, M. 1977. Attack on a colobus monkey. *East Africa Natural History Society* Vol. 5.

Cloudsley-Thompson, J. 1994. *Predation and Defence Amongst Reptiles*. R & A Publishing Ltd., England.

Coimbra-Filho, A. 1978. Natural shelters of *Leontopithecus rosalia* and some ecological implications (Callitrichidae: Primates). In: *The Biology and Conservation of the Callitrichidae*, D. Kleiman (ed.). Smithsonian Institution Press, Washington, D.C. pp. 79–89.

Colquhoun, I. 1993. The socioecology of *Eulemur macaco*: a preliminary report. In: *Lemur Social Systems and Their Ecological Basis*, P. Kappeler and J. Ganzhorn (eds.). Plenum Press, New York. pp. 11–23.

Collar, J. 1989. Harpy eagle. *World Birdwatch* 11(3):5.

Conroy, G. 1990. *Primate Evolution*. W. W. Norton, New York.

———. [in press] *Reconstructing Human Origins: A Modern Synthesis*, Second Edition. W. W. Norton, New York.

Cook, M. and S. Mineka. 1990. Selective associations in the observational conditioning of fear in rhesus monkeys. *Journal of Experimental Psychology: Animal Behavior Processes* 16(4):372–389.

Cooke, C., S. Shultz, and W. McGraw. 2004. A taphonomic analysis of crowned hawk-eagle nests from Tai National Forest, Ivory Coast. *American Journal of Physical Anthropology*, Suppl. 38:79.

Cooper, S. 1990. The hunting behaviour of spotted hyenas (*Crocuta crocuta*) in a region containing both sedentary and migratory populations of herbivores. *African Journal of Ecology* 28:131–141.

Corbett, J. 1954. *The Temple Tiger and More Man-Eaters of Kumaon*. Oxford University Press, New Delhi.

Coryndon, S. 1964. Bone remains in the caves. *Studies in Speleology* 1(1):60–63.

Cott, H. 1961. Scientific results of an inquiry into the ecology and economic status of the Nile crocodile (*Crocodilus niloticus*) in Uganda and Northern Rhodesia. *Trans. Zool. Soc. London* 29:211–356.

Cowlishaw, G. 1994. Vulnerability to predation in baboon populations. *Behaviour* 131(3–4):293–304.

———. 1997. Alarm calling and implications for risk perception in a desert baboon population. *Ethology* 103(5):384–394.

Crook, J. 1970. The socioecology of primates. In: *Social Behaviour in Birds and Mammals*, J. Crook (ed.). Academic Press, London. pp. 103–159.

Crook, J. and J. Gartlan. 1966. Evolution of primate societies. *Nature* 210:1200–1203.

Curio, E. 1976. *The Ethology of Predation*. Springer-Verlag, Berlin.

Dahlberg, F. 1981. *Woman the Gatherer*. Yale University Press, New Haven, Connecticut.

Daneel, A. 1979. Prey size and hunting methods of the crowned eagle. *Ostrich* 50:120–121.

Dart, R. 1953. The predatory transition from ape to man. *International Anthropological and Linguistic Review* 1:201–217.

Dart, R. and D. Craig. 1959. *Adventures with the Missing Link*. Harper, New York.

Darwin, C. 1874. *The Descent of Man*, Revised Edition. The Henneberry Company, Chicago.

Dawkins, R. 1976. *The Selfish Gene*. Oxford University Press, Oxford.

Defenders of Wildlife. 2001. Wolves around the world.
http://www.defenders.org/publications/wolvesarworld.pdf

Degler, C. 1991. *In Search of Human Nature*. Oxford University Press, New York.

Deurbrouck, J. and D. Miller. 2001. As cougar attacks grow, coexistence is key. *The Christian Science Monitor* 5/9/01. p. 9.

DeVore, I. and S. Washburn. 1963. Baboon ecology and human evolution. In: *African Ecology and Human Evolution*, C. Howell and F. Bourliere (eds.). Aldine, New York. pp. 335–367.

De Waal, F. and F. Lanting. 1997. *Bonobo: The Forgotten Ape*. University of California Press, Berkeley, California.

Discovery Channel. 1996. *Dragons of Komodo* [video]. Discovery Communications, Bethesda, Maryland.

Dittus, W. 1974. The ecology and behavior of the toque monkey, *Macaca sinica*. Ph.D. dissertation, University of Maryland, College Park, Maryland.

_____. 1975. Population dynamics of the toque monkey, *Macaca sinica*. In: *Socioecology and Psychology of Primates*, R. Tuttle (ed.). Mouton, The Hague. pp. 125–152.

_____. 1977. The socioecological basis for the conservation of the toque monkey (*Macaca sinica*) of Sri Lanka (Ceylon). In: *Primate Conservation*, HRH Rainier III and G. Bourne (eds.). Academic Press, New York. pp. 237–265.

_____. 1979. The evolution of behaviors regulating density and age-specific sex ratios in a primate population. *Behaviour* 69:265–302.

Domico, T. 1988. *Bears of the World*. Facts on File, New York.

Dunbar, R. 1988. *Primate Social Systems*. Comstock Publications, Ithaca.

Eason, P. 1989. Harpy eagle attempts predation on adult howler monkey. *Condor* 91(2):469–470.

Eaton, R. 1974. *The Cheetah: The Biology, Ecology, and Behavior of an Endangered Species*. Van Nostrand Reinhold, New York. pp. 41–87.

Ehrenreich, B. 1997. *Blood Rites: Origins and History of the Passions of War*. Henry Holt, New York.

Eisenberg, J., N. Muckenhirn and R. Rudran. 1972. The relation between ecology and social structure in primates. *Science* 176:863–874.

Eliot, J. 2003. What's for dinner? We are. *National Geographic* 8/03. [unnumbered page]

Elliott, J., I. Cowan, and C. Holling. 1977. Prey capture in the African lion. *Canadian Journal of Zoology* 55:1811–1828.

Ellis, R. 1996. *The Book of Sharks*. Alfred A. Knopf, New York.

Emmons, L. 1987. Comparative feeding ecology of felids in a neotropical rainforest. *Behavioural Ecology and Sociobiology* 20:271–283.

Endler, J. 1991. Interactions between predators and prey. In: *Behavioural Ecology: An Evolutionary Approach, Third Edition*, J. Krebs and N. Davies (ed.). Blackwell Scientific Publications, New York. pp. 169–196.

Estes, R. 1967. Predators and scavengers. *Natural History* 76:21–29.

Estes, R. and J. Goddard. 1967. Prey selection and hunting behavior of the African wild dog. *Journal of Wildlife Management* 31:52–70.

Everett, M. 1977. *A Natural History of Owls*. The Hamlyn Publishing Group, Ltd., London.

Ewer, R. 1954. Sabre-toothed tigers. *New Biology* 17:27–40.

_____. 1973. *The Carnivores*. Cornell University Press, New York.

Fay, J., R. Carroll, J. Kerbis Peterhans, and D. Harris. 1995. Leopard attack on and consumption of gorillas in the Central African Republic. *Journal of Human Evolution* 29(1):93–99.

Fedigan, L. 1974. The classification of predators by Japanese macaques (*Macaca fuscata*) in the mesquite chaparral habitat of south Texas. *American Journal of Physical Anthropology* 40(1):135.

_____. 1992. *Primate Paradigms*. University of Chicago Press, Chicago.

Fedigan, L., A. Rosenberger, S. Boinski, M. Norconk, and P. Garber. 1996. Critical issues in cebine evolution and behavior. In: *Adaptive Radiation of Neotropical Primates*, M. Norconk, A. Rosenberger, and P. Garber (eds.). Plenum Press, New York. pp. 219–228.

Feibel, C., F. Brown, and I. McDougall. 1989. Stratigraphic context of fossil hominids from the Omo Group deposits: northern Turkana basin, Kenya and Ethiopia. *American Journal of Physical Anthropology* 78:595–623.

Fowler, J. and J. Cope. 1964. Notes on harpy eagle in British Guiana. *Auk* 81:257–273.

Fox, R. 1967. In the beginning: aspects of hominid behavioural evolution. *Man* 2:415–433.

Fuller, T. and P. Kat. 1990. Movements, activity, and prey relationships of African wild dogs (*Lycaon pictus*) near Aitong, southwestern Kenya. *African Journal of Ecology* 28:330–350.

Gabunia, L., A. Vekua, D. Lordkipanidze et al. 2000. Earliest Pleistocene hominid cranial remains from Dmanisi, Republic of Georgia: taxonomy, geological setting, and age. *Science* 288:1019–1025.

Galdikas, B. 1985. Crocodile predation on a proboscis monkey in Borneo. *Primates* 26(4):495–496.

_____. 1995. *Reflections of Eden: My Years with the Orangutans of Borneo*. Little, Brown, New York.

Galdikas, B. and C. Yeager. 1984. Crocodile predation on a crab-eating macaque in Borneo. *American Journal of Primatology* 6(1):49–51.

Gandini, G. and P. Baldwin. 1978. An encounter between chimpanzees (*Pan troglodytes*) and a leopard (*Panthera pardus*) in Senegal. *Carnivore* 1(1):107–121.

Gargett, V. 1971. Some observations on black eagles in the Matopos, Rhodesia. *Ostrich,* Suppl. 9:91–124.

_____. 1990. *The Black Eagle: A Study of Verreaux's Eagle in Southern Africa*. Academic Press, London.

Gautier-Hion, A., R. Quris, and J. Gautier. 1983. Monospecific vs. polyspecific life: a comparative study of foraging and anti-predatory tactics in a community of *Cercopithecus* monkeys. *Behavioural Ecology and Sociobiology* 12(4):325–335.

Gautier-Hion, A. and C. Tutin. 1988. Mutual attack by a polyspecific association of monkeys against a crowned hawk eagle. *Folia Primatologica* 51:149–151.

Gebo, D. and E. Simons. 1984. Puncture marks on early African anthropoids. *American Journal of Physical Anthropology* 65(1):31–36.

Ghiglieri, M. 1984. *The Chimpanzees of Kibale Forest: A Field Study of Ecology and Social Structure*. Columbia University Press, New York.

_____. 1999. *The Dark Side of Man: Tracing the Origins of Male Violence*. Perseus Books, Reading, Massachusetts.

Gillard, L. 1979. Giant eagle owl. *Witwatersrand Bird Club News* 104:5–6.

Goldizen, A. 1987. Tamarins and marmosets: Communal care of offspring. In: *Primate Societies*, B. Smuts, D. Cheney, R. Seyfarth, R. Wrangham and T. Struhsaker (eds.). University of Chicago Press, Chicago. pp. 34–43.

Gonzales, R. 1968. A study of the breeding biology and ecology of the monkey-eating eagle. *Silliman Journal* 15:461–491.

Goodall, J. 1965. Chimpanzees of the Gombe Stream Reserve. In: *Primate Behavior: Field Studies of Monkeys and Apes*, I. De Vore (ed.). Holt, Rinehart, and Winston, New York. pp. 425–473.

_____. 1968. The behaviour of free-living chimpanzees in the Gombe Stream Reserve. *Animal Behaviour Monographs* 1:165–311.

_____. 1971. *In the Shadow of Man*. Houghton Mifflin, Boston.

_____. 1986. *The Chimpanzees of Gombe: Patterns of Behavior*. Harvard University Press, Cambridge, Massachusetts.

Goodman, S. 1994. Description of a new species of subfossil eagle from Madagascar: *Stephanoaetus* (Aves: Falconiformes) from the deposits of Ampasambazimba. *Proceedings of the Biological Society of Washington* 107:421–428.

Goodman, S., S. O'Connor, and O. Langrand. 1993. A review of predation on lemurs: implications for the evolution of social behavior in small, nocturnal primates. In: *Lemur Social Systems and Their Ecological Basis*, P. Kappeler and J. Ganzhorn (eds.). Plenum Press, New York. pp. 51–66.

Gore, R. 2002. New find: the first pioneer? *National Geographic* 8/02. [unnumbered addition to issue]

Goren-Inbar, N., N. Alperson, M. Kislev, O. Simchoni, Y. Melamed, A. Ben-Nun, and E. Werker. 2004. Evidence of hominin control of fire at Gesher Benot Ya'aqov, Israel. *Science* 304:725–727.

Greene, H. 1997. *Snakes: The Evolution of Mystery in Nature*. University of California Press, Berkeley, California.

Grzimek, B. 1975. *Grzimek's Animal Life Encyclopedia, Volume 6: Reptiles*. Van Nostrand Reinhold Company, New York.

_____. 1975. *Grzimek's Animal Life Encyclopedia, Volume 12: Mammals III*. Van Nostrand Reinhold Company, New York.

Guggisberg, C. 1975. *Wild Cats of the World*. Taplinger Publishing Company, New York.

Hall, K. 1965. Ecology and behavior of baboons, patas and vervet monkeys in Uganda. In: *The Baboon in Medical Research*, H. Vagtborg (ed.). University of Texas Press, San Antonio. pp. 43–61.

_____. 1966. Distribution and adaptation of baboons. *Symposium of the Zoological Society of London* 17:49.73.

Hamburg, D. 1971. Aggressive behavior of chimpanzees and baboons in natural habitats. *Journal of Psychiatric Research* 8:385–398.

Hamilton, P. 1981. The leopard *Panthera pardus* and the cheetah *Acinonyx jubatus* in Kenya. Unpublished report for the U.S. Fish and Wildlife Service, the African Wildlife Leadership Foundation and the Government of Kenya.

Hamilton, W., R. Buskirk, and W. Buskirk. 1975. Defensive stoning by baboons. *Nature* 256:488–489.

Hanif, M. 1970. The harpy eagle (*Harpia harpyja*) at Georgetown Zoo. In: *International Zoo Yearbook*, Vol. 10, J. Lucas (ed.). Zoological Society of London. pp. 24–25.

Harding, R. 1981. An order of omnivores: nonhuman primate diets in the wild. In: *Omnivorous Primates: Gathering and Hunting in Human Evolution*, R. Harding and G. Teleki (eds.). Columbia University Press, New York. pp. 191–214.

Harrison, G., J. Tanner, D. Pilbeam, and P. Baker. 1989. *Human Biology: An Introduction to Human Evolution, Variation, Growth, and Adaptability*. Oxford University Press, Oxford.

Hart, D. 2000. Primates as prey: ecological, morphological, and behavioral relationships between primate species and their predators. Ph.D. dissertation, Washington University, St. Louis, Missouri.

Hart, J., M. Katembo and K. Punga. 1996. Diet, prey selection and ecological relations of leopard and golden cat in the Ituri Forest, Zaire. *African Journal of Ecology* 34:364–379.

Hartstone-Rose, A., D. de Ruiter, L. Berger, and S. Churchill. [in press] A saber-tooth felid from Coopers Cave (Gauteng, South Africa) and its implications for *Megantereon* (Felidae Machairodontinae) taxonomy. *Journal of Systematic Paleontology of the Museum of Natural History, London.*

Harvey, P. and P. Greenwood. 1978. Anti-predator defense strategies: Some evolutionary problems. In: *Behavioural Ecology: An Evolutionary Approach*, First Edition, J. Krebs and N. Davies (eds.). Blackwell Scientific Publications, Oxford, London. pp. 129–151.

Harvey, P., M. Kavanagh, and T. Clutton-Brock. 1978. Sexual dimorphism in primate teeth. *Journal of Zoology, London* 186:475–485.

Hauser, M. 1988. How infant vervet monkeys learn to recognize starling alarm calls: the role of experience. *Behaviour* 105(3- 4):187–201.

Hausfater, G. 1975. *Dominance and Reproduction in Baboons (Papio cynocephalus).* S. Karger, Basel.

Hausfater, G. and S. Hrdy (eds.). 1984. *Infanticide: Comparative and Evolutionary Perspectives.* Aldine Publishing, New York.

Heald, F. and C. Shaw. 1991. Sabertooth cats. In: *Great Cats: Majestic Creatures of the Wild*, J. Seidensticker and S. Lumpkin (eds.). Rodale Press, Emmaus, Pennsylvania. pp. 24–25.

Herrero, S. 2002. *Bear Attacks: Their Causes and Avoidance.* The Lyons Press, Guilford, Connecticut.

Heymann, E. 1987. A field observation of predation on a moustached tamarin (*Saguinas mystax*) by an anaconda. *International Journal of Primatology* 8(2):193–195.

Hill, R. and R. Dunbar. 1998. An evaluation of the roles of predation rate and predation risk as selective pressures on primate grouping behaviour. *Behaviour* 135(4):411–430.

Hiraiwa-Hasegawa, M., R. Byrne, H. Takasaki, and J. Byrne. 1986. Aggression toward large carnivores by wild chimpanzees of Mahale Mountains National Park, Tanzania. *Folia Primatologica* 47(1):8- 13.

Hoogerwerf, A. 1970. *Udjung Kulon, The Land of the Last Javan Rhinoceros.* E. J. Brill, Leiden.

Hoppe-Dominik, B. 1984. Prey frequency of the leopard (*Panthera pardus*) in the Tai National Park of the Ivory Coast. *Mammalia* 48(4):477–488.

Howell, F. and G. Petter. 1976. Carnivora from the Omo Group Formations, Southern Ethiopia. In: *Earliest Man and Environments in the Lake Rudolf Basin*, Y. Coppens, F. Howell, G. Isaac, and R. Leakey (eds.). University of Chicago Press, Chicago. pp. 314–331.

Hrdy, S., C. Janson, and C. van Schaik. 1995. Infantcide: Let's not throw out the baby with the bath water. *Evolutionary Anthropology* 3(5):151–154.

Isbell, L. 1990. Sudden short-term increase in mortality of vervet monkeys (*Cercopithecus aethiops*) due to leopard predation in Amboseli National Park, Kenya. *American Journal of Primatology* 21(1):41–52.

_____. 1994. Predation on primates: Ecological patterns and evolutionary consequences. *Evolutionary Anthropology* 3(2):61- 71.

Isbell, L., D. Cheney, and R. Seyfarth. 1990. Costs and benefits of home range shifts among vervet monkeys (*Cercopithecus aethiops*) in Amboseli National Park, Kenya. *Behavioral Ecology and Sociobiology* 27:351–358.

_____. 1993. Are immigrant vervet monkeys, *Cercopithecus aethiops*, at greater risk of mortality than residents? *Animal Behaviour* 45:729–734.

Isemonger, R. 1962. *Snakes of Africa: Southern, Central and East.* Thomas Nelson and Sons, Johannesburg.

Iwamoto, T., A. Mori, and M. Kawai. 1995. [Antipredatory behaviour of gelada baboon.] *Reichorui Kenkyu/Primate Research* 11(3):286.

Izor, R. 1985. Sloths and other mammalian prey of the harpy eagle. In: *The Evolution and Ecology of Armadillos, Sloths, and Vermilinguas*, G. Montgomery (ed.). Smithsonian Institution Press, Washington, D.C. pp. 343–346.

Jackson, P. 1991. Man versus man-eaters. In: *Great Cats: Majestic Creatures of the Wild*, J. Seidensticker and S. Lumpkin (eds.). Rodale Press, Emmaus, Pennsylvania. pp. 212–213.

Janzen, D. 1980. When is it coevolution? *Evolution* 34:611–612.

Johanson, D. and M. Edey. 1981. *Lucy: The Beginnings of Humankind.* Simon and Schuster, New York.

Johanson, D. and J. Shreeve. 1989. *Lucy's Child.* William Morrow, New York.

Johnsingh, A. 1980. Ecology and behavior of the dhole or Indian wild dog, *Cuon alpinus* Pallas 1811, with special reference to predator-prey relations at Bandipur. Ph.D. dissertation, Madurai University, Tamil Nadu, India.

_____. 1983. Large mammalian prey-predators in Bandipur. *Journal of the Bombay Natural History Society* 80(1):1–57.

Johnson, S. 2003. The brain + emotions: fear. *Discover* 3/03. pp. 32–39.

Jolly, A. 1972. Hour of birth in primates and man. *Folia Primatologica* 18:108–121.

_____. 1985. *The Evolution of Primate Behavior*, Second Edition. Macmillan Publishing Company, New York.

Jones, H. and M. Jones. 1928. Maturation and emotion: fear of snakes. *Childhood Education* 5:136–143.

Joslin, J., H. Fletcher, and J. Emlen. 1964. A comparison of the responses to snakes of lab and wild reared rhesus monkeys. *Animal Behaviour* 22:348–352.

Jouventin, P. 1975. Observations sur le socio-ecologie du mandrill. *Terre Vie* 29:493–532.

Junshi, C. et al. 1990. *Diet, Lifestyle, and Mortality in China: A Study of the Characteristics of 65 Chinese Counties*. Cornell University Press, Ithaca, New York.

Jurmain, R., L. Kilgore, W. Trevathan, and H. Nelson. 2003. *Introduction to Physical Anthropology*, Ninth Edition. Wadsworth/Thomson Learning, Belmont, California.

Kala, A. 1998. Killers on the loose. *Asiaweek* 4/24/98. Environment section.

Kemp, A. 1990. What is a raptor? In: *Birds of Prey*, I. Newton (ed.). Facts on File, New York. pp. 14–31.

Kennedy, R. 1977. Notes on the biology and population status of the monkey-eating eagle of the Philippines. *Wilson Bulletin* 89(1):1–20.

_____. 1981. The air's noblest flier. *The Filipinas Journal of Science and Culture* 2:33–48.

_____. 1985. Conservation research of the Philippine eagle. *National Geographic Society Research Reports* 18:401–414.

Kingdon, J. 1974. *East African Mammals, Volume 1*. University of Chicago Press, Chicago.

_____. 1989. *East African Mammals, Volume III Part A (Carnivores)*. University of Chicago Press, Chicago.

Kitchener, A. 1991. *The Natural History of the Wild Cats*. Comstock Publishing Associates, Ithaca.

Klein, L. 1974. Agonistic behavior in neotropical primates. In: *Primate Aggression, Territoriality, and Xenophobia*, R. Holloway (ed.). Academic Press, New York. pp. 77–122.

Klein, L. F. 2004. *Women and Men in World Cultures*. McGraw Hill, Boston.

Klein, R. 1989. *The Human Career: Human Biological and Cultural Origins*. University of Chicago Press, Chicago.

_____. 1999. *The Human Career: Human Biological and Cultural Origins*, Second Edition. University of Chicago Press, Chicago.

Klein, R. and B. Edgar. 2002. *The Dawn of Human Culture*. John Wiley & Sons, New York.

Kortlandt, A. 1967. Experimentation with chimpanzees in the wild. In: *Neue Ergenbnisse der Primatologie Progress in Primatology*, First Congress of the International Primatological Society, Frankfurt (May 26–July 30, 1966), D. Starck, R. Schneider, and H. Kuhn (eds.). Gustav Fischer Verlag, Stuttgart. pp. 208–224.

Kruuk, H. 1970. Interactions between populations of spotted hyaenas (*Crocuta crocuta*, Erxleben) and their prey species. In: *Animal Populations in Relation to Their Food Resources*, A. Watson (ed.). Blackwell Scientific, Oxford. pp. 359–374.

_____. 1972. *The Spotted Hyena: A Study of Predation and Social Behavior*. University of Chicago Press, Chicago.

_____. 1975. Functional aspects of social hunting by carnivores. In: *Function and Evolution in Behaviour*, G. Baerends, C. Beer, and A. Manning (eds.). Clarendon Press, Oxford. pp. 119–141.

_____. 1986. Interactions between Felidae and their prey species: a review. In: *Cats of the World: Biology, Conservation and Management*, S. Miller and D. Everett (eds.). National Wildlife Federation, Washington, D.C. pp. 353–374.

_____. 2002. *Hunter and Hunted: Relationships between Carnivores and People*. Cambridge University Press, Cambridge, U.K.

Kruuk, H. and M. Turner. 1967. Comparative notes on predation by lion, leopard, cheetah, and wild dog in the Serengeti area, East Africa. *Mammalia* 31(1):1–27.

Kummer, H. 1971. *Primate Societies*. Aldine-Atherton, Chicago.

Lamprecht, J. 1978. The relationship between food competition and foraging group size in some large carnivores: a hypothesis. *Zeitschrift fuer Tierpsychologie* 46:337–343.

Leakey, M. 1976. Carnivora of the East Rudolf Succession. In: *Earliest Man and Environments in the Lake Rudolf Basin*, Y. Coppens, F. Howell, G. Isaac, and R. Leakey (eds.). University of Chicago Press, Chicago. pp. 302–313.

Lee, R. 1969. !Kung bushman subsistence: an input-output analysis. In: *Environment and Cultural Behavior*, A. Vayda (ed.). Natural History Press, New York. pp. 47–79.

_____. 2003. Eating Christmas in the Kalahari. In: *Annual Editions: Anthropology 03/04*, E. Angeloni (ed.). McGraw-Hill/Dushkin, Guilford, Connecticut. pp. 31–34.

Le Gros Clark, W. 1959. *The Antecedents of Man*. Edinburgh University Press, Edinburgh.

Leland, L. and T. Struhsaker. 1993. Teamwork tactics: Kibale forest's monkeys and eagles each depend on strategic cooperation for survival. *Natural History* 102(4):42–48.

Leutenegger, W. and J. Kelley. 1977. Relationship of sexual dimorphism in canine size and body size to social, behavioral, and ecological correlates in anthropoid primates. *Primates* 18:117–136.

Lévi-Strauss, C. 1966. *The Savage Mind*. University of Chicago Press, Chicago.

Lindburg, D. 1977. Feeding behaviour and diet of rhesus (*Macaca mulatta*) in a Siwalik Forest in North India. In: *Primate Ecology*, T. Clutton-Brock (ed.). Academic Press, London. pp. 223–249.

Lineaweaver, T. and R. Backus. 1970. *The Natural History of Sharks*. Lyons & Burford Publishers, New York.

Lovejoy, C. 1981. The origin of man. *Science* 211(4480):341–350.

Lumpkin, S. 1993. *Great Creatures of the World: Big Cats*. Facts on File, New York.

Macdonald, D. (ed.). 1984. *The Encyclopedia of Mammals*. Facts on File, New York.

_____. 1992. *The Velvet Claw: A Natural History of the Carnivores*. BBC Books, London.

Macedonia, J. 1990. What is communicated in the anti-predator calls of lemurs: evidence from playback experiments with ringtailed and ruffed lemurs. *Ethology* 86(3):177–190.

_____. 1993. Adaptation and phylogenetic constraints in the antipredator behavior of ringtailed and ruffed lemurs. In: *Lemur Social Systems and Their Ecological Basis*, P. Kappeler and J. Ganzhorn (eds.). Plenum Press, New York. pp. 67–84.

MacKinnon, J. and K. MacKinnon. 1978. Comparative feeding ecology of six sympatric primates in west Malaysia. In: *Recent Advances in Primatology, Volume 1*, D. Chivers and J. Herbert (eds.). Academic Press, London. pp. 305–322.

Maclatchey, A. 1937. Etude des oiseau de Gabon. *Oiseau* 7:71- 76.

Maclean, G. 1993. *Roberts' Birds of Southern Africa,* Sixth Edition. John Voelcker Bird Book Fund, Capetown.

Maglio, V. 1975. Pleistocene faunal evolution in Africa and Eurasia. In: *After the Australopithecines: Stratigraphy, Ecology, and Culture Change in the Middle Pleistocene*, K. Butzer and G. Isaac (eds.). Mouton Publishers, The Hague. pp. 419–476.

Makacha, S. and G. Schaller. 1969. Observations on lions in the Lake Manyara National Park, Tanzania. *East African Wildlife Journal* 7:99–103.

Man-Eating Snakes I and Man-Eating Snakes II. 2004. Not for the squeamish. http://home.att.net/~crinaustin/Snake1.htm and http://home.att.net/~crinaustin/Snake2.htm

Marean, C. 1989. Sabertooth cats and their relevance to early hominid diet and evolution. *Journal of Human Evolution* 18:559–582.

Marks, J. 1991. What's old and new in molecular phylogenetics. *American Journal of Physical Anthropology* 84:207–219.

_____. 2002. *What It Means to Be 98% Chimpanzee: Apes, People, and Their Genes*. University of California Press, Berkeley, California.

Marks, J., C. Schmid, and V. Sarich. 1988. DNA hybridization as a guide to phylogeny: relations of the Hominoidea. *Journal of Human Evolution* 17:769–786.

Martin, L. 1989. Fossil history of the terrestrial carnivora. In: *Carnivore Behavior, Ecology, and Evolution*, J. Gittleman (ed.). Comstock/Cornell University Press, Ithaca. pp. 536–568.

Martin, R. 1972. A preliminary field study of the lesser mouse lemur (*Microcebus murinus* J. Miller 1777). *Zeitschrift für Tierpsychologie* 9:43–89.

_____. 1990. *Primate Origins and Evolution: A Phylogenetic Reconstruction*. Princeton University Press. Princeton, New Jersey.

Masataka, N. 1993. Categorical responses to natural and synthesized alarm calls in Goeldi's monkeys (*Callimico goeldii*). *Primates* 24:40–51.

Mattison, C. 1995. *The Encyclopedia of Snakes*. Facts on File, New York.

Maurer, A. 1965. What children fear. *Journal of Genetic Psychology* 106:167–177.

McDougal, C. 1977. *The Face of the Tiger*. Rivington Books, London.

———. 1991. Man-eaters. In: *Great Cats: Majestic Creatures of the Wild*, J. Seidensticker and S. Lumpkin (eds.). Rodale Press, Emmaus, Pennsylvania. pp. 204–211.

McGrew, W. 1976. An encounter between a leopard and a group of chimpanzees at Gombe National Park. [unpublished report] 11 pp.

McKenzie, A. 1991. Co-operative hunting in the black-backed jackal *Canis mesomelas*. *Dissertation Abstracts International, Science and English* B52(4):1902.

Mech, L. D. 1970. *The Wolf*. The Natural History Press, Garden City, New York.

Mehrtens, J. 1987. *Living Snakes of the World*. Sterling Publications, New York.

Meshach, J. 2004. All about feathers. *Mews News* 24(1):7–8.

Mills, M. 1978. Foraging behaviour of the brown hyena (*Hyaena brunnea* Thunberg, 1820) in the southern Kalahari. *Zeitschrift für Tierpshychologie* 48:113–141.

———. 1989. The comparative behavioral ecology of hyenas: The importance of diet and food dispersion. In: *Carnivore Behavior, Ecology and Evolution*, J. Gittleman (ed.). Cornell University Press, Ithaca. pp. 125–142.

Mills, M. and H. Biggs. 1993. Prey apportionment and related ecological relationships between large carnivores in Kruger National Park. In: *Mammals as Predators*, N. Dunstone and M. Gorman (eds.) Clarendon Press, Oxford. pp. 253–268.

Milton, K. 1999. A hypothesis to explain the role of meat eating in human evolution. *Evolutionary Anthropology* 8:11–21.

Mineka, S., R. Keir, and V. Price. 1980. Fear of snakes in wild- and laboratory-reared rhesus monkeys (*Macaca mulata*). *Animal Learning Behavior* 8:653–663.

Minton, S. and M. Minton. 1973. *Giant Reptiles*. Charles Scribner's Sons, New York.

Mitchell, C., S. Boinski, and C. van Schaik. 1991. Competitive regimes and female bonding in two species of squirrel monkeys (*Saimiri oerstedi* and *S. sciureus*). *Behavioral Ecology and Sociobiology* 28:55–60.

Moody, M. and E. Menzel. 1976. Vocalizations and their behavioral contexts in the tamarin, *Saguinus fuscicollis*. *Folia Primatologica* 25:73–94.

Moore, J. 1984. Female transfer in primates. *International Journal of Primatology* 5:537–589.

Montgomery, G. and A. Rand. 1978. Movements, body temperature and hunting strategy of a boa constrictor. *Copeia* 1978:532–533.

Mourer-Chauvire, C. 1981. Première indication de la présence de phorusracidés, famille d'oiseaux géants d'Amerique du Sud, dans le Tertiaire Européen: Ameghinornis nov. gen. (Aves, Ralliformes) des Phosphorites du Quercy, France. *Géobios* 14:637–647.

Msuya, C. 1993. Feeding habits of crowned eagles, *Stephanoaetus coronatus*, in Kiwengoma Forest Reserve, Matumbi Hills, Tanzania. In: *Proceedings of the 8th Pan-African Ornithological Congress: Birds and the Environment*, R. Trevor Wilson (ed.). pp. 118–120.

Mukherjee, A. and S. Gupta. 1965. Habits of the rhesus macaque *Macaca mulatta* (Zimmermann) in the Sundarbans, 24-Parganas, West Bengal. *Journal of the Bombay Natural History Society* 62:145–146.

Murphy, J. and R. Henderson. 1997. *Tales of Giant Snakes: A Historical Natural History of Anacondas and Pythons*. Krieger Publishing Company, Malabar, Florida.

Nagel, C. 1973. A comparison of anubis baboons, hamadryas baboons, and their hybrids at a species border in Ethiopia. *Folia Primatologica* 19:104–165.

Napier, J. and P. Napier. 1985. *The Natural History of the Primates*. MIT Press, Cambridge, Massachusetts.

National Public Radio. 2004. Bicyclist saved from mountain lion attack. *All Things Considered* 1/9/04.

Newman, K. 1970. Giant eagle owl. *Witwatersrand Bird Club News Sheet* 71:16.

Newton, P. 1985. A note on golden jackals (*Canis aureus*) and their relationship with langurs (*Presbytis entellus*) in Kanha Tiger Reserve. *Journal of the Bombay Natural History Society* 82:633–636.

Neyman, P. 1977. Aspects of the ecology and social organization of free-ranging cotton-top tamarins (*Saguinus oedipus*) and the conservation status of the species. In: *The Biology and Conservation of the Callitrichidae*, D. Kleiman (ed.). Smithsonian Institution Press, Washington, D.C. pp. 39–72.

Nicastro, N. 2001. Habitats for humanity: effects of visual affordance on the evolution of hominid antipredator communication. *Evolutionary Anthropology* 10:153–157.

Nishida, T., M. Hiraiwa-Hasegawa, and Y. Takahata. 1985. Group extinction and female transfer in wild chimpanzees in the Mahale National Park, Tanzania. *Zeitschrift für Tierpsychologie* 67:281–301.

Norris, J. 1990. The semantics of *Cebus olivaceus* alarm calls: object designation and attribution. *Dissertation Abstracts International* B52(3):1160.

Nowak, R. 1991. *Walker's Mammals of the World, Volumes I and II*. The Johns Hopkins University Press, Baltimore.

Nunes, C., J. Bicca-Marques, K. Schacht, and A. de Alencar Araripe. 1998. Reaction of wild emperor tamarins to the presence of snakes. *Neotropical Primates* 6(1):20.

Oda, R. and N. Masataka. 1996. Interspecific responses of ringtailed lemurs to playbacks of antipredator alarm calls given by sifakas. *International Primatological Society/American Society of Primatologists Congressional Abstracts* #501.

Oliwenstein, L. 2000. Dr. Darwin. In: *Physical Anthropology 00/01*, E. Angeloni (ed.). Dushkin McGraw-Hill, Guilford, Connecticut. pp. 219–222.

Olson, S. 1985. The fossil record of birds. In: *Avian Biology*, D. Farner, J. King, and K. Parker (eds.). Academic Press, New York. pp. 79–238.

Oppenheimer, J. 1977. *Presbytis entellus*, the Hanuman langur. In: *Primate Conservation*, HRH Rainier III and G. Bourne (eds.). Academic Press, New York. pp. 469–512.

Osada, Y. 1991. [A comparison of fear responses to snakes of wild- and lab-reared squirrel monkeys.] *Reichorui Kenkyu Nempo* 7(2):131.

Owen, D. 1980. *Survival in the Wild: Camouflage and Mimicry*. The University of Chicago Press, Chicago.

Owens, M. and D. Owens. 1978. Feeding ecology and its influence on social organization in brown hyenas (*Hyaena brunnea*) of the central Kalahari Desert. *East African Wildlife Journal* 16(2):113–136.

Packer, D. and J. Clottes. 2000. When lions ruled France. *Natural History* 11/00. pp. 52–57.

Packer, C., D. Scheel, and A. Pusey. 1990. Why lions form groups: food is not enough. *American Naturalist* 136(1):1–19.

Park, M. 2002. *Biological Anthropology*, Third Edition. McGraw-Hill Mayfield, Boston.

Passamani, M. 1995. Field observation of a group of Geoffroy's marmosets mobbing a margay cat. *Folia Primatologica* 64:163–166.

Patterson, J. 1925. *The Man-Eating Lions of Tsavo*. Field Museum of Natural History, Chicago.

Paulraj, S. 1995. Prey-predator relationships with special reference to the tiger, panther and dhole competitions in Kalakad-Mundanthurai Tiger Reserve (Tirunelveli District Tamil Nadu). *Indian Forester* (October):922–930.

Peetz, A., M. Norconk, and W. Kinzey. 1992. Predation by jaguar on howler monkeys (*Alouatta seniculus*) in Venezuela. *American Journal of Primatology* 28:223–228.

Pereira, M. and J. Macedonia. 1991. Ringtailed lemur anti-predator calls denote predator class not response urgency. *Animal Behaviour* 41(3):543–544.

Peres, C. 1990. A harpy eagle successfully captures an adult male red howler monkey. *Wilson Bulletin* 102(3):560–561.

———. 1991. Ecology of mixed-species groups of tamarins in Amazonian terra firme forests. Ph.D. dissertation, University of Cambridge, Cambridge, U.K.

Petter, G. 1973. Carnivores Pleistocènes du ravin d'Olduvai (Tanzanie). In: *Fossil Vertebrates of Africa, Volume 3*, L. Leakey, R. Savage, and S. Coryndon (eds.). Academic Press, New York. pp. 43–100.

Pfeffer, P. (ed.). 1989. *Predators and Predation: The Struggle for Life in the Animal World*. Facts on File, New York.

Phillips, K. 1995. Differing responses to a predator (*Eira barbara*) by *Alouatta* and *Cebus*. *Neotropical Primates* 3(2):45–46.

Phythian-Adams, E. 1939. Behaviour of monkeys when attacked. *Journal of Bombay Natural History Society* 41:653.

Pienaar, U. 1969. Predator-prey relationships among the larger mammals of the Kruger National Park. *Koedoe* (12):108–176.

Pitman, C. and J. Adamson. 1978. Notes on the ecology and ethology of the giant eagle owl, *Bubo lacteus*. *Honeyguide* 96:26–43.

Pola, Y. and C. Snowdon. 1975. The vocalizations of pygmy marmosets (*Cebuella pygmaea*). *Animal Behaviour* 23:826–842.

Pooley, A. and C. Gans. 1976. The Nile crocodile. *Scientific American* 234:114–124.

Pooley, A., T. Hines, and J. Shield. 1989. Attacks on humans. In: *Crocodiles and Alligators*, C. Ross (ed.). Facts on File, New York. pp. 172–186.

Pope, C. 1980. *The Giant Snakes: The Natural History of the Boa Constrictor, the Anaconda, and the Largest Pythons*. Alfred A. Knopf, New York.

Power, M. 1991. *The Egalitarians, Human and Chimpanzee: An Anthropological View of Social Organization*. Cambridge University Press, Cambridge, U.K.

Prater, S. 1971. *The Book of Indian Animals*, Third Edition. Bombay Natural History Society, Bombay, India.

Quammen, D. 2003. *Monster of God*. W. W. Norton, New York.

Quiatt, D. and V. Reynolds. 1995. *Primate Behaviour: Information, Social Knowledge, and the Evolution of Culture*. Cambridge University Press, Cambridge, U.K.

Rabinowitz, A. 1988. The clouded leopard in Taiwan. *Oryx* 22:46–47.

———. 1991. *Chasing the Dragon's Tail: The Struggle to Save Thailand's Wild Cats*. Doubleday, New York.

Raemaekers, J. and D. Chivers. 1980. Socioecology of Malayan forest primates. In: *Malayan Forest Primates: Ten Years' Study in Tropical Rain Forest*, D. Chivers (ed.). Plenum Press, New York. pp. 279–331.

Rak, Y. 1991. Lucy's pelvic anatomy: its role in bidpedal gait. *Journal of Human Evolution* 20:283–290.

Rakotondravony, D., S. Goodman, and V. Soarimalala. 1998. Predation on *Hapalemur griseus griseus* by *Boa manditra* (Boidae) in the littoral forest of eastern Madagascar. *Folia Primatologica* 69(6):405–408.

Rasoloarison, R., B. Rasolonandrasana, J. Ganzhorn, and S. Goodman. 1995. Predation on vertebrates in the Kirindy Forest, Western Madagascar. *Ecotropica* 1:59–65.

Rautenbach, I. and J. Nel. 1978. Coexistence in Transvaal carnivora. *Bulletin of the Carnegie Museum of Natural History* 6:138–145.

Rettig, N. 1977. In quest of the snatcher. *Audubon Magazine* 79:26–49.

———. 1978. Breeding behavior of the harpy eagle (*Harpia harpyja*). *Auk* 95:629–643.

_____. 1995. Remote world of the harpy eagle. *National Geographic* 187(2):40–49.

Reynolds, V. and F. Reynolds. 1965. Chimpanzees of Budongo Forest. In: *Primate Behavior: Field Studies of Monkeys and Apes*, I. DeVore (ed.). Holt, Rinehart and Winston, New York. pp. 368–424.

Rice, C. 1986. Observations on predators and prey at Eravikulam National Park, Kerala, India. *Journal of the Bombay Natural History Society* 83(2):283–305.

Rijksen, H. 1978. *A Field Study on Sumatran Orangutans, (Pongo pygmaeus abelii): Ecology, Behaviour and Conservation*. Veenman and Zonen, Wageningen, The Netherlands.

Rijksen, H. and A. Rijksen-Graatsma. 1975. Orang-utan rescue work in north Sumatra. *Oryx* 13(1):63–73.

Romer, A. 1955. *Vertebrate Paleontology*. University of Chicago Press, Chicago.

Rose, L. and F. Marshall. 1996. Meat eating, hominid sociality, and home bases revisited. *Current Anthropology* 37(2):307–319.

Rose, W. 1962. *The Reptiles and Amphibians of Southern Africa*. Maskew Miller, Cape Town, South Africa.

Rosevear, D. 1974. *The Carnivores of West Africa*. British Museum of Natural History, London.

Ross, C. 1993. Predator mobbing by an all-male band of Hanuman langurs (*Presbytis entellus*). *Primates* 34(1):105–107.

Ross, C. A. (ed.) 1989. *Crocodiles and Alligators*. Facts on File, New York.

Roughgarden, J. 1983. The theory of coevolution. In: *Coevolution*, D. Futuyma and M. Slatkin (eds.). Sinauer Associates, Sunderland. pp. 33–64.

Ruse, M. 1993. Evolution and ethics: the sociobiological approach. In: *Environmental Ethics: Readings in Theory and Application*, L. Pojman (ed.). Jones and Bartlett, Boston. pp. 91–109.

Ruse, M. and E. O. Wilson. 1985. The evolution of ethics. *New Scientist* 108:50–52.

Saayman, G. 1971. Baboons responses to predators. *African Wild Life* 25(2):46–49.

Saberwal, V., J. Gibbs, R. Chellam, and A. Johnsingh. 1994. Lion-human conflict in the Gir Forest, India. *Conservation Biology* 8(2):501–507.

Sanders, W., J. Trapani, and J. Mitani. 2003. Taphonomic aspects of crowned hawk-eagle predation on monkeys. *Journal of Human Evolution* 44:87–105.

Sanz, C. 2004. Behavioral ecology of chimpanzees in a central African forest: *Pan troglodytes troglodytes* in the Goualougo Triangle, Republic of Congo. Ph.D. dissertation, Washington University, St. Louis, Missouri.

Sauther, M. 1989. Anti-predation behavior in troops of free-ranging *Lemur catta* at Beza Mahafaly Special Reserve, Madagascar. *International Journal of Primatology* 10(6):595–606.

Schaller, G. 1963. *The Mountain Gorilla*. University of Chicago Press, Chicago.

————. 1967. *The Deer and the Tiger*. University of Chicago Press, Chicago.

————. 1972. *The Serengeti Lion: A Study of Predator-Prey Relations*. University of Chicago Press, Chicago.

Schaller, G., H. Jinchu, P. Wenshi, and Z. Jing. 1985. *The Giant Pandas of Wolong*. University of Chicago Press, Chicago.

Schaller, G., H. Li, J. Ren, M. Qiu, and H. Wang. 1987. Status of large mammals in the Taxkorgan Reserve, Xinjiang, China. *Biological Conservation* 42:53–71.

Schaller, G. and G. Lowther. 1969. The relevance of carnivore behavior to the study of early hominids. *Southwest Journal of Anthropology* 25:307–341.

Schaller, G. and J. Vasconcelos. 1978. Jaguar predation on capybara. *Zeitschrift für Saugetierkunde* 43:296–301.

Searcy, Y. and N. Caine. 1998. Reactions of captive Geoffroy's marmosets to experimentally presented calls of a raptorial and non-raptorial bird. *American Journal of Primatology* 45(2):206.

Seidensticker, J. 1985. Primates as prey of *Panthera* cats in South Asian habitats. Paper given at the seventh annual meeting of the American Society of Primatology, University of Buffalo State University of New York, Niagara Falls, New York, June 1–4, 1985.

————. 1991. Leopards. In: *Great Cats: Majestic Creatures of the Wild*, J. Seidensticker and S. Lumpkin (eds.). Rodale Press, Emmaus, Pennsylvania. pp. 106–115.

Seidensticker, J., R. Lahiri, K. Das, and A. Wright. 1976. Problem tiger in the Sundarbans. *Oryx* 11:267–273.

Seidensticker, J. and I. Suyono. 1980. *The Javan Tiger and the Meru-Betiri Reserve, a Plan for Management*. International Union for Conservation of Nature and Natural Resources, Gland, Switzerland.

Seyfarth, R. and D. Cheney. 1980. The ontogeny of vervet monkey (*Cercopithecus aethiops*) alarm calling behavior: a preliminary report. *Zeitschrift für Tierpsychologie* 54(1):37–56.

————. 1986. Vocal development in vervet monkeys. *Animal Behaviour* 34:1640–1658.

Seyfarth, R., D. Cheney, and P. Marler. 1980. Monkey responses to three different alarm calls: Evidence for predator classification and semantic communication. *Science* 210:801–803.

Sherman, P. 1991. Harpy eagle predation on a red howler. *Folia Primatologica* 56(1):53–56.

Shine, R. 1991. Why do larger snakes eat larger prey items? *Functional Ecology* 5(4):493–502.

Shine, R., P. Harlow, J. Keogh, and Boeadi. 1998. The influence of sex and body size on food habits of a giant tropical snake, *Python reticulatus*. *Functional Ecology* 12(2):248–258.

Shipman, P. 1983. Early hominid lifestyle: hunting and gathering or foraging and scavenging? In: *Animals and Archaeology: Hunters and Their Prey*, J. Clutton-Brock and C. Grigson (eds.). BAR, International Series 163, Oxford. pp. 31–47.

———. 2000. Scavenger hunt. In: *Physical Anthropology 00/01*, E. Angeloni (ed.). Dushkin McGraw-Hill, Guilford, Connecticut. pp. 118–121.

Sigg, H. 1980. Differentiation of female positions in hamadryas one-male units. *Zeitschrift fuer Tierpsychologie* 53:265–302.

Simons, E. 1997. Lemurs: old and new. In: *Natural Change and Human Impact in Madagascar*, S. Goodman and B. Patterson (eds.). Smithsonian Institution, Washington, D.C. pp. 142–166.

Simons, E., L. Godfrey, W. Jungers, P. Chatrath, and J. Ravaoarisoa. 1995. A new species of *Mesopithecus* (Primates, Palaeopropithecidae) from northern Madagascar. *International Journal of Primatology* 16:653–682.

Simons, J. 1966. The presence of leopard and a study of food debris in the leopard lairs of the Mount Suswa Caves, Kenya. *Bulletin of Cave Exploration Group East Africa* 1:51–69.

Skinner, J. 1976. Ecology of the brown hyaena, *Hyaena brunnea*, in the Transvaal with a distribution map for Southern Africa. *South African Journal of Science* 72:262–269.

Skorupa, J. 1989. Crowned eagles, *Stephanoaetus coronatus*, in rainforest: observations on breeding chronology and diet at a nest in Uganda. *Ibis* 131:294–298.

Small, M. 1997. The good, the bad, and the ugly. *Evolutionary Anthropology* 5:143–147.

Smuts, B. 1987. Gender, aggression, and influence. In: Primate Societies, B. Smuts, D. Cheney, R. Seyfarth, R. Wrangham, and T. Struhsaker (eds.). University of Chicago Press, Chicago. pp. 400–412.

Sommer, V., D. Mendoza-Grandados, and U. Reichard. 1998. Predation risk causes grouping pattern in Hanuman langurs (*Presbytis entellus*). *Folia Primatologica* 69(4):223–224.

Speth, J. 1987. Early hominid subsistence strategies in seasonal habitats. *Journal of Archaeological Science* 14:13–29.

Srivastava, A. 1991. Cultural transmission of snake-mobbing in free-ranging hanuman langurs. *Folia Primatologica* 56(2):117–120.

Srivastava, K., A. Bhardwaj, C. Abraham, and V. Zacharias. 1996. Food habits of mammalian predators in Periyar Tiger Reserve, South India. *Indian Forester* 122(10):877–883.

Stacey, P. 1986. Group size and foraging efficiency in yellow baboons. *Behavioural Ecology and Sociobiology* 18:175–187.

Stafford-Deitsch, J. 1987. *Sharks: A Photographer's Story*. Sierra Club Books, San Francisco.

Stanford, C. 1989. Predation on capped langurs (*Presbytis pileata*) by cooperatively hunting jackals (*Canis aureus*). *American Journal of Primatology* 19:53–56.

_____. 1995. The influence of chimpanzee predation on group size and anti-predator behaviour in red colobus monkeys. *Animal Behaviour* 49(3):577–587.

_____. 1999. *The Hunting Ape: Meat Eating and the Origins of Human Behavior.* Princeton University Press, Princeton, New Jersey.

Stanford, C. and J. Allen. 1991. On strategic storytelling: current models of human behavioral evolution. *Current Anthropology* 32(1):58–61.

Stanford, C., J. Wallis, H. Matama, and J. Goodall. 1994. Patterns of predation by chimpanzee on red colobus monkeys in Gombe National Park, 1982–1991. *American Journal of Physical Anthropology* 94(2):213–228.

Stanford, C. and R. Wrangham. 1998. *Chimpanzee and Red Colobus: The Ecology of Predator and Prey.* Harvard University Press, Cambridge, Massachusetts.

Starin, E. 1991. Socioecology of the red colobus monkey in The Gambia with particular reference to female-male differences and transfer patterns. Ph.D. dissertation, The City University of New York, New York.

Starin, E. and G. Burghardt. 1992. African rock pythons in the Gambia: observations on natural history and interactions with primates. *Snake* 24(1):50–62.

Stelzner, J. and K. Strier. 1981. Hyena predation on an adult male baboon. *Mammalia* 45:259–260.

Stevenson-Hamilton, J. 1947. *Wildlife in South Africa.* Cassell and Co., London.

Steyn, P. 1983. *Birds of Prey of Southern Africa.* Tanager Books, Dover, New Hampshire.

Stjernstedt, B. 1975. Eagle attack. *Black Lechwe* 12:18–22.

Stoltz, L. 1977. The population dynamics of baboons *(Papio* ursinus Kerr 1792) in the Transvaal. Ph.D. dissertation, University of Pretoria, Pretoria, South Africa.

Stoltz, L. and G. Saayman. 1970. Ecology and behaviour of baboons in the Northern Transvaal. *Annals of the Transvaal Museum* 26:99–143.

Struhsaker, T. 1967. Auditory communication among vervet monkeys (*Cercopithecus aethiops*). In: *Social Communication Among Primates*, S. Altmann (ed.). University of Chicago Press, Chicago. pp. 281–324.

_____. 1975. *The Red Colobus Monkey.* University of Chicago Press, Chicago.

Struhsaker, T. and J. Gartlan. 1970. Observations on the behaviour and ecology of the patas monkey (*Erythrocebus patas*) in the Waza Reserve, Cameroon. *Journal of the Zoological Society, London* 161:49–63.

Struhsaker, T. and M. Leakey. 1990. Prey selectivity by crowned hawk-eagles on monkeys in the Kibale Forest, Uganda. *Behavioural Ecology and Sociobiology* 26(6):435–443.

Strum, S. 2001. *Almost Human: A Journey into the World of Baboons*. University of Chicago Press, Chicago.

Sugiyama, Y. 1972. Social characteristics and socialization of wild chimpanzees. In: *Primate Socialization*, F. Poirier (ed.). Random House, New York. pp. 145–163.

Sunquist, F. and M. Sunquist. 1988. *Tiger Moon*. University of Chicago Press, Chicago.

Sunquist, M. and F. Sunquist. 1989. Ecological constraints on predation by large felids. In: *Carnivore Behavior, Ecology, and Evolution*, J. Gittleman (ed.). Cornell University Press, Ithaca. pp. 283–301.

Sussman, R. 1974. Ecological distinctions in sympatric species of *Lemur*. In: *Prosimian Biology*, R. Martin, G. Doyle and A. Walker (eds.). Duckworth, London. pp. 75–108.

————. 1977. Feeding behaviour of *Lemur catta* and *Lemur fulvus*. In: *Primate Ecology*, T. Clutton-Brock (ed.). Academic Press, London. pp. 1–37.

————. 1999. Species-specific dietary patterns in primates and human dietary adaptations. In: The Biological Basis of Human Behavior, R. Sussman (ed.). Prentice Hall, Upper Saddle River, New Jersey. pp. 143–157.

————. 2000. Piltdown man: the father of American field primatology. In: *Primate Encounters: Models of Science, Gender, and Society*, S. Strum and L. Fedigan (eds.). University of Chicago Press, Chicago. pp. 85–103.

————. 2003a. *Primate Ecology and Social Structure, Volume I: Lorises, Lemurs and Tarsiers*. Pearson Custom Publishing, Needham Heights, Massachusetts.

————. 2003b. *Primate Ecology and Social Structure, Volume II: New World Monkeys*. Pearson Custom Publishing, Needham Heights, Massachusetts.

————. 2004. Are humans inherently violent? In: *Anthropology Explored: Revised and Expanded*, R. Selig, M. London, and P. Kaupp (eds.). Smithsonian Books, Washington, D.C. pp. 30–45.

Sussman, R. and A. Chapman. 2004. *The Origins and Nature of Sociality*. Aldine de Gruyter, New York.

Sussman, R. and W. Kinzey. 1984. The ecological role of the Callitrichidae: a review. *American Journal of Physical Anthropology* 64:419–449.

Sussman, R. and I. Tattersall. 1981. Behavior and ecology of *Macaca fascicularis* in Mauritius: a preliminary study. *Primates* 22(2):192–205.

————. 1986. Distribution, abundance, and putative ecological strategy of *Macaca fascicularis* on the island of Mauritius, southwestern Indian Ocean. *Folia Primatologica* 46:28–43.

Suzuki, A. 1969. An ecological study of chimpanzees in a savanna woodland. *Primates* 10:103–148.

Swedell, L. 2005. *Strategies of Sex and Survival in Female Hamadryas Baboons*. Prentice Hall, Upper Saddle River, New Jersey.

Tanaka, J. 1976. Subsistence ecology of Central Kalahari San. In: *Kalahari Hunter-Gatherers: Studies of the !Kung San and Their Neighbors*, R. Lee and I. De Vore (eds.). Harvard University Press, Cambridge, Massachusetts. pp. 98–119.

Tanner, N. and A. Zihlman. 1976. Women in evolution: innovation and selection in human origins. *Signs* 1:585–608.

Tarboton, W. l989. *African Birds of Prey*. Cornell University Press, Ithaca.

Tattersall, I. 1982. *The Primates of Madagascar*. Columbia University Press, New York.

———. 1998. *Becoming Human*. Harcourt Brace, New York.

———. 1999. The major features of human evolution. In: *The Biological Basis of Human Behavior*, Second Edition, R. Sussman (ed.). Prentice-Hall, Upper Saddle River, New Jersey. pp. 45–54.

Tattersall, I. and J. Schwartz. 2000. *Extinct Humans*. Westview Press, Boulder, Colorado.

Teaford, M. and P. Ungar. 2000. Diet and the evolution of the earliest human ancestors. *Proceedings of the National Academy of Science* 97(25):13,506–13,511.

Tenaza, R. and R. Tilson. 1977. Evolution of long-distance alarm calls in Kloss's gibbon. *Nature* 268:233–235.

Terborgh, J. 1983. *Five New World Primates: A Study in Comparative Ecology*. Princeton University Press, Princeton.

———. 1990. Mixed flocks and polyspecific associations: cost and benefits of mixed groups to birds and monkeys. *American Journal of Primatology* 21(2):87–100.

Terborgh, J. and C. Janson. 1986. The socioecology of primate groups. *Annual Review of Ecology and Systematics* 17:111–135.

Thapar, V. 1986. *Tiger: Portrait of a Predator*. Facts on File Publications, New York.

Thiollay, J. l985. Species diversity and comparative ecology of rainforest falconiforms on three continents. In: *Conservation Studies on Raptors*, I. Newton and R. Chancellor (eds.). ICBP Technical Publication No. 5, Cambridge, U.K. pp. 55–166.

Tilson, R. 1977. Social organization of simakobu monkeys (*Nasalis concolor*) in Siberut Island, Indonesia. *Journal of Mammalogy* 58:202–212.

Tooby, J. and I. De Vore. 1987. The reconstruction of hominid behavioral evolution through strategic modeling. In: *The Evolution of Human Behavior: Primate Models*, W. Kinzey (ed.). State University of New York Press, Albany. pp. 183–238.

Treves, A. 1999. Has predation shaped the social systems of arboreal primates? *International Journal of Primatology* 20(1):35–67.

Tsukahara, T. 1993. Lions eat chimpanzees: the first evidence of predation by lions on wild chimpanzees. *American Journal of Primatology* 29(1):1–11.

Turnbull-Kemp, P. 1967. *The Leopard*. Howard Timmins, Capetown.

Turner, A. 1997. *The Big Cats and Their Fossil Relatives*. Columbia University Press, New York.

Tutin, C. and K. Benirschke. 1991. Possible osteomyelitis of skull causes death of a wild lowland gorilla in the Lopé Reserve, Gabon. *Journal of Medical Primatology* 20:357–360.

Tutin, C., W. McGrew, and P. Baldwin. 1983. Social organization of savanna-dwelling chimpanzees, *Pan troglodytes verus*, at Mt. Assirik, Senegal. *Primates* 24:154–173.

Tylor, E. 1871. *Primitive Culture*. John Murray, London.

Uehara, S., T. Nishida, M. Hamai, T. Hasegawa, H. Hayaki, M. Huffman, K. Kawanaka, S. Kobayashi, J. Mitani, U. Takahata, H. Takasaki, and T. Tsukahara. 1992. Characteristics of predation by the chimpanzees in the Mahale Mountains National Park, Tanzania. In: *Topics in Primatology, Human Origins, Volume 1*, T. Nishida, W. McGrew, P. Marler, M. Pickford, and F. de Waal (eds.). University of Tokyo Press, Tokyo. pp. 143–158.

Uhde, N. and V. Sommer. 1998. The importance of predation risk for gibbon behavior and evolution. *Folia Primatologica* 69(4):224.

_____. 2002. Antipredatory behavior in gibbons (*Hylobates lar*, Khao Yai/Thailand). In: *Eat or Be Eaten: Predation Sensitive Foraging among Primates*, L. Miller (ed.). Cambridge University Press, Cambridge, U.K. pp. 268–291.

Uprety, A. 1998. Killers on the prowl. *The Week* 8/2/98.

van Schaik, C. 1983. Why are diurnal primates living in groups? *Behaviour* 87(1–2):120–143.

van Schaik, C. and T. Mitrasetia. 1990. Changes in the behaviour of wild long-tailed macaques (*Macaca fascicularis*) after encounters with a model python. *Folia Primatologica* 55(2):104–108.

Vekua, A., D. Lordkipanidze, G. Rightmire et al. 2002. A new skull of early *Homo* from Dmanisi, Georgia. *Science* 297:85–89.

Vencl, F. 1977. A case of convergence in vocal signals between marmosets and birds. *American Naturalist* 111:777–782.

Vermeij, G. 1982. Unsuccessful predation and evolution. *American Naturalist* 120:701–720.

Vernon, C. 1965. The black eagle survey in the Matopos, Rhodesia. *Arnoldia* (*Rhodesia*) 2(6):1–9.

Verschuren, J. 1958. Ecologie et biologie des grandes mammiferes. Exploration du Pare National de Garamba. Inst. Parcs Nat. Congo Belge: Brussels. 9 pp.

Vezina, A. 1985. Empirical relationships between predator and prey size among terrestrial vertebrate predators. *Oecologia* 67:555–565.

Vitale, A., E. Visalberghi, and C. de Lillo. 1991. Responses to a snake model in captive crab-eating macaques (*Macaca fascicularis*) and captive tufted capuchins (*Cebus apella*). *International Journal of Primatology* 12(3):277–286.

von Hippel, F. 1998. Use of sleeping trees by black and white colobus monkeys (*Colobus guereza*) in the Kakamega Forest, Kenya. *American Journal of Primatology* 45(3):281–290.

Voorhies, M. 2002. *Nebraska Wildlife Ten Million Years Ago*. University of Nebraska State Museum, Lincoln, Nebraska.

Voous, K. 1969. Predation potential in birds of prey from Surinam. *Ardea* 57:117–148.

Walters, J. and R. Seyfarth. 1987. Conflict and cooperation. In: *Primate Societies*, B. Smuts, D. Cheney, R. Seyfarth, R. Wrangham, and T. Struhsaker. University of Chicago Press, Chicago. pp. 306–317.

Waser, P. and R. Wiley. 1980. Mechanisms and evolution of spacing in animals. In: *Handbook of Behavioral Neurobiology, Volume 3*, P. Marler and J. Vandenbergh (eds.). Plenum Press, New York. pp. 159–233.

Washburn, S. 1957. Australopithecines: the hunters or the hunted? *American Anthropology* 59(4):612–614.

Washburn, S. and V. Avis. 1958. Evolution of human behavior. In: *Behavior and Evolution*, A. Roe and G. Simpson (eds.). Yale University Press, New Haven. pp. 421–436.

Washburn, S. and C. Lancaster. 1968. The evolution of hunting. In: *Man the Hunter*, R. Lee and I. DeVore (eds.). Aldine, Chicago. pp. 293–303.

Werdelin, L. and M. Lewis. 2000. Carnivora from the South Turkwel hominid site, northern Kenya. *Journal of Paleontology* 74(6):1173–1180.

Werdelin, L. and N. Solounias. 1991. The Hyaenidae: taxonomy, systematics and evolution. *Fossils and Strata* 30:1–104.

Westergaard, G. and S. Suomi. 1994. Aimed throwing of stones by tufted capuchin monkeys (*Cebus apella*). *Human Evolution* 9(4):323–329.

White, J. 2000. Bites and stings from venomous animals: a global overview. *Therapeutic Drug Monitoring* 22:65–68.

Whitfield, P. 1978. *The Hunters*. Simon and Schuster, New York.

Wiens, F., and A. Zitzmann. 1999. Predation on a wild slow loris, *Nycticebus coucang*, by a reticulated python, *Python reticulatus*. *Folia Primatologica* 70:362–364.

Wilford, J. 2001. Skull may alter experts' view of human descent's branches. *The New York Times* 3/22/01. p. A1.

Willett, W., M. Stampfer, G. Colditz et al. 1990. Relation of meat, fat, and fiber intake to the risk of colon cancer in a prospective study among women. *New England Journal of Medicine* 323:1664–1672.

Wilson, E. O. 1975. *Sociobiology: The New Synthesis*. Harvard University Press, Cambridge, Massachusetts.

_____. 1976. Sociobiology: a new approach to understanding the basis of human nature. *New Scientist* 70:342–345.

Wolfheim, J. 1983. *Primates of the World: Distribution, Abundance, and Conservation.* University of Washington Press, Seattle.

Wong, K. 2003. Stranger in a new land. *Scientific American* 289(5):74–83.

Wood, B. 2002. Paleoanthropology: hominid revelations from Chad. *Nature* 418:133–135.

Worster, D. 1994. *Nature's Economy: A History of Ecological Ideas*, Second Edition. Cambridge University Press, Cambridge, U.K.

Wrangham, R. 1974. Predation by chimpanzees in the Gombe National Park, Tanzania. *Primate Eye* 2:6.

_____. 1979. On the evolution of ape social systems. *Social Science Inf.* 18:335–368.

_____. 1980. An ecological model of female-bonded primate groups. *Behaviour* 75:262–300.

_____. 1995. Ape culture and missing links. *Symbols* (Spring): 2–9, 20.

Wrangham, R. and D. Peterson. 1996. *Demonic Males: Apes and the Origins of Human Violence.* Houghton Mifflin, Boston.

Wright, P. 1985. The costs and benefits of nocturnality of *Aotus trivirgatus* (the night monkey). Ph.D. dissertation, The City University of New York, New York.

Wright, P., S. Heckscher and A. Dunham. 1997. Predation on Milne-Edward's sifaka (*Propithecus diadema edwardsi*) by the fossa (*Cryptoprocta ferox*) in the rain forest of southeastern Madagascar. *Folia Primatologica* 68(1):34–43.

Yeager, C. 1991. Possible anti-predator behavior associated with river crossings by proboscis monkeys (*Nasalis larvatus*). *American Journal of Primatology* 24(1):61–66.

Young, T. 1994. Predation risk, predation rate, and the effectiveness of anti-predator traits. *Evolutionary Anthropology* 3(2):67.

Zahl, P. 1960. Face to face with gorillas in Central Africa. *National Geographic* 117:114–137.

Zapfe, H. 1981. Ein schadel von *Mesopithecus* mit biss-spuren. [A skull of *Mesopithecus* with bite marks.] *Folia Primatologica* 35:248–258.

Ziegler, T., and E. Heymann. 1996. Response to snake models in different species of Callitrichidae. *Primate Report* 44:58–59.

Zihlman, A. 1997. The Paleolithic glass ceiling: women in human evolution. In: *Women in Human Evolution*, L. Hager (ed.). Routledge, London. pp. 91–113.

_____. 2000. *The Human Evolution Coloring Book*, Second Edition. HarperCollins, New York.

Zinner, D. and F. Peláez. 1999. Verreaux's eagles (*Aquila verreauxi*) as potential predators of hamadryas baboons (*Papio hamadryas*) in Eritrea. *American Journal of Primatology* 47:61–66.

Zuberbuhler, K. and D. Jenny. 2002. Leopard predation and primate evolution. *Journal of Human Evolution* 43:873–886.

INDEX